A Very English Family

A Very English Family

(1945–1954)

The First Volume of a Memoir by
Richard Perceval Graves

Troubador Publishing Ltd
Unit E2 Airfield Business Park
Harrison Road, Market Harborough
Leicestershire LE16 7UL
Tel: 0116 279 2299
Email: books@troubador.co.uk
Web: www.troubador.co.uk

ISBN 978 1 8051 4504 2

British Library Cataloguing in Publication Data.
A catalogue record for this book is available from the British Library.

Printed and bound by CPI Group (UK) Ltd, Croydon, CR0 4YY
Typeset in 12pt Adobe Jenson Pro by Troubador Publishing Ltd, Leicester, UK

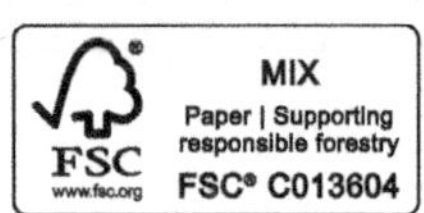

For my family, and especially for my children
David, Philip and Lucia;
and my grandchildren Natalie, Hallam and Asta

Also, for anyone wishing to visit or revisit
that vanished world of the 1940s and 1950s
in which I was lucky enough to spend my early childhood.

Contents

Acknowledgements

The author and publishers would like to thank the following for kind permission to reproduce copyright material:

The Betjeman Estate for an extract from Murray's Berkshire Architectural Guide (1949) by John Betjeman and John Piper (Ed.)

The family of Anthony Buckeridge for an extract from his wonderful Jennings and Darbyshire novels

Orion Publishing Group Limited for an extract from *The Little Princesses* by Marion Crawford as it originally appeared in *Sunny Stories*. Reproduced with permission of the Licensor through PLSclear; and acknowledging the help given by Helen Jennings of PLSclear Helpdesk

Cheryl Thomas and Macmillan Children's Books for an extract from *Still William* by Richmal Crompton, first published in 1925 and copyright Edward Ashbee and Catherine Massey; acknowledging the help given by Emily Talbot of United Agents.

Constance Egan's grand-daughter Clare J.M. Brooke-Little for extracts from *Epaminondas Helps in the House* by Constance Egan

The Carcanet Press for extracts from the published work of Robert von Ranke Graves

David Higham Associates for an extract from *The Fox in the Attic* by Richard Hughes, published by Chatto & Windus (1961)

In respect of extracts from the works of A.A. Milne:

1. 'Disobedience' from When We Were Very Young by A.A. Milne
Copyright © Pooh Properties Trust 1924
Reproduced with permission from Curtis Brown Group Ltd on behalf of The Pooh Properties Trust.
2. The House at Pooh Corner by A.A. Milne
Copyright © Pooh Properties Trust 1928
Reproduced with permission from Curtis Brown Group Ltd on behalf of The Pooh Properties Trust.
3. From Winnie-the-Pooh by A.A. Milne
Copyright ©Pooh Properties Trust 1926
Reproduced with permission from Curtis Brown Group Ltd on behalf of The Pooh Properties Trust.

A.M. Heath & Co Ltd. for an extract from *White Boots* by Noel Streatfeild (Copyright © Noel Streatfeild, 1951)

Reach Publishing Services Limited for an extract from *The Wokingham Times* of 1953

In addition, the author acknowledges the use of unpublished words by the following people whom it has been impossible to trace: Alfred Vines of Rottingdean, and six teachers from Holme Grange School: Miss Goad, Mr. Noble, Miss Robinson, Mr. Hinton, Mr. Craig and Mr. Rushton

The author and publishers acknowledge the use of material from the following publications:

1. One of the 'Think-and do' books by William S. Gray published in the 1940s or 1950s.
2. *The Bad Old Days* by Charles Graves (Faber and Faber 1951).
3. *Robert Graves and the White Goddess 1940-1985*, by Richard Perceval

Graves (Weidenfeld & Nicolson 1995), for an extract from a letter of Jenny Nicholson.

4. *Who's Who in Sport 1935* for its entry on J.T.R.Graves.
5. Mail Online 8 May 2020, for an extract of 11 words.
6. The Daily Mail of 2 June 1953 for an extract of 46 words

The Photographs all come from my personal collection apart from photographs of Richard Graves and Simon Graves professionally taken in October 1950 by J. Fowler Smith of 45 The Canal, Salisbury; and a Graves family photograph taken on 12 July 1910 by Russell & Sons of Wimbledon.

Prologue: Somewhere Out There

> Nothing dies, not even the Present. Time is a tricky thing; and its sister, Space, preserves our voices and our gestures for all eternity. It is simply a matter of the point of view we take. Somewhere in space, I am still in that awkward position on the turf of a Lucknow polo-ground. Somewhere, also, the thunders of Trafalgar are echoing, and further back, the roars of a sabre-toothed tiger.
>
> F. Yeats-Brown, Chapter XV *Bengal Lancer* 1930

Somewhere out there, according not only to the brilliant Yeats-Brown but also to many 21st century physicists, every particle of past history still exists. Indeed, if you believe in God, as I do, how could it be otherwise? So, as you read these words, please imagine that you are looking over my shoulder and observing what I observe as we travel together through the appropriate worm-hole in the space-time continuum and find ourselves looking down upon what, somewhere out there, *still exists*, and is now being always lovingly if at times painfully revisited.

In the course of this shared adventure, even if in your current world I am now dead while you must obviously still be alive, you will get to know me very well. Whether you come to think of me as a good friend, or whether you decide after a while that you can't stand being in the same room as me, I hope that I may one day know. In the meantime, it is only fair of me to warn you that you are certain to come across a great deal of poetry, and you should definitely abandon this memoir and go elsewhere if (for example) you dislike James Elroy Flecker's *To a Poet a Thousand Years Hence*:

> I who am dead a thousand years,
> And wrote this sweet archaic song,
> Send you my words for messengers
> The way I shall not pass along.
>
> I care not if you bridge the seas,
> Or ride secure the cruel sky,
> Or build consummate palaces
> Of metal or of masonry.
>
> But have you wine and music still,
> And statues and a bright-eyed love,
> And foolish thoughts of good and ill,
> And prayers to them who sit above?
>
> How shall we conquer? Like a wind
> That falls at eve our fancies blow,
> And old Mæonides the blind
> Said it three thousand years ago.
>
> O friend unseen, unborn, unknown,
> Student of our sweet English tongue,
> Read out my words at night, alone:
> I was a poet, I was young.
>
> Since I can never see your face,
> And never shake you by the hand,
> I send my soul through time and space
> To greet you. You will understand.

You don't like it? Well then, no hard feelings, but it might be better for you to abandon this memoir now, because what follows almost certainly won't suit you. But do come along for the ride if you feel ready for change! You will be most welcome.

Oh, you do like it? Perhaps you already know it? That's good. I can tell you now that I have admired Flecker ever since as a schoolboy I was excited by *The War Song of the Saracens*. Then as an Oxford undergraduate I bought the Folio edition of *Hassan*, his play ending with Hassan as a pilgrim taking the Golden Road to Samarkand. There will be space enough later on for those two. But for now, before we begin to take the first steps together upon our own Golden Road, let me give you the present (or simply remind you) of one of Flecker's lesser-known poems, *Tenebris Lucentem*, or *Shining out of the Darkness*.

A linnet who had lost her way
Sang on a blackened bough in Hell,
Till all the ghosts remembered well
The trees, the wind, the golden day.

At last they knew that they had died
When they heard music in that land,
And someone there stole forth a hand
To draw a brother to his side.

And now dear reader, wherever and whenever you are: perhaps on a commuter train dashing at high speed through the London or New York or Sydney suburbs in the summer of 2030; perhaps in a space-freighter on its three-week journey home across the 600 light years from Kepler 22-b, in the year 2525 (if we are still alive); imagine that you are closing your eyes, that they are tight shut, and that by a supreme effort of will you plunge most daringly through time and space, (a little like John Carter on his fictional journeys between Earth and Mars) and open them again to find yourself looking down on a twentieth-century English landscape of fields and low hills.

Between these fields runs and bends to the left and straightens briefly and then bends again to the right, one of those rolling English roads described by G.K. Chesterton:

Before the Roman came to Rye or out to Severn strode,
The rolling English drunkard made the rolling English road.
A reeling road, a rolling road, that rambles round the shire,
And after him the parson ran, the sexton and the squire;
A merry road, a mazy road, and such as we did tread
The night we went to Birmingham by way of Beachy Head.

It is the summer of 1952, and this is the main road from London to Brighton. It is a narrow road, just wide enough for one car in each direction and, as we go down further, following the road southward, we can see that the cars are almost all coloured black.

Closer still, and we are now just above the road, looking at the back of one of these black cars. There is a rack on the top of the car, covered with trunks and cases – and is that a box of vegetables?

Beneath the spare tyre, safely attached to the back of the car, a number-plate reads EPB 223. It is a squarely-built two-door Ford 7Y (sometimes called a Ford 8) with running-boards and a cramped interior and a floor through which, if sitting in one of the two front seats, the road is clearly visible. Bought for £100 back in 1936 or 1937, it was laid up throughout the Second World War (1939-1945), and finds steep hills difficult, especially with its current load; but it is still doing sterling service as it voyages towards Brighton with its five occupants, four of whom are lovingly described by my father, the driver, as his 'precious cargo'.

My father! 'Daddy' as we call him. John Tiarks Ranke Graves, a good Christian gentleman of 49, is a preparatory-school Headmaster, utterly commanding, fiercely knowledgeable, deeply sensitive and perhaps a little eccentric. He drives us on this beautiful summer's day wearing a three-piece suit and a long winter overcoat and a scarf and a trilby hat.

That excited seven-year-old boy with curly brown hair sitting on his left in the front passenger seat, wearing T-shirt and shorts and sandals and longing to be at his journey's end, that's me, that's Ricky. Behind me sits my mother, 'Mummy' to us, Mary Graves née Wickens, a beautiful woman of 35, a Graduate of the Royal College of Music, another good Christian and a fiercely loyal and protective wife and mother. She adores my father and loves us all very dearly – but sometimes displays the expression of noble suffering by which my father recognised her as his soul-mate when he first saw her at a concert at Harrow School. He commented 'Quelle triste visage', and then a moment later: 'That's the woman I'm going to marry!'

Mummy carries on her lap one-year-old Elizabeth, plump and clever and sickly survivor of twins. Next to them sits my brother Simon, within a few weeks of his fifth birthday, a formidably intelligent child with straight hair and large brown eyes who is my closest friend and constant companion. However, he combines underlying physical strength and apparent fearlessness with the delicate psychological balance of a cuckoo clock, and from the pained expression on his face you can tell how much he hates travelling.

But how exciting it is for me, driving into Brighton! At first, we pass by some almost incredibly well-manicured public gardens full of blooming flowers. Daddy comments approvingly, though it is most unlike the wild beauty of our own grounds at Holme Grange, grounds which were planted towards the end of the nineteenth century with specimen trees and shrubs and with thousands upon thousands of bulbs. We travel on into the busy town centre, where at last we catch between tall buildings our first sight of the sea.

"θαλασσα!" Daddy cries out in Ancient Greek, reliving that famous moment from 401 BC when Xenophon and his exhausted 10,000 warriors, having been stranded deep in enemy territory, and having had to fight their way to freedom across desert and mountain, finally, from a mountain-top thirty miles away, catch their first sight of the Black Sea. "θαλασσα! θαλασσα! Thalassa! Thalassa! The sea! The sea!" And beneath the light blue of the sky there is that desperately exciting patch of darker, deeper blue.

We drive towards it. To the right of us appear for a while the green somewhat sinister domes of the Brighton Pavilion. Ahead of us, soon afterwards, a view of Brighton Pier, shining white and beautiful in the sunshine; and already this part of the town is full of memories of slot-machines and large round pennies and collecting my tricycle and then we sweep round to the left and begin to take the coast road for Rottingdean.

As always at this point in our journey my father, who has been keeping up his usual unvaried but always interesting running commentary, suddenly sweeps his hat from his head. This is in my honour. We are briefly close to the place where I was born, in a Brighton nursing home on 21 December 1945, within sight and smell of the sea, within earshot of the breaking of the waves, of the crying of the gulls, and of the unforgettable and wonderfully evocative crunching noise made at each step that one takes upon that shingled shore.

Observing all this, I find myself longing to continue towards Rottingdean, towards Braemar, the tall terraced house half-way-up Steyning Road where Grandad with his flat cap and his golden watch-chain and Aunt Joan with her tremendous hug and Solomon the dachshund are all eagerly waiting for us. [Noony the cat has already sensed that we are on our way and has slunk off to hide.] But perhaps, after all, we had better begin at the beginning.

BOOK ONE

CROYDON 1945–1949

CHAPTER ONE

An Unexpected Arrival

To begin at the beginning – and immediately those words tug me sideways, not least because in due course we will be revisiting both Laugharne and *Under Milk Wood*. 'To begin at the beginning' writes Dylan Thomas,

> It is spring, moonless night in the small town, starless and
> bible-black, the cobblestreets silent and the hunched courters'
> -and rabbits' wood limping invisible down to the sloeblack,
> slow, black, fishingboatbobbing sea.

Some of Dylan's past I know as well as my own. Fragments of his and other lives are so deeply intertwined with my own, that it is as though I am dreaming, and I see a montage of apparently random images: Dylan Thomas in the grounds of Laugharne Castle, levering open a wooden cover and stealing a bottle of Nuits St. Georges from Richard Hughes's makeshift wine-cellar, while Hughes observes from the shadows with a wry and somewhat sinister smile; Richard Hughes again, walking along a Harlech road deep in conversation with Robert Graves, utterly betraying his friendship with my Uncle Charles; Robert, diving into the Mediterranean sea and striking out strongly for a distant rock; and then the ghost of an ancient sailing-ship at twilight rushing through deep waters with no-one immediately visible on deck.

I thought it a ship of death, but see, quite plainly
Lashed to the mast, a man who is weak and blind
Who sails over a sea of desolation,
Seeking the tideless harbours of the mind.

Whenever my birth was mentioned on those childhood journeys to Rottingdean, it brought into my mind, though I kept it to myself, and surely no-one can remember the hours immediately after their own birth, an image of white-washed walls and figures wearing white uniforms and a bed and the warmth of my mother's body and soft milky sweetness and enduring and powerful love.

Later on, I would be told that my birth in 1945 was considered by my Grandmother Amy to be a great event in the family. Amy was the saintly stepmother of five and the mother in her own right of five more by Alfred Perceval Graves, the Anglo-Irish poet and Inspector of Schools who had died in his sleep a few days after Christmas 1931.

On his 85th birthday, earlier that year, APG had been so happy to have his daughter Molly visiting that he had danced a few steps of his Irish jig and sung *Father O'Flynn*, the song for which he had become famous throughout late-Victorian Great Britain, and which begins:

Of priests we can offer a charmin' variety
Far renowned for larnin' and piety;
Still, I'd advance ye widout impropriety
Father O'Flynn as the flower of them all.
[Chorus]
Here's a health to you, Father O'Flynn,
Slainté and slainté and slainté agin;
Powerfulest preacher, and
Tinderest teacher, and
Kindliest creature in ould Donegal.

Don't talk of your Provost and Fellows of Trinity
Famous for ever at Greek and Latinity,
Faix, and the divels and all at Divinity,
Father O'Flynn'd make hares of them all!

But so far, despite APG's being the father of ten, there had been only two legitimate grandsons born with the surname Graves. These were David and Sam Graves, my uncle Robert's sons by the artist Nancy Nicholson. David (another poet) had died as recently as March 1943, fighting with what his commanding officer had described as 'most conspicuous gallantry' against the Japanese in the far-distant jungles of Burma. There, trying to retrieve a hopeless situation, he had single-handedly bombed his way into two enemy posts before being shot down while advancing undaunted upon the third. As for Sam: he was still unmarried.

It's true that by this time Robert had two more sons by Beryl Hodge; but unfortunately, with Nancy refusing a divorce, Robert and Beryl had been unable to marry, so Beryl was technically Robert's mistress and both six-year-old William and one-year-old Juan were technically bastards. Legitimacy still counted for something in those days; and although Amy will have known of Shakespeare's impassioned plea: 'Now Gods stand up for bastards!' their names certainly couldn't be entered into the family Bible.

So, my birth caused great joy as well as great excitement – I was the first living Graves grandson born in wedlock since Sam back in 1924 – even if Amy was a little concerned that John had married beneath him. For Mary Wickens was a butcher's daughter; and even though Amy Graves (previously von Ranke) had met and been charmed by Mary, she had still felt it necessary to write to John warning him not to risk inviting any of his brothers or sisters to the wedding in case they were horribly shocked by the low status of their fellow-invitees.

This was purely pragmatic. Amy herself was too good a Christian to have any innate prejudice against Mary; but she could not answer for her children and step-children, and it must have been immediately clear to her that Mary came from a lower social class: not only was her father in trade, but the Wickens family tree, unlike that of the von Rankes or the Graveses, contained no very distinguished ancestors, no famous historians or Bishops or Prime Ministers or Kings and Queens or friends of the Kaiser, not a single person whose family had come over with William the Conqueror in 1066, only humble shepherds walking across the South Downs or the Isle of Wight in all weathers watching over their flocks by day and by night.

George Bernard Shaw famously wrote in *Pygmalion*: 'It is impossible for an Englishman to open his mouth, without making some other Englishman despise him'; and a few signs of social inferiority were evident in the language they used. They were never so vulgar as to call the lavatory 'the toilet'; but Mary's father, Sidney William Wickens, encouraged me and my siblings to call him not 'Grandfather', or 'Grandpapa' as he would have done in an upper-class family; but the common or garden 'Grandad'.

I was enough of a snob to flinch inwardly whenever my mother or one of her sisters referred to magazines as 'books'; but I never minded the word Grandad (though I could tell that others did), because my Grandad was a man with the kindest heart I have ever known. I loved him when I was a young child and in many ways he seemed to me like another child, sometimes more in need of my protection than I was of his; and I love him still now that I am an old man, and in his honour I insist upon being called Grandad by my own Grandchildren. It must be at least sixty years since we were together in the same room: probably that dark front room in Chyngton with its drawn curtains, its antique brass carriage-clock ticking on the mantelpiece, and the high brass bed in which during his final illness Grandad lay unable to speak; yet the merest memory of him still brings tears flooding into my eyes and running down my cheeks.

Incidentally, if Mary had married above her, then so in a way had her father. The Wickens family business was so successful that it had expanded beyond Southsea and had an outpost in Rottingdean; and here it was that the handsome Sidney Wickens, in his spare time a dashing young subaltern in the Hampshire Yeomanry, had won the heart of Ellen Hilder. The Hilders too were in business – one of them ran a local bakery – but through her mother, Ellen was descended from a wealthy family of French Huguenots. Back in the 1690s, members of the de la Chambre family had fled to England in a desperate effort to escape from the murderous religious persecution of Louis XIV. There they had purchased lands in the Seaford area and anglicized their name from de la Chambre to Chambers.

They brought with them their aristocratic high standards, their deep and unshakeable Protestant faith, and their fierce hatred of the Roman Catholics who had driven them into exile. These high standards and religious prejudices were passed on through the female line from generation to generation; and, thanks to Ellen, Mary and her three elder sisters Betty, Ruth and Joan, despite Amy's anxiety, were all well enough brought-up to be able to pass muster in any rank of society.

Particularly important was the fact that they all spoke the King's English flawlessly and without any regional accent, the slightest trace of which would have been fatal to their chances of being acceptable in polite society. Moreover, despite being girls, they had been given a first-class education at the Portsmouth High School under the diminutive but formidable Miss Cossey until 1932, and then under Miss Watt, with her great love of music and the arts. And as daughters of a butcher, I have no doubt that during their History lessons they will have listened with particular interest (as I would do later) when they came to the well-known story of Thomas Wolsey, notable not merely for his great loyalty back in the 1520s to his master King Henry VIII, but for having risen to the great height of being Lord Chancellor and Roman Catholic Cardinal despite his father being only an Ipswich butcher.

Like Wolsey's mother Joan Daundy, Ellen Hilder had raised some remarkable children. I have always felt sad never to have met her, though I know her appearance well enough, chiefly from the locket with her picture which always stood upon my mother's dressing-table, and which I am now holding in my hand. It shows Ellen, possibly on her way to church, wearing a light brown coat fastened with an orange clasp and with a narrow fur trim at the neck. On her head is a hat of a much darker brown with a broad brim and a blue band round it just above the brim. Between the hat which comes low over her forehead and the coat which comes up to her neck, she is smiling with a conspiratorial sense of fun. With her lovely brown eyes, a good complexion and an excellent set of teeth between red lips, Ellen is a handsome woman, despite the very determined chin of her Chambers ancestry.

It was partly this Chambers determination which meant that although she had married for love, Ellen retained the respect of her own kith and kin; that she successfully brought up her four daughters to be good Christian folk; and that she inspired them with such personal adoration that I never heard a single one of them refer to her (even in the most argumentatively smoky rooms) with anything but the very deepest love and affection.

However, she taught them not to be hoarders, so only one of her letters survives, a wartime letter written to 'My darling Mary' on 15 July 1943, when Ellen was just 60 years old. Her letter is lively and although it is mainly about her plans to visit Mary who was then a music teacher up at St. Andrews in Scotland, it is full of family news. She is anxious about Daddy, who seems to have an attack of catarrh, possibly brought on by spending too much time in the garden during rainy weather; Ruth has 'just gone on duty'; she and Joan and her sister Effie are going to a 'do' at the Convent in aid of the Waifs and Strays fund: 'I only hope', she writes, 'there are not too many encores'; and before she ends 'with much love & many kisses. God bless you. Yours ever, Mummie' she adds that:

> I washed my hair yesterday, so you can imagine what it is like today to keep up. Effie had hers shampooed this morning & it is like shock-headed Peter. Our lodger got wet through this morning & he came home at 1:15 & had a bath & changed his clothes & put the others on the line to dry. We cannot find out if he is going tomorrow or not, yet. He told us last night he is in no hurry to leave, & does not care about Winchester much. I think he is getting pretty good attention here. – Still he is a nice lad.

Her comparison of Effie to a character from Struwelpeter, and her very slightly acid comments about both the encores and the lodger, suggest to me that she would have been excellent company; but as I said, I never met her: less than two years after writing this letter she had died of cancer.

It was because of her impending death that my parents were married on 3 February 1945 having only known each other for a few months, so that Ellen could live to see their wedding-day. This took place at Rottingdean Church; and I have a photograph taken that day of 41-year-old John and 27-year-old Mary, standing just outside the church porch. My father, tall, thin and handsome, with an authoritative but kindly face, is every inch a gentleman with his well-polished black shoes and his morning dress which is worn both elegantly and naturally, and has clearly not been hired for the day. In his right hand he carries his silk top hat, there is a handkerchief in his breast pocket and a large carnation in his lapel, and tucked into his left arm is my mother's arm, with only her hand showing. She herself looks beautiful and happy, but (remember this was still wartime) she is dressed not in any long white creation down to her ankles, but, in a simple formal dress with a pleated skirt which comes down to just below the knees, a high neck, and an open jacket, to which, over her left breast, is pinned a spray of lilies. She wears a plain hat, the front of which is also decorated with flowers; on her feet are court shoes; and in her left hand she carries a pair of gloves.

Yes, this was still wartime, though the Nazi swastika no longer dominated Europe. Thanks largely to the military genius of General George Patton, the last major German breakout in the West has recently been defeated in the Battle of the Bulge; Auschwitz concentration camp has been liberated by Soviet troops; and, with heavy bombing over Berlin itself, Hitler and Eva Braun are already living underground in their final refuge in Berlin. But V2 rockets are still reaching England and causing immense destruction and loss of life; American troops have not yet crossed the Rhine into Germany; US Marines have not yet raised the American flag over Iwo Jima; and many fierce battles lie ahead, especially in the Far East.

John, like his journalist elder brother Charles and many others of their generation, was marked for the rest of his life by having been too young for one war, the Great War, the 1914-1918 war; but too old for the next major conflict.

Charles had joined up in 1918, but had never seen active service: exactly like his friend Richard Hughes, with whom Charles had shared a desk at Charterhouse. Charles had been 'completely flabbergasted' by the idea that he might 'go on living' and wondered uneasily for the rest of his life whether or not he would have turned out to be a coward. For Hughes also, 'the shock was stupendous. No one', as he later wrote of his fictional alter ego Augustine Penry-Jones in *The Fox in the Attic*,

> No one had warned him that he might after all find himself with his life to live out: with sixty years still to spend, perhaps, instead of the bare six months he thought was all he had in his pocket. Peace was a condition unknown to him and scarcely imaginable. The whole real-seeming world in which he had grown to manhood had melted round him.

John, born in 1903, three years later than Charles, was still only fifteen when the Great War ended; and when Hitler invaded Poland in September 1939, John had been a schoolmaster of 36, an age which, in a reserved occupation, meant that although he tried to enlist he was compelled to go on teaching at Malvern College: fortunately for me, because in 1942 (having already had a spell at Blenheim Palace while it was taken over by the Admiralty as a possible retreat should their London headquarters be bombed) Malvern College was compelled to move in with Harrow School while their premises were used by the Telecommunications Research Establishment: hence my father's meeting with my mother in the autumn of 1944, not long after she had begun teaching music at Harrow School.

He first saw her when he was sitting a row or two behind her at a school concert. She turned her head to look around, and he was instantly smitten. "That's the girl I'm going to marry!' he told the member-of-staff sitting next to him. And within a few weeks he had found out who she was, secured an introduction, and swept her off her feet.

The prospect of marriage made my father think seriously about his financial future, and he acted rapidly and decisively. By the time of his wedding, he had thrown up his teaching career and taken a much better-paid job as Assistant Editor of the Times Educational Supplement; and before long he and my mother had moved into a small terraced house at 3 Moreton Road, Croydon, from where John could commute daily to his London office. And when the job at the TES began to seem less interesting than he had hoped, John continued to commute, having metamorphosed into a senior official within the Ministry of Education, at that time facing the formidable task of implementing the Butler Education Act of 1944.

It was not long before I was conceived; and during my mother's pregnancy, the most momentous events were happening in the outside world. On 30 April 1945, Hitler and Eva Braun committed suicide; on 7 May, Germany surrendered unconditionally and on 14 August, only a few days after the dropping of atomic bombs on Hiroshima and Nagasaki, Emperor Hirohito announced the surrender of Japan. These events, which seemed so utterly remote to me as a child, such very ancient history, would nevertheless cast their shadow forward across at least the first twenty years of my life.

I arrived several weeks before I was expected, and Mummy and Daddy often told me that this was because I was so keen to see what was going on in the outside world. I might also point out that by appearing as early as 21 December I had narrowly avoided being born under the reliable but somewhat stodgy Earth sign of Capricorn. Instead, I am proud to be a Sagittarian; and my son Philip, an expert in astrological matters, assures me that I have all the traditional virtues and vices of this creative but somewhat volatile Fire sign.

As for my being born in Brighton, so far away from my parents' Croydon home, this came about because in the run-up to their first Christmas together, they were faced with the usual dilemma of young married couples with two sets of relatives, both of whom hope and expect that they will be the ones to be favoured with a visit on Christmas Day. Many and various were the solutions which I would employ when I myself was a young married man: not one of them was ever wholly satisfactory, and they mostly involved hellish journeys from one household to another on Boxing Day.

However, Harlech in North Wales is very far from Croydon, and still further from Rottingdean, and in those pre-motorway days it was too long and exhausting a journey for a woman in a late stage of pregnancy, especially with such a formidable mother-in-law at the end of it. So, it was decided that John would travel alone all the way up to North Wales to visit his 88-year-old mother Amy at Erinfa, her large rambling house looking out over the Irish Sea; while Mary would spend Christmas in Rottingdean with her beloved sisters and their 69-year-old father Sidney at Braemar, the narrow, terraced house they owned half-way up Steyning Road. Hence my birth in a Brighton nursing-home within the sound of the sea breaking on that inimitable shingle shore.

CHAPTER TWO
Early Days in Croydon

A telegram was sent to my father, who hurried southward as fast as the railways would allow; and since he found that there were no buses running over Christmas between Rottingdean and Brighton, he walked the four miles in and out each day to visit his wife and to visit me, his first-born child.

Soon I had been named: *Richard,* after my half-uncle Dick Graves, Graves Supérieur, a senior official in the Consular Service; *Perceval* because it had become a family tradition since my great-grandfather's day to give the eldest son of the family Perceval as his middle name out of regard for our great-great-grandmother Helena Perceval, the Dublin beauty who could trace her lineage back to an ancestor of William the Conqueror; and the combination *Richard Perceval* possibly because that was the name of one of Helena's ancestors who was famous for having deciphered secret Spanish documents and had therefore been able back in 1588 to give Queen Elizabeth I 'the first certain intelligence' about the impending arrival of the Spanish Armada.

Before long I had also received an envelope addressed to:

Mr. Richard Graves
"Braemar"
Steyning Road
Rottingdean

It had been stamped with a blue 2 ½d stamp bearing a portrait of King George VI; and inside was my very first letter, from a family friend called Alfred Vines, who wrote to welcome me to Rottingdean and to tell me that: 'I wish you very many happy years – and only give you one bit of advice – "be kind to your Mother"'.

As soon as possible, I was brought home to 3 Moreton Road, South Croydon; where the joyful day of arrival was soon followed by months of anxiety as I steadfastly refused to put on weight. At one time I was so sickly that I was hardly expected to live, and so on 3 March 1946 I was removed for observation to the Children's Hospital in Great Ormonde Street.

My problem was that I had great difficulty in keeping down the milk that I swallowed – a difficulty with unmixed milk that has plagued me ever since. Shredded Wheat with milk – yes! Chocolate-flavoured milk – yes! But how I hated free school milk, which pursued me implacably through my childhood until, when a milk monitor myself at Charterhouse, and in charge of those vile third-of-a-pint bottles which clanged and rattled in their crates with loathsome cheerfulness, I devised a scheme which I will tell you about later, and which meant that I never had to drink a single drop of the wretched stuff myself.

Fortunately for me, an eminently practical doctor at Great Ormonde Street, to whom I undoubtedly owe my life, had the excellent idea of thickening my feed, after which I began to prosper; and by 13 April I was well enough to be carried to the local St. Peter's Church in South Croydon to be baptized: not by the local vicar, but by the distinguished Reverend F.W. Dillistone, who happened to be visiting England from the USA, where he was currently the Professor of Theology at the Episcopal Divinity School in Cambridge, Massachusetts.

Always known as 'Dilly' by my mother, who adored him, Frederick Dillistone had become a family friend after his ordination back in 1928, when he had begun his glittering career as a humble curate at St. Jude's in Southsea; and now it was he who presided over my baptism. So far as all present were concerned, this was a critically important ceremony since, in the opening words of the service, 'all men are conceived and born in sin, and .... none can enter into the kingdom of God, except he be regenerate and born anew of Water and of the Holy Ghost'.

My three Godparents, chosen very properly for the strength of their religious convictions, were Cyril Lace and Nigel Pickstone, respectively a fellow-teacher and an ex-pupil from my father's days at Malvern College; and Nancy Biddle, who had studied alongside my mother at the Royal College of Music; and it was these three of whom Dillistone demanded:

> DOST thou, in the name of this Child, renounce the devil and all his works, the vain pomp and glory of the world, with all covetous desires of the same, and the carnal desires of the flesh, so that thou wilt not follow nor be led by them?

A little later, having received satisfactory replies to these and other questions, Dillistone took me in his arms and baptized me on the forehead with water taken from the Font in the name of the Father, and of the Son and of the Holy Ghost, before declaring:

> 'WE receive this Child into the Congregation of Christ's flock, and do sign him with the sign of the Cross, in token that hereafter he shall not be ashamed to confess the faith of Christ crucified, and manfully to fight under his banner against sin, the world, and the devil, and to continue Christ's faithful soldier and servant unto his life's end.'

My new Godfathers and Godmother were then solemnly enjoined to teach me 'what a solemn vow, promise and profession he hath here made by you', to call upon me to hear sermons, and in due course 'to take care that this child be brought to the Bishop to be confirmed by him, so soon as he can say the Creed, the Lord's Prayer and the Ten Commandments in the vulgar tongue, and be further instructed in the Church Catechism set forth for that purpose.'

With both my immortal soul and my perishable body in safe hands, my father was able to turn more of his attention to the wider world, where for a while imperial and family difficulties ran alongside each other in distant Palestine.

Those Imperial difficulties were everywhere evident. Although we had finally won the War just a few months before I was born, it had seriously weakened us. We could justifiably pride ourselves on having fought on to victory, but despite our glorious single-handed successes in the Battle of Britain and at El Alamein, that victory had ultimately been possible only with American help. This unpalatable fact plummeted deep down into the British psyche where it festered horribly – no-one likes to be helped too much – and was responsible for generations of anti-American sentiment.

Worse still, the calamitous and disgraceful fall of Singapore had permanently damaged our credibility. The days were now over when a single British officer, like some Roman centurion, could stand up and by his mere presence quell a thousand rioters single-handed, representing as he did the might of a vast and unassailable Empire. We had not only lost face but we were also impoverished and heavily in debt. And alongside food rationing and hard winters and power-cuts and shortages of coal, we retained Imperial responsibilities, especially in India, which it began to seem impossible for us to sustain.

For the Graveses, Palestine was a particular concern. On 24 July 1946, just over three months after my christening, it was the centenary of my grandfather's birth. His widow Amy placed flowers on his Harlech grave, and my Aunt Susan and a group of their friends had supper at Erinfa where they listened to a wireless recital of APG's poems and songs. But these centenary celebrations had already been overshadowed by events far away.

Two days previously, my Uncle Dick Graves, then Director of the Labour Department in Palestine, had arranged to meet my Aunt Clarissa at the King David Hotel in Jerusalem for a slightly early APG centenary lunch. They were both on the way there when by chance they met in the street about half a block away, and stopped to talk. As anyone who knows us will tell you, we Graveses are fond of talking; and a few minutes later, still too engrossed in conversation to have resumed their walk towards the King David Hotel, they were shocked to hear the loud roar of a huge explosion as the hotel was blown up by Jewish terrorists. It was a successful attack, with 91 killed and 49 injured; and had they not met and stopped to talk, Dick and Clarissa would almost certainly have been among the dead.

It was then only three months since Clarissa, thanks to my Uncle Robert paying for her air fare, had been able to return to Palestine after a year-long visit to her mother. This visit had not been a great success, because Amy enjoyed her independence and found Clarissa's efforts to look after her 'very kind, but trying'. Clarissa herself had been delighted to have been able to escape from Harlech and to resume the somewhat eccentric life she lived in 'By a Fig Tree', her little house in the Arab Quarter of Jerusalem, the place where she hoped to spend the rest of her days. She had even become a Palestinian citizen in order to confirm that this was now her real home; and she seemed sublimely unaware of the danger she was in as a close relative of one of the senior members of the colonial administration.

Only seven months later, on 2 February 1947, the situation in Palestine had deteriorated to such an extent that Clarissa was forcibly included among the British woman and children who were suddenly given 48 hours' notice to leave Palestine, and told that they could take only two suitcases and £20 for the journey home. It was a journey which broke Clarissa's already fractured heart.

This remarkable but highly sensitive creature, now remembered in the family chiefly for the eccentricities of her old age, was a woman of great spiritual insight, one of the very few people upon whose poetic judgment her brother Robert felt that he could rely, and the author herself of a fine collection of poems, *Seven Days*. In her youth she had studied as an artist, before suffering a complete nervous breakdown, brought on by the discovery that the Professor at the Slade with whom she had held hands in Lyons Corner Houses was already married, and intended her to be not his wife but his mistress. On her recovery, she had led a curious but reasonably independent life. At one time she had become Secretary to a leading Christian Scientist, whose beliefs she had wholeheartedly embraced; and before the War she had risen to be head of Children's Broadcasting in Palestine; but the shock of losing her home in Jerusalem was extreme.

Clarissa arrived back in England to find us all suffering from the bitterly cold winter of 1947, of which my mother's diary gives a vivid impression. It had begun innocuously enough, and she describes very lovingly how I woke up from my morning sleep on 6 January that year, was 'much fascinated' to discover that the world outside had turned white, and made 'funny clucking noises' of appreciation. It was less amusing when it continued to snow for much of January and February, the cold became intense, it was occasionally impossible to get out of the house, there were electricity cuts, my father went down with acute bronchitis (his chest was always his weak point), and the pipes in the house froze more than once.

Dick also returned to England for an operation and some leave – but it was not a long leave. 'Graves Supérieur' as he was known in the family because of a taste for good living which meant that he wore unusually good suits and drank unusually good wine, had been asked to become the Mayor of Jerusalem. As it turned out, he would be the last British Mayor, and he filled his new position with great courage, travelling about Jerusalem with an armed bodyguard in a car whose windscreen was shattered at least once by a would-be assassin's bullet.

And then in August 1947 came the final days of the British Raj. George VI remained by the Grace of God King of England, Northern Ireland, and the Territories beyond the seas; but he was no longer Emperor of India. That vast subcontinent had been violently partitioned into Muslim Pakistan and Hindu India, at a cost of hundreds of thousands of dead, most of them massacred by men who not so long ago had been their fellow-subjects. It was a brutal end to 89 years of a largely benevolent imperial rule which had for the most part kept India peaceful and had given her, among other things, her common language, her civil service, her railways and the rule of law.

I was completely unaware of these events, though they would cast their own particular shadows across my early life; and it is from about this time, in the summer of 1947, when I was one-and-a-half years old, that I can date my own first memories. These are fragmentary, but each fragment is exceptionally clear.

CHAPTER THREE
Waving to the Crowds

The even tenor of our life may have been disturbed from time to time by darker currents from the outside world, but on the whole everything was very secure and predictable. 3, Moreton Road (we never gave it a name) is a semi-detached three-storey red-brick Victorian property on a steeply sloping road in a quiet part of South Croydon. There was at first more room than was needed for our small family, EPB 223 had its own garage just to one side, and there was a delightful garden at the back with well-tended flower-beds, a thriving vegetable-garden and a lawn on which Mummy and Daddy would sit in deck-chairs while I played happily at their feet. It was only a few minutes' walk away from St. Peter's church where I was christened, from Lloyd Park where I was often taken to play, from the shops to which Mummy pushed me in my perambulator, and from the railway station where Daddy caught a train into London every weekday, including Saturdays.

But although Daddy is away a great deal, Mummy is rarely lonely. Through the Young Wives Group at St. Peter's, she has soon befriended other young mothers in the area, including a couple in Moreton Road itself; a cleaner arrives most mornings, sturdy and cheerful and often seen by me with a mop in one hand and a bucket in the other and a cigarette between her lips; tradesmen regularly come to the door to ask for orders; and before long there will be a succession of mostly foreign girls who come as au pairs to help out for a few months at a time.

By now, in this very hot summer of 1947, I am not yet talking myself, but I understand most of what other people are saying: though my parents have the irritating habit of breaking into French if they want to say something private, just as the Welsh villagers of my father's youth would break into Welsh whenever they wanted to say something uncomplimentary about their English overlords.

In any case, I feel safest and happiest as an observer, and there seems to be no pressing need to for me to speak. If I want something, I simply point at it while making a noise: "Errhh" This is mild enough when the need is not urgent, but if I want something badly then the noise becomes louder and more violent: "EEEEERRRRRGH!" I find this most effective. Perhaps I sense that once I begin speaking, I will be opening myself up to a more coercive pattern of parental control. More important, I am very much afraid of making a fool of myself by trying to speak and getting something wrong. In this situation speech may be silver, but 'Silentium est aureum': silence, as the ancient Romans wisely observe, is golden.

During this observational phase of my life, there is a handful of incidents that swim sharply into focus. The first of these occurs during an afternoon when Mummy is planning to take me out to a children's party. Having washed and dressed me, she sits me down in my playpen in the drawing-room and then, after telling me very firmly to sit still until she returns, she goes off to change into her own party finery.

I don't mind being put in my playpen: in fact it is one of my favourite places. Let me explain why. Never having seen anyone else crawl, I have never wanted to crawl myself. My aim is to be like Mummy and Daddy, whom I love so dearly. I never see Mummy crawling around the kitchen. Daddy doesn't crawl into the house when he returns from the office. No, they walk, and I am determined to walk just like them. And being put in my playpen enables me to undertake some serious training in this respect.

Normally, I would think: 'watch me!' as I haul myself up on the inside of the playpen, clutching onto the wooden bars; and then, when I am standing up, 'continue watching me!' as I begin to move sideways, hand by hand, bar by bar, step by step, doing the closest thing to walking that I can manage. You will see that I only stop for a few minutes when I come to the place where set into the upright bars is a special oblong section. Into this have been placed, one above the other, two metal bars along which two rows of six coloured wooden balls can be slid: three yellow, three red, three blue and three green. Moving these as far as possible in one direction, and then back again in the other, I find a strangely absorbing pursuit.

But on this occasion, I have been explicitly commanded to sit still; and you can tell that I must be an obedient child, because for a while I do remain sitting still, looking at the door through which Mummy has gone, shutting it behind her; and wondering how long it will be before her return. After waiting for ages and ages (perhaps as much as a minute) I look away from the door and through the bars to my right. There, very close to my playpen, sitting like me on the carpet, is a shining brass scuttle brimming over with large black objects. These are extraordinarily interesting to me. I have seen them before, but I have never been able to study them at close quarters. They are clearly made of the same material, yet they are all different shapes and sizes, with some smooth and some jagged or serrated edges. After a while, I realize that I can learn nothing more by observation alone and so, putting my hands through the bars, I reach out towards them.

Sometime later, the door opens and Mummy reappears. As I watch her, I am struck for a moment by how very beautiful she looks in her party best. But then, a fraction of a second later, a look of shock and horror appears on her face. "Ooooh Richie!" is all she can manage to say at first. So thorough have been my investigations that I am covered from head to toe in black smears of coal. "Ooooh Richie!" But then an understanding, I might almost say a *conspiratorial* smile crosses her face and uncomplainingly she picks me up and washes and dresses me all over again, and off we go to the party.

Apart from the playpen, by the way, my favourite article of furniture is my high-chair. As with all high-chairs, its primary function is to contain and control a small child at the table. I can easily be lifted up into it, have a bib tied round my neck, and have food put on the wooden tray in front of me in a round china bowl whose interior and tall sides are covered with characters from the tales of Beatrix Potter. But although my high-chair is an absolutely standard item of wooden Utility wartime construction, it has been beautifully designed and is quite magical in its operation. So cleverly is it hooked and hinged and jointed and wheeled that by unhooking it and swinging it open, its two connected parts can be brought back together in such a way that it is completely transformed. What had been a high-chair on four firm wooden legs becomes a low-chair running on wheels with a wooden tray in front of it on which toys can be pushed around or small jigsaws made.

One more incident, this time a dangerous one. Those playpen exercises resulting from my determination to walk have borne fruit and, since mid-May 1947, very pleased with myself according to my mother's diary, I have been 'walking everywhere and not liking to be confined to one room – He likes all the doors open so that he can wander!' And now, on the morning of Sunday 10 August, Mummy is doing something extremely boring in the kitchen, and Daddy is somewhere upstairs and since he is not often at home I have decided that I will go and find him. I therefore make my way out of the kitchen into the deserted hallway and begin climbing up the stairs.

This is an entirely new experience and, as climbs go, it is an epic of heroism, of endurance, and of blind determination to win through. Each huge step looks to me as I approach it like the side of a cliff. Each huge step, carpeted in the fashion of the day down the middle, but not at the sides, and held in place by stair-rods at the back of each step, involves an entirely separate struggle. First, I have to get myself into position, standing upright and leaning against the step; then, with my hands on top of it, I have to begin scrabbling with my arms and legs until I am safely over the edge and lying down on the rough carpet and can begin getting myself into position ready for my assault on the next step. Up and up, step after step, up and up until I have reached the landing at the top of the first very long flight of steps. Filled with pride, I turn to look back at what I have achieved.

"Amazing!" I think to myself. "All that way!" Wishing to savour my triumph to the full, I lean over so that I can see more clearly the distance that I have come. "Who would have believed it!" I think to myself; and then I lean over just a little more, and suddenly I have lost my footing and I am turning over and over as I hurtle downwards until I have landed on my head at the very foot of the stairs with a terrible thud. I suppose the sound of my fall must have been heard throughout the house, because as I look up from my prone position, not yet feeling any pain but quite annoyed at my wasted effort, I can see Daddy leaning over the upstairs banisters and staring down at me with a look of horror on his face. This is exactly matched by the look of horror on the face of Mummy, who has simultaneously rushed out from the kitchen to find me lying on my back at the foot of that steep flight of stairs.

Fortunately, the Graveses have good thick skulls: any small weakness and I would have died there and then. The doctor who came out to the house to examine me could find nothing wrong with the rest of me – no broken bones at any rate, it was my skull which had taken the full force of that tremendous fall. He left with various vague warnings and in the short term the only major difference was that, as if some wizard had waved a magic wand, the next time that I remember stepping into the hallway, wooden gates had suddenly appeared at both the foot and the head of the staircase.

At the time, I was chiefly impressed by how kindly my parents had treated me after an incident that was, after all, entirely my own fault. In later life, however, I have often wondered whether that severe shock might not have caused permanent damage. Because although there are some areas in which I believe that I am in the first rank, from time to time throughout my life I have been horribly aware of odd and inexplicable gaps in my intellectual armoury.

Almost as soon as the doctor had left, Daddy drove Mummy and me down to Rottingdean. On the way, while we were driving rather slowly through the outskirts of Brighton, my parents were surprised to find that everyone was waving to us. When they glanced over their shoulders they could see why. I was kneeling on the back seat looking out through the window and waving to the crowds of passers-by in a splendidly regal manner, and they were waving back. To me, this seemed perfectly natural as well as highly enjoyable, but it seemed to give Mummy in particular a rather unpleasant shock.

On our arrival at Braemar, where Daddy had lunch with us before driving back to Croydon, Mummy was so anxious both about my odd behaviour in waving to the crowds and about the large soft area that had now appeared on my skull, that over the next ten days she took me twice to visit a Rottingdean GP. Much to her annoyance, however, he had 'No helpful advice at all'.

By now, in any case, Mummy was once again heavily pregnant and, as she records in her diary, was feeling so 'very lifeless' that I spent a good deal of our holiday being looked after by my Aunts Ruth and Joan. With the two of them I made numerous visits to the beach and the village duck-pond, went blackberrying up Whiteway, and was enjoying myself so much that my happiness bubbled over and apparently my 'latest trick' was to begin dancing, which I did for the sheer pleasure of being alive.

CHAPTER FOUR
The Arrival of Simon

We had only been back at 3 Moreton Road for just over a fortnight when my mother's waters broke and she was taken into a Croydon nursing home where on the following day, 16 September 1947, she gave birth to my brother Simon William. He was a far healthier child then me and had no trouble in putting on weight; but as was normal in those days my mother stayed with him in the nursing home for another fortnight. As for me: I had been sent down to Rottingdean once again to stay for almost a month with Grandad and my Aunt Joan.

Joan was pretty, with curly brown hair, a cheerful, kindly face and a good figure. She was also extremely practical, a good cook, and a prudent housekeeper: how well I remember the large red housekeeping purse whose contents were guarded so carefully and used so wisely. She was also a keen gardener like Grandad, who was famous for his chrysanthemums, for which in his Southsea days he had won several large silver cups. Joan would have made an excellent wife and mother but she was now an old maid well over the age of thirty and had almost certainly missed her chance of marriage. However, she was a good Christian, and for several years she had been living a life of devoted family service: first as her mother's nurse and now as her father's housekeeper.

It was not until 12 October that I returned home to 3a Moreton Road and finally met my new brother. By the following day, my mother was able to record in her diary that I was 'perfectly sweet with Simon, watching him and giving him sweet little kisses on his forehead'.

Simon did indeed become a very dear friend of mine; but appropriately enough, in view of what happened later on, my first actual memory of Simon is not of happily kissing his forehead, but of him being a source of great anxiety. Look, there we are, Mummy and me, at the foot of Moreton Road, walking home from a shopping expedition in Croydon. Sometimes Mummy would take us out together, pushing us in our formidable Victoria perambulator, so vast that we could sit one at each end and either make happy gurgling noises to each other or entertain any interested passers-by while we were briefly left parked outside any shop in which Mummy had business to transact. But on this occasion, she and I are walking alone together. Simon has been left sleeping in that same large Victoria pram just outside the front door.

Now you can hear that, as we draw close to home, the world is full of almost unbearably loud noise, because a workman in a red shirt and blue dungarees and no ear muffs is stabbing again and again into the tarmac surface of the road just opposite our house with a pneumatic drill. Mummy, who has been happy up to this moment, is suddenly fearful, and while the noise of the pneumatic drill reverberates in waves of brutal and repetitive sound which burst upon my ears with almost shattering force, she leans over me and says: "Richie – be very quiet- we don't want to wake up Sily!".

This came as a great shock to me. I said nothing, but I wondered how on earth any noise we could possibly make could be louder than the sound of the drilling. This was the first time in my life that I had thought of my mother as behaving absurdly; and because I loved her so dearly it also occurred to me for the first time that she like me was a vulnerable person who was sometimes in need of protection. The result was that a few years later, when I heard it for the first time, I would identify very strongly with the hero of A.A. Milne's 'Disobedience', which begins:

> James James
> Morrison Morrison
> Weatherby George Dupree
> Took great
> Care of his Mother,

Though he was only three.
James James Said to his Mother,
"Mother," he said, said he;
"You must never go down
to the end of the town,
if you don't go down with me."

Why did I say nothing? Because my stubborn pride still prevented me from saying a word, as I had no wish to make a fool of myself by speaking incorrectly. Indeed, every effort by grown-ups to persuade me to speak only made me all the more determined not to do so, even when it landed me in hot water, as it had done on 10 September, less than a week before Simon's birth. Only the previous day Mummy and I had met a family called the Lucases on one of our frequent visits to Lloyd Park; and Mrs. Lucas, very likely an acquaintance from St. Peter's, had been invited by Mummy to bring her two boys, 15-month-old Stephen and nearly 3-year-old Grahame, round to tea. There was something on the table, perhaps a chocolate biscuit (I was very partial to chocolate biscuits) which I could not reach and which I particularly wanted, so after a while I pointed at it and uttered such a ferocious "EEEEERRRRRRGH!" that Grahame was immediately reduced to floods of tears.

I guess that had I been born more recently, this refusal to speak would have made me an exciting case study for the child psychologists; and clearly it could not go on for ever. As it was, the turning-point did not come until my second birthday on 21 December 1947, when my Aunt Ruth came up for the day from Rottingdean to help my mother celebrate.

Ruth, who was just as cheerful and as practical as her sister Joan, was an altogether stronger character and appropriately enough she had inherited Ellen's somewhat formidable chin. Her wartime career in the Women's Royal Naval Service (the Wrens) had been distinguished – her Chief had wanted her to go with him as his Principal Secretary to the Potsdam Conference, but she had declined owing to her mother's terminal illness – and in March 1947 she had succeeded in ensconcing herself at the Girl's High School in Portsmouth where in due course she would be Secretary to several Headmistresses.

So formidable was she in this capacity that by the time she retired many years later, the role of Headmistress had been reduced in power, if not in status, to being that of a kind of constitutional monarch compelled to obey the wishes of her Prime Minister. Ruth officially deferred to the Headmistress of the day, while actually running the school. This suited most Headmistresses, for whom in those days teaching was likely to be a genuine vocation, while administration was tedious. They could educate their pupils, which was their duty, their passion, their purpose in life; while the admirable Miss Wickens saw to everything else.

I call her admirable deliberately, because she was undoubtedly a kind of female version of the hero of J.M. Barrie's *The Admirable Crichton*, the Butler who effectively runs an Edwardian household and whose superior qualities are only recognised when members of that household are shipwrecked on a remote island in the South Seas. The principal difference is that Ruth would have been far less deferential than Crichton: the navy had taught her plain speaking, heavy smoking and a good deal of salty language. However, she kept off the rum: she and her sisters had all been brought up to fear 'the Hilder thirst' of which more later.

So: to the morning of my second birthday. Ruth and Mummy are sitting drinking tea near the French windows in the drawing-room. I am standing in the middle of the room, watching them. Behind me, the door into the hall has been left ajar. The two women are laughing and joking and I am suddenly aware that I have become the subject of their conversation.

"It's *time* he was talking, isn't it?" Ruth is teasing Mummy, and I don't like it.

Mummy is flustered and embarrassed and eventually she says: "But I tell you, he understands everything I say!"

"No, he doesn't!"

"Yes, he does!" She turns to me in desperation. "Richie! Richie, go and shut the door!"

I am now absolutely furious with my aunt. I stride over to the door, and slam it shut, and then I turn round and shout out at the top of my voice "Yeth!"

The two of them look at me in utter astonishment. Then they burst out laughing and crying. I have done the right thing – Mummy's embarrassment is over. "I told you", she says proudly.

As for me, now that I have started talking, there is no stopping me; any word that I hear for the first time I immediately repeat, and by the end of January I have acquired a considerable vocabulary. I have even started calling after our new daily maid Miss Page in a somewhat lordly fashion: "Page! Page!"

The winter is once again cruel, with thick snow, some of which Daddy transforms into a snow-lady called Tabitha Topplebody in whom I show a keen interest; and when towards the end of March 1948 the weather improves, Mummy takes Simon and me by train down to Rottingdean for an Easter holiday, which I mention only because it begins with an utterly terrifying experience.

We have hardly stepped onto one of the platforms at East Croydon Station when I see a monstrous black dragon-like steam-engine roaring into the station as though maddened beyond endurance and looking for victims. It is coming too fast to escape, and there is no time to warn the others, but I can see some iron seating close by and I run as fast as I can and hide behind it, expecting that at any moment the engine will leave the tracks and hurl itself across the platforms and crush us all to death.

The next moment it races powerfully past, a huge fire raging in its belly and thick loud bursts of steam escaping from its head and sides. Amazingly no-one has been hurt, but I feel that I have been wise to take evasive action, and it takes some time for Mummy to persuade me to emerge from my place of safety.

Not long after we return home again, I find that I am expected to sit up to table at all meals and that, slightly to my annoyance, Simon has permanently replaced me in the high-chair which, though I no longer use it, I have always thought of as mine. As the year goes on, I have other reasons to be jealous. Most obvious, I notice that Simon receives a great deal of praise when in June he begins to crawl. As you know, I have always despised crawling and I have been proudly walking everywhere since the previous summer before Simon was even born. But now, seeing all the admiring glances and hearing the kindly comments, I throw off my anti-crawling prejudices, hurl myself to the ground, and began crawling too. Once again, what a case-study I would have made for any developmental psychologist!

No-one seems to have much minded my crawling around, and my jealousy carried its own nemesis: it is while I am crawling experimentally round the drawing-room one day that I find an electric point into which I stick my fingers and receive such a nasty shock that I am frightened of power points for years afterwards.

My only other attempt to imitate my young brother was still more of a failure, in that it led to my receiving one of the only really severe rebukes of my entire childhood. It happened like this: one afternoon Simon and I were out in the garden, when it suddenly became clear from the revolting stench that Simon had just done what we called 'dupides' in his nappy. By this time, I myself was well past the nappy stage, but I decided to follow his example. Daddy, who happened to be in charge of us that afternoon, cleaned us both up, but made it very clear to me that this was *never* to happen again!

One more glimpse of that summer of 1948 when I was two-and-a-half years old: my mother's eldest sister Barbara, always known as Betty, and happily married for some years to Geoffrey Brockhurst, a banker, was staying with us together with her young daughter Judith, and they joined Mummy and me in an expedition to one of Croydon's most famous shops, Kennards. We often visited this massive Department Store and, on this occasion, when the shopping was done, we all descended to a basement area in which a number of children, all of whom seemed older than me, were being given pony-rides.

How exciting it looks! And it becomes more exciting still when I am lifted up onto one of the ponies, which is being led round by a young woman whose job it is to keep a careful eye on me, so she puts her arm round my waist. Each pony has somehow been attached to a central spindle, so that it can only walk round in a circle in the centre of this large basement; and this curious arrangement meant that for many, many years afterwards I felt uncertain as to whether I had been riding on a real horse, or whether I had in fact been drawn round on a roundabout, like the one hosted in *Carousel* by Billy Bigelow, with the wooden horses magically transformed by my imagination into creatures of panting, snorting, hot-breathed flesh and blood.

There was never any such doubt in my mind about the small wooden horse which was given to me at about the same time by Iwa Blomqvists' mother. Iwa was a Swedish au pair who lived with us for much of 1948; and when her mother came to visit, she presented me with a traditional hand-carved Swedish Dala horse, painted blue and with a flower-patterned saddle. After more than seventy years it is a little the worse for wear, and since our dog Rostov (of whom more later) chewed one of its legs it can no longer stand up unaided; but I have loved it all my life and perhaps I will have it buried with me, my own personal 'Rosebud', a memento from a time when all that was expected of me was to be happy.

CHAPTER FIVE

Waiting for the Tide to Come In and Other Incidents

That summer we went down again to Rottingdean (an Anglo-Saxon name, as Howard Colvin will later teach me, meaning the valley [dean] of the followers [-ing or -ingas] of Rott).

Three glimpses are all that we have here.

Glimpse the first: there I am, standing with my mother on the village Green, not far from the War Memorial, looking out over the village pond. This boasts a small central island and a colony of half-a-dozen ducks. As a great treat I am sometimes given a white paper bag full of crusts of bread which I can break up and throw into the water and watch as the ducks, full of quacking, splashing excitement, thrust their beaks into the water and gobble them up.

On this occasion however we have brought no bread, and I am simply standing at the edge of the water and waiting patiently and expectantly. "Come on", says Mummy, holding out her hand, "it's time to go."

"I can't go yet, I'm waiting."

"What are you waiting for, Richie darling?"

"I'm waiting for the tide to come in."

Glimpse the second: we are being visited by the boy next door. He is about the same age as me and I think his name may have been Hubert; and when he is sent off with me and finds that there is nothing very interesting for us to do in Braemar, he invites me on what he says will be a secret journey back to his house, the one just above us on Steyning Road. The secrecy, the not asking anyone for permission, make this very exciting. Both our front doors are unlocked, and soon Hubert is letting me in through his front door where I find myself in a territory of which I know nothing. I begin to explore. I enter a darkened front room (the curtains are still drawn) full of heavy wooden furniture.

Then I hear Hubert's mother calling out to him, and I notice that Hubert has run off, leaving me alone in the dark. I know that I am here without permission, so Hubert's mother is the enemy: she mustn't find me! Now I can hear footsteps coming along the corridor. Quickly I dive down onto the carpet and hide myself underneath a convenient chair. From this position I can look out and soon I see that feet with gaily-decorated house-slippers on them have come into the room and are advancing in my direction. I hope that I am too well-hidden for their owner to find me – but she does!

Without saying a word, Hubert's mother unceremoniously picks me up, takes me out into the back garden and lowers me over the wall into the arms of my waiting family like an inconvenient sack of potatoes. "This is yours, I think!" she says with a curl of her lips. What ignominy! Though they all seem to find it very amusing. Why couldn't I have been allowed to walk back home like a normal person? In any case, it has been one of my first real adventures, and I often think of it and wonder how it can be repeated.

Glimpse the third: Simon and I are sitting in our pram outside the greengrocer's shop in the High Street when the proprietor's wife comes out with Mummy in tow and says 'It's ever so lovely to see you!' To which, little vermin that I am, I reply grandly: 'My Daddy says that you mustn't say 'ever so!' My poor mother is covered with confusion.

There is no further sight of us to be had until almost the end of the year. Swoop down on 3 Moreton Road on the afternoon of Christmas Day 1948, pass magically through the closed drawing-room windows, and you will find several of us relaxing in front of a blazing coal fire. Simon is out of the room having his afternoon nap, but Mummy sits reading in an armchair on the left-hand side of the fire, Daddy sits reading in another on the right-hand side, and I am playing happily at their feet.

There is a real Christmas Tree in the corner of the room, covered with streamers and tinsel and lighted candles in little tin holders; and since it is only a few days since my third birthday, and Mummy and Daddy have been kind enough to give me separate presents for birthday and Christmas, there are toys and jigsaws and little cloth reading-books all around.

Trains have fascinated me ever since my frightening encounter with that steam-engine at East Croydon station, and my principal birthday present has been a Hornby-Dublo train set. There it is in the middle of the drawing-room carpet. Daddy has helped me to put the track together, its curves and straights forming a large oblong; and when the clockwork engine has been wound up and set down carefully on the track, the three carriages and the Guard's Van have been attached, and the clockwork release lever has been pushed over, to my great joy the train runs happily round and along and round and along for several minutes before needing to be wound up all over again.

My favourite new jigsaw is of a traditional farmyard. It has very thick wooden pieces, which form a framework into which individual pieces showing farmers and farm animals and farm vehicles can be dropped. Just one of these still survives. I am holding it now in the palm of my left hand. It shows a 1940s farmer with a genial and untroubled face beneath a large broad-brimmed hat. He is wearing brown trousers fastened by a broad belt, a white shirt with sleeves rolled-up and open at the neck, and above his shirt a kind of jerkin or unbuttoned rough waistcoat like those worn by cowboys in the Wild West. And since it is the haymaking season, in his right hand he holds a pitchfork, and above his head towers a huge mass of hay, recently speared, which he is carrying towards a new haystack, exactly as he and his predecessors have done for hundreds of years.

But now my attention is focused elsewhere. Metal Humming Tops must have been fashionable this year, because I have been given three of them. Pressing on the central handle of one of them, and then lifting it up and pressing it down again, and then again, harder and harder, to make the Top spin faster and faster, is an engrossing pursuit, especially when each Top gives off its own particular hum; and my aim, my ambition, is to get all three Tops spinning and humming as fast and as loudly as possible at the same time.

I have also been given a box with hundreds of letters in it. I am fascinated by these letters, seeing something magical in them as they dance through my fingers in all kinds of combinations and permutations. But after a while, much to my sorrow, my parents tell me that this present is too grown-up for me. Their word is law, so I make no protest. Much to my sorrow my box of letters is taken away, and I never see it again, though I often wonder what has become of it.

Simon too had received a number of presents, but they were mostly appropriately babyish so I took little notice of them, except for one. The previous year, I had been presented with a stuffed toy called simply Blue Boy, made of stuffing and cloth to which had been glued a coating of fuzzy wool dyed light blue. Because Blue Boy was mine, I loved him, though he was a wholly unrealistic-looking creature, with unnaturally straight arms and straight legs with no fingers or toes, and a flat head with little black buttons for eyes, no proper ears, and no easily discernible mouth or nose. And now Simon was given Panda, the most wonderfully cuddly stuffed toy imaginable, a realistic-looking animal made of black velvet with patches of vivid white and huge black floppy ears and huge smiling eyes. I did my best not to show that I was jealous, but how I wished that Panda was mine!

Still, I had been given a ball which I very much enjoyed bouncing, and when we went out to Lloyd Park, with Simon in the pram and me walking, I insisted on taking three balls with me. One was for Mummy, one was for our current au pair Therese Hoare, described by my mother as 'not at all domesticated but Richard appears to like her'; and one was for me, so that no-one who was old enough to play ball could possibly feel left-out.

CHAPTER SIX

My Lovely Green Tricycle

The scene changes abruptly to the Braemar kitchen, where you can see me sitting at the kitchen table while Aunt Joan tidies away the last of the breakfast. If you look out through the kitchen window, you can see that it's a fine April morning, not a cloud in the sky. Daddy drove us down here to Rottingdean a week ago, on Good Friday, had a bad attack of asthma, and only stayed a night before returning to Croydon. Grandad is sitting at his desk in the front room, doing some paperwork. Mummy and Aunt Ruth have taken Simon out with them to show him off to their Hilder cousins at Whipping Post Cottage. And Aunt Joan and I are about to set out on an expedition to Brighton, with the aim of finding me a tricycle.

First, we walk all the way down to the bottom of Steyning Road, where we turn left along Rottingdean High Street in the direction of the sea. The pavement is excitingly punctuated by numerous large stone steps leading up to the shops and houses, and whenever we reach a new step, I jump up onto it, as I always do, before leaping down to the pavement on the other side. Then there is the dangerous main coast road to cross, and we have to wait for the lights to change, says Aunt Joan, so as not to be knocked down and killed by the cars which go racing past. Then there are more shops, and a café with, just outside it, an intriguing row of low wooden posts, intriguing because most of them are topped by the wooden head-and-shoulders of strange-looking individuals, and one of them by a still more beautifully carved miniature coach-and-horses.

Now we are very close to the sea. We can begin to smell the ozone and to hear the gulls crying and see them winging their way overhead. From here, there are two routes down to the Underwalk just above the sea. The one I prefer involves climbing down some steps to one side of the main roadway. These steps are set behind a flinty wall so high that I know from past experience that I can walk up or down completely hidden and unobserved. But today Joan is wheeling along a push-chair, in case I feel tired.

'Me, tired!' I think to myself scornfully, determined not to use it.

However, because of the pushchair we have to take the main way down, a smooth tarmacadam slope of no possible interest, except that it provides a good view of the forbidden levels of the private hotel grounds over to our right.

And now, here we are on the broad path of the Underwalk, stretching out to the left and to the right as far as the eye can see. I run straight across the Underwalk until I am leaning happily against the low wall (with a broad curved coping along the top) which edges the seaward side. Far down below, some eight or ten feet, is a rocky beach with patches of sand here and there, and a scattering of families with rugs and deckchairs; beyond them the sea; and to left and right old somewhat broken-down breakwaters or groynes separating this beach from the ones on either side.

"Come along", calls Joan. "We've got a long way to go. Would you like to ride in your pushchair for a while?"

I wouldn't like to ride in the pushchair, which I consider to be for babies, and this is 1949 and I will soon be three-and-a-half for goodness' sake. But I run back towards her, and we set off westward towards Brighton.

To begin with the Underwalk remains broad, and to the right (as we pass beneath the hotel) there is a cavernous space with hundreds of deckchairs for rent at 4d per day. But then the Underwalk narrows again to an average width of only ten or twelve feet. To our right, white chalk cliffs begin to loom, held in for the first four or five feet by brick walls in which there are very occasional mysterious doorways set into the cliff face. Above us, in a perfectly blue sky, sea-gulls wheel and cry out and sometimes land on the paving-stones in front of us hoping for food. To our left, there are regular gaps in the sea-wall where flights of steps lead down to the beaches below.

Although I am wearing a sun-hat, the sun is beating down so fiercely that I am becoming very hot and thirsty. I am also a little tired, and at times the pushchair begins to look tempting, but I am far too stubborn to give in to its blandishments, and I keep on walking. Occasionally we meet other holidaymakers, usually a mother with several excited children carrying buckets and spades; until we are so far from Rottingdean that almost the only passers-by are elderly folk out walking their dogs. These, totally uncontrolled, run up and down at top speed, yelping loudly and occasionally providing a little diversion by getting into fights with other dogs and having to be restrained.

At long last, we can see Brighton Pier in the distance; and gradually there are more and more people around us until at last we are in Brighton itself; and here, not far from the Pier, Joan finds a long narrow shop crammed with bicycles and tricycles of every shape and size and asks me to choose which one I would like.

Almost immediately I single out a wonderfully sturdy-looking green tricycle with three large wheels and, most exciting of all, a bell, which I ring several times to make sure that it works. Joan makes the purchase, and before long there I am, in a state of undiluted joy, sitting on my new tricycle and riding it back along the Underwalk towards Rottingdean, smiling broadly and ringing the bell as loudly as possible whenever I am close enough to a potential audience.

Joy is infectious and people grin back at me, and wave to me and shout out encouraging comments. I have almost completely forgotten Joan, the cause of all my happiness, who is still pushing along the redundant push-chair, and who sometimes has to break into a run to keep up with me. I have abandoned myself to the excitement of finding myself in a new and wonderfully independent world in which I have the freedom to choose where to turn my wheels.

Tricycling has instantly become my principal passion. When we return to 3 Moreton Road a couple of days later, my green tricycle is strapped by Daddy to the roof of EPB 223 and comes with us. I want to cycle everywhere. Mummy says that I would cycle upstairs to bed if I could! And the third Sunday in May is a real red-letter day. Not only is Daddy home from the office, but he has promised to take me out tricycling.

Look! There he is, in his long dark overcoat and furry hat, striding masterfully through Lloyd Park. There am I, by his side, riding my lovely green tricycle along a broad path at the very edge of the park: to our left only railings, to our right a long line of trees and beyond them a huge expanse of grass.

It is disappointingly cloudy and cool for mid-May, but this does not matter to me in the least. There I am, pedaling happily away, enjoying, as I have done from the first, the comfortable feel of the rubber grips on the handlebars, the way in which my pressure on the pedals sends the machine forwards in a highly satisfactory manner so disproportionate to the effort involved, and the independence of charting my own course forward. I am also pleased to have Daddy to myself. It's a rare treat to have his undivided attention, and in his presence, I feel fearless and utterly secure.

Then I notice in the distance some rough-looking boys playing a makeshift game of cricket with only some chalk on a tree-trunk for their wicket. As we draw closer, a ball is bowled, the batsman takes a wild swing, connects, and the cricket ball races through the air at top speed in my direction.

Closer it comes, closer – and suddenly there is a loud crash.

Some guardian angel must be watching over me, because I am untouched, but my lovely new tricycle has been struck so hard amidships that several spokes on its front wheel have been bent and one has been knocked right out. The boys rush up to see what damage has been done. To me it is all a great adventure, but they are chastened, apologetic, like naughty children in a Headmaster's study.

Fortunately for them, the damage to my tricycle is outweighed in Daddy's mind by his pleasure in seeing these boys spending part of their weekend playing cricket. APG, a great believer in the importance of sport, had been a pioneer advocate of providing playing-fields for all secondary-school pupils; and my father likes to see a new generation of children playing football or cricket, having himself been a very remarkable sportsman. I have on my shelves a 1935 edition of *Who's Who in Sport* in which he is listed as follows:

GRAVES, John. b: London. c: Old Carthusians, Oxford Univ Centaurs, Brentford, & Casuals A.F.C., Royal St. David's G.C.,

> Hon. Sec. Oxford Univ. Skating Club. Publ: The Boy's Book of Association Football; Herbert Chapman on Football. Has written the scenario of F.A. Instructional Film, instructional articles on Association football, & cricket articles in National dailies. Rec Golf. a: Sandroyd, Cobham, Surrey

In the days when it was still possible for an amateur to play for a football team, he had played for several years for Brentford United; once, because the family home was in Harlech, he had even been tried out as a left-winger for Wales; and as late as the 1980s, in the company of Richard Hughes's former secretary Lucy McEntee, I met a very old man on the streets of Harlech whose eyes lit up when he learned whose son I was. "Ah yes", he said in a vigorous Welsh sing-song of lilting memory: 'Johnny Graves, with his red hair, running down the wing, running like the wind!'

So Daddy had a good deal of sympathy with these amateur cricketers, even if they had been careless and stupid. And fortunately, as I mentioned, I was completely unhurt. As we make our way home, with me on foot and Daddy pushing along my damaged tricycle, I feel only excitement at having been a key player in so dramatic a confrontation.

Nor is my lovely green tricycle out of action for long. The very next morning Mummy walks with the tricycle and me to a bicycle repair shop. Here, amid a welter of damaged machines, the elderly owner listens attentively while Mummy explains what has happened, and tells him how upset I have been (at this I do my best to look suitably depressed) and how lucky it is that I wasn't seriously injured. Then she smiles at him very sweetly and asks what is the best that he can do for us. After carefully examining the damage, he tells her that he will fix it all then and there and make it as good as new for the grand sum of only 1/- (one shilling); and to my mother's delight and mine he is as good as his word.

CHAPTER SEVEN
Gabriele

Therese had now left us, and had soon been forgotten by me just as completely as her predecessor. However, our next au pair was far too memorable ever to be forgotten. She was a distant German cousin of my father's, her name was Gabriele (pronounced Gabriéle) Heim, and on her arrival at 3 Moreton Road on 3 June 1949, my mother commented in her diary: 'Gabriele arrived late in the evening. She is a pretty girl and speaks English quite well and understands very well'.

Calling Gabriele pretty was an epic understatement on the scale of describing Michelangelo as a competent sculptor or Mozart as a reasonably good composer. This young woman of eighteen or nineteen was not merely pretty but, to me at least (since they say that beauty is in the eye of the beholder) very beautiful with her long dark hair and her kind and loving face and the most expressive eyes I have ever seen; and so it was not at all surprising that I fell in love with her at once and have remained in love with her ever since.

Because although infatuation has a very limited life-span, true love, though it may appear to fade a little over the years, never ever dies; a part of oneself remains forever attached to each individual one has truly loved; and this is a case in point. I may as well tell you now the story of how I would meet Gabriele again after an interval of some forty-six years, when she came to pay her respects to my then elderly mother at 26 Hills Lane, Shrewsbury.

Gabriele was still a very handsome woman; and by then she had lived a full and somewhat exotic life, which had included being married for some time to a man whom we would now call a native American, but who in those days was still referred to in the family as a Red Indian. I was delighted to see her again, though I regret to say that meeting me again embarrassed her a little, because although in what I said to her I was simply welcoming and polite, her most unusual depths of perception enabled her to see that I was just as much in love with her as a man of fifty as I had been as a child of three or four.

But then one of my greatest gifts and greatest weaknesses has always been to fall too easily in love; and since, as I remarked just now, a part of oneself remains permanently attached to every true love, the more of these one has, the more fragmented is the outer core of one's personality. Not the inner core, fortunately, unless one is unlucky enough to suffer from a major nervous breakdown and it becomes irretrievably damaged.

In the meantime, there is Gabriele kneeling beside me on the carpet in the living-room and showing me how to arrange thirty or forty conkers in the shape of a magical spiral. This creates a curving road along which I am soon driving my toy cars one by one into a kind of garage in the very centre of the spiral. It must have been Iwa who gathered these conkers the previous September, but for the rest of my childhood I assume that it is Gabriele who has knocked them from the trees, or found them already lying on the ground, and picked them up; and that it is she who has used her fingers to tear open the spiky outer green casings and reveal the beautiful brown conkers with their little intimate patch of white so neatly concealed within.

There is another unusual place for me to push my cars, not quite so magical as Gabriele's spiral of conkers, but exciting all the same. Follow me into the downstairs dining-room, and here you will find a pedestal oval dining-table made of walnut with exquisitely designed marquetry inlays. Beneath the table-top, and just above the point at which four sculpted feet join themselves to the central pedestal, there is a wooden circular curved track that is just wide enough for the smallest of my toy cars to be pushed round it.

It is round this table that one evening (having heard voices and stolen down from my bedroom) I find my parents playing cards with some visitors. As a great treat, I am allowed to sit on Daddy's lap while he plays; but the excitement of this unexpected party is a little too much for me, and later that night I wake again with some terrible nightmare, and I am taken along the corridor into my parents' bed, where I am deeply comforted by the soft maternal warmth of Mummy's arm around me.

Despite being surrounded by so much love, it was in Croydon that1 I first experienced a deep awareness of evil. This emanated from nowhere within or close to 3a Moreton Road, which was always a safe and kindly place. Just over the road, for example, was a house to which I was once taken for a party at which there were lots of delicious things to eat. And a little further up the slope on our side of Moreton Road was another house where my mother had made friends whom we visited occasionally. It had a back garden that seemed to be larger than ours, with room on its lawn for several huge round mysterious stone mushrooms; and there was a girl living there, about my own age, to whom I became secretively and silently attached. But somewhere beyond the top of the hill, where the road branches in two directions, there was a house the very sight of which filled me with terror.

I never mentioned this terror either to Mummy or to Gabriele; but I hated it when our walks turned in that direction, and I always hurried past it, eyes averted, as quickly as I could. To others it may have been just another large detached brick-built house, rather dark, perhaps, in the shadow of huge trees; but whenever I looked upon it, I saw a scene of pure horror, of transcendent malignance. I knew for certain that terrible things had happened in that house and I felt that from it there still emanated some terrifying spiritual evil.

I said nothing about it, because I knew that whatever I said on the subject would almost certainly be treated as a childish delusion, and if there was anything I hated most passionately it was to be treated by some grown-up as being much younger than I felt. Sometime that year, for example, I entered my little bedroom at the top of the stairs and discovered that the plainly painted walls, of which I had approved, had been covered over with a desperately babyish wallpaper showing fairies on a light blue background. "Look, isn't that lovely?" said Mummy, pointing it out.

I held my tongue; but that very night, as soon as I had been safely left alone, and before the paste at the back of the wallpaper had had time to dry, I got out of my bed and tore down as much of it as I could reach. The next morning, I didn't want Mummy and Daddy coming in to see what I had done, so I tried to keep the door shut to bar their way, but they pushed their way in anyway. They seemed a little taken-aback by the scene of destruction that greeted them, but Mummy could not hide the fact that she was also a little amused. "But why did you do, it darling?" she asked me in quite a sympathetic tone of voice. I explained how babyish it had been, and how much I hated it; and she and Daddy very kindly accepted my explanation. There were no recriminations, as there would have been in most families, and the rest of the wallpaper was quietly removed and never spoken of again.

Special children's services at St. Peter's, to which Mummy took me from time to time, had also begun to seem quite annoyingly babyish. Which reminds me that one Sunday afternoon, Gabriele and Simon and I were just setting out down Moreton Road on our way to Lloyd Park, with Gabriele pushing Simon in his pram, when I saw my parents slip out of the house behind us, and cross over the road in the direction of St. Peter's. They looked happy and excited and they were carrying prayer-books and wearing their smartest coats and hats, and so were clearly on their way out to an early Sunday evening service. I protested loudly about not being taken with them. "Are you sure you want to go?" asked Daddy. "It's not a children's service, you know. Are you sure?" I was adamant, and after a while they gave way. So, the three of us went off to church together, while Simon was taken on his walk by Gabriele without me.

Mummy and Daddy were both devout Christians, so perhaps they thought that God was calling me. We are always being told that He moves in a mysterious way His wonders to perform, so perhaps He was. It was certainly a far more memorable experience than any of the children's services I normally attended, though I soon realised that in a way Mummy and Daddy had been completely right to have tried to dissuade me, because the service wasn't at all suitable for children.

For one thing, when we all stood up in our pews for hymn-singing, they and the other grown-ups all towered over me to such an extent that instead of feeling an integral part of the congregation, I felt almost entirely cut off from everything that was happening around me. I knew that it would have been rude to turn round and look at the people in the pew behind; and in front of me I could see nothing at all apart from the soberly-clad backs of the next row of adults. After a while I gave up trying to take part, and when I thought that no-one was looking, I began playing trains with the prayer-books on the shelf at the back of the pew in front of me. Still, I felt glad to have been able to accompany Mummy and Daddy and not to have been cruelly left behind.

I am still not at all sure that it was from anything I learned at St. Peter's that I derived that strong sense of spiritual evil to which I have just referred, though I am sure that evil exists and I believe that, just as Nigel Kneale suggests in his 1972 play *The Stone Tape*, evil deeds and powerful events can somehow be recorded in the very fabric of the houses where they have occurred, and that some sensitive souls are lucky or unlucky enough to be compelled by their proximity to play back that recording.

On a closely related subject, I believe it is important for all children to learn the difference between good and evil, and to develop a conscience – though things can be taken too far, at times a pragmatic streak is essential, and my father was always very scathing about anyone with what he called 'a gouty conscience'. Personally, I have always been one of those sensitive souls who only need a little encouragement to behave reasonably well, at least while we are children, and whose main danger at that age is becoming unbearably priggish; but there are large numbers of people for whom something more is needed; and a small but dangerous minority who can be deterred from evil only by the near-certainty of swift and on occasion merciless retribution. This is simply human nature, and in this respect the doctrine of original sin can be a useful corrective to those who suffer from the happy but misguided delusion that all children are born naturally good.

At the age of three-and-a-half, I certainly suffered from at least three of the so-called Seven Deadly Sins: Greed, Envy and Pride; but my worst fault was most probably possessiveness, which led to the only occasion during my early childhood when I had to endure the shameful horror of having my mother make it clear that she was seriously disappointed in me.

Let me explain: somewhere in the house, I can't see exactly where, there is a glass-fronted toy-cupboard that is mine; and here is the day when a family of visitors arrives, bringing with them a particular boy and a particular girl whom I have never met before, but whom I distrust on sight. I don't mind their being a few years older than me. What I mind is that I only have to meet them to know them to be exactly the kind of careless blundering children who will damage anything they touch. So, when Mummy says to me encouragingly: 'Richie, do show them your toys!' I do what I think is the only sensible thing. This is to run as fast as possible to my toy-cupboard, to stand in front of it with both arms stretched out protectively; and then, when the boy and girl have caught up with me, to shout out as loudly as I can: "They're mine! They're mine!"

Mummy comes up and is clearly shocked. 'Oh Richie', she said, 'That's not kind. You must learn to share.' I stand aside reluctantly, feeling so deeply ashamed that when what I had known would happen does happen, and between them the boy and girl manage to completely ruin several of my toys, I cannot bring myself to say "I told you so!" but suffer the loss in silence, feeling that perhaps I have deserved it.

At least their visit is mercifully short, while Gabriele's seems delightfully long.

Lately, she has been encouraging me to build. First, she fetches from the toy-cupboard my red, wooden cart. This has a wheel at each corner and a string to pull it along and is laden with four rows of large wooden building blocks: green, red, blue, and yellow. [By the way, I still have one of these blocks to hand: it is now a rather faded red, but then it was very bright.] Gabriéle shows me how to lay out a straight row of six blocks with gaps between them, gaps which are just narrow enough for it to be possible to lay on top of them, carefully balanced across the gaps, a new row of five blocks. Above these come further rows of four, three and two blocks; and finally, one block is placed right on the top, completing a grand triangular structure full of power and strength like the cross-section of a pyramid.

Then came our 1949 summer holiday at Erinfa, the large house a little beyond the northern edge of Harlech on the coast of Merionethshire, which Amy and Alfred had built as a holiday home back in 1897 and to which they had later retired. Gabriele went on ahead by train, to make more room for the rest of us when we set out from 3 Moreton Road in EPB 223 on our lengthy drive to North Wales.

CHAPTER EIGHT
Erinfa

Our journey was memorable both for the time it took – some seven or eight hours – and for a very dangerous incident. I was sitting on the front seat next to Daddy, not wearing any kind of restraint; while Mummy was looking after Simon in the back. We had already been travelling for what felt to me like days when, as were climbing a steep hill, we reached a large open tarmacked area with a substantial hotel at its back. EPB 223 didn't like hills much, and we were forced to slow down to such an extent that I somehow got it into my head that we were about to stop for lunch. To my parents' horror, and without any warning, I opened the car door, lost my balance, and rolled out onto the tarmac.

Almost immediately, it seemed, Daddy had picked me up and was rushing me into the hotel in case an ambulance needed to be telephoned. Fortunately, although slightly shaken, I had simply rolled over a few times and was completely unscathed; but I could see that Mummy and Daddy were terribly shocked, realizing (as I did not) that I might easily have rolled under the back wheels and been killed.

Before long (not, much to my disappointment, having stopped for lunch) we were once more on our way north-westward. Our route lay for many miles along the old A5 which eventually reached Shropshire. Here it took us right through the bustling centre of Shrewsbury and later on through the little village of Whittington, where it narrowed almost to a thread as it ran round in a half-circle at the Three Trees Junction beside the stone wall of the Rectory gardens. From Shropshire we headed across the Welsh border where we were briefly in Montgomeryshire; and then we skirted the edge of Llangollen in Denbighshire, still on the A5, before finally, a few miles beyond Corwen, turning south-westward along the A494 towards Bala in Merionethshire. By now I was drifting in and out of sleep, and I'm no longer sure of the exact route we took; but I recall passing the edge of a long lake, perhaps Llyn Trawsfynedd; and then we could see the sea over to our right with a mountainside on our left; and finally there were trees overhead and we turned sharply to the left up a steep driveway and parked on the terrace in front of Erinfa, not far from where a spring of clear water gushed from the hillside.

Aunt Clarissa had heard us arriving, and rushed out and waved at us cheerily. She had a friendly, eager face, with an aquiline nose; her long hair was done up in a bun; and she was wearing what I came to know as her characteristic attire of a skirt, a blouse, a cardigan and sensible shoes. Whenever she was out-of-doors she added a broad-brimmed hat, attached to the hair on her head with a lethal-looking hatpin, twelve inches of sharpened cold steel; and in cold weather she added mittens and a coat. "Welcome welcome John, Mary – and here are the boys! This must be Richard. Let me look at you!" And she bent down and fixed me for a few seconds with a sharp enquiring gaze. "Now then, Mother's waiting for us inside! Come on in!" And she pushed the heavy front door further open and ushered us in.

I have written elsewhere about my first remembered meeting with my grandmother, this old lady in her nineties who:

> Known chiefly to the world as Robert Graves's mother...was still mentally alert, with a commanding physical presence that was all her own.
>
> Standing to welcome us beside the massive oak bookcase in Erinfa's gloomy hall, she might easily have appeared terrifying to me, for besides being tall she was dressed from head to foot in black. However, she radiated such a warm and unselfish love that I felt instantly at home and utterly secure in her presence. Later,

at tea in the dining-room, where I was allowed for the first time to hold a toasting-fork up to a blazing fire, I turned proudly to the table where she sat with my mother and father and several aunts and uncles, and it was clear to me that she was the presiding genius of the company. At the same time, she was strangely unlike anyone I had ever met before: there was something about her that was not quite of this world.

Had I known and been able to appreciate her history, this would not have surprised me. Born in London but then brought up in Bavaria by her German father Heinrich von Ranke, she had returned to London to look after an elderly relative; and after that relative had died, but before Amy von Ranke had been swept off her feet by Alfred Perceval Graves, this saintly woman had wanted to become a missionary. Instead, she had taken on the burden of looking after Alfred's five children, and had then added five more of her own; and now she seemed deeply happy to have so many members of her family around her. She watched me lovingly as, with help from Daddy, I wielded that gleaming brass toasting-fork, and she promised me that before I went to bed, as a reward for making some excellent toast, I should be allowed to choose a treat from the box of chocolates Mummy and Daddy had just given her.

Gabriele had now reappeared; and in a little while she left the room taking Simon with her. Then it was time for me too to say goodnight, and Mummy led me from that brightly-lit and happy gathering by the fire out into the dark and chilly hallway where I immediately burst into tears. "Richie, what on earth is the matter?" I explained that I had been promised a chocolate, but that now it was too late. "It's never too late!" And she took me back again into that brightly-lit world of the grown-ups, where I stood feeling rather shame-faced while she explained what had happened. Grandmother was apologetic and kindly offered me a chocolate, and I took it gratefully.

Mummy and I went out into the dark hallway a second time, and then she led the way up the wooden uncarpeted stairs so that I could be bathed and made ready for bed. The most exciting thing in the bathroom was a large white bathmat, bordered by red pictures of wild animals, on which I stood to be dried. Amy had lived a very frugal life at Erinfa since moving up from London during the Great War, spending nothing at all on maintaining or refurbishing the property, so everything was much as it had always been, and I later found out that it was the very same bathmat on which my father and his siblings had stood to be dried when they themselves were children some forty-five or fifty years previously.

I was then taken to a nearby bedroom of my own, a small dark room very simply furnished with a bed, a chest-of-drawers and a wardrobe. I remember it well because late one evening, I awoke from a nightmare in this strange room and began crying out for Mummy and Daddy. Grandmother came to my rescue, turning on the light and explaining in the kindest possible way that my parents had gone out for the evening. "Don't worry, they'll be back before long!"

But I felt that perhaps they would never find their way back to Erinfa, perhaps I would never see them again- why hadn't they told me that they were going out? And I would not be comforted until much later when they had returned, smart and talkative, bringing with them the happy atmosphere of their outing. At once I felt safe again, and almost immediately I was back in bed, safely tucked up, and fast asleep.

The 'aunts and uncles' who had joined us for tea, included not only my Aunt Clarissa but also my Aunt Susan, and Susan's elderly husband Kenneth Macaulay. Susan herself was a warm-hearted and sprightly woman in her mid-60s whom I immediately loved. Born back in 1885 as the youngest child of APG's first wife, she had no recollection of her mother, the beautiful Janie, who had died of tuberculosis within a few months of Susan's birth. So, when Alfred remarried in 1892, this slight but spirited six-year-old girl was happy to treat Amy as the mother she had never known. She and Kenneth (who between the wars had been a colonial official in the 'Delta Light Railways' in Egypt) had no children of their own and had now retired to a cottage in Harlech where one morning Mummy and I paid them a visit.

I remember a garden full of flowers and a wide colonial-type verandah with red and white roses climbing across it in great profusion. My mother clearly adored Susan, and sparkled in her company; and Susan seemed very fond of my mother, perhaps because she shared and appreciated her mildly subversive tendencies. All I know for certain is that I was wholly captivated by her. Every day for the rest of our holiday I found myself hoping beyond hope that we would visit her again. Sadly, we never did; but many years later, when I was researching my biography of Robert, it was always a great pleasure to come across one of Susan's letters, written in her clear and careful hand, always thoughtful but never dull, with many a witty and illuminating insight showing how well she understood each of the members of her extensive family.

As for Clarissa, whom I had soon begun calling 'Aunt Kwissa', I did not love her as I loved Susan, but I liked her because she seemed to know who I really was and she treated me, if not quite as an equal then at least as an ally; and one morning she woke me up early so that I could join her in an adventure. First, she dressed me up warmly, because it was cold in the mornings; and then we went out through the heavy front door and walked round to the back of Erinfa and there, set in the hedge, was a small iron gate that I had never noticed before. Aunt Kwissa unlatched it and ushered me through.

Immediately we entered into a very different world of closely-cropped green grass, and sloping fields on green hills. Clarissa took my hand and led me along a path which climbed up steeply. After a while we could look back over the top of Erinfa towards the sea, or ahead of us to the mountains. Clarissa had already told me that we were searching for mushrooms, just as she and Daddy had done when *they* were children; and after half-an-hour or so we came to a field where she grew suddenly excited and held her right arm out and pointed with her mitten-covered finger: "Look, look there!"

At first I saw nothing; but then, as we drew closer, I began to see a small circle of white growths upon the grass. "We're lucky – we must be the first people here this morning – look how fresh they are!" And she picked a medium-sized mushroom for me to examine. "It's easy to see that they're white on top", she said; "and the stems are white too. But always look at the gills." She showed me the crinkly underside. "They start out pink, just like this, and then they gradually go dark brown. If the gills are white underneath, they could be poisonous, but these are perfectly safe. Have a look round, and see if you can find any more!" I scampered off excitedly, and she called after me: "Whatever you do, don't touch them if they have any red spots!"

Before long we had returned to Erinfa with a small wicker basket piled high with mushrooms, some of which we ate for breakfast. Having helped to pick them, I thought they tasted wonderful; and I have loved mushrooms ever since.

I never remember seeing either the kitchen or the cook, though both must have existed; but I once caught a glimpse of Amy, all in black as usual, standing in a dark and gloomy room on the other side of the hall from the dining-room. I guess this must have been her drawing-room, and in retrospect I can see that it is a typically Victorian room, crowded with old furniture, the walls covered with family portraits and the windows framed with heavy curtains which reach all the way down to the floor.

Dear, dear Amy – as with all old people she had outlived her own era and most of those whom she had known and cared for in her youth. However, she kept herself so busy with village and family matters (she wrote letters to all her children and step-children at least once every week, sometimes twice) that she had little time to worry about herself. Indeed, so busy was she that by the time of my birth in 1945 she had apparently quite forgotten that before the War she had been diagnosed with breast cancer, and told that she was not expected to live more than another two or three years.

If Amy had a fault, it was that she sometimes gave her children too little room to breathe. They themselves would have disputed this. Whenever Clarissa or Rosaleen or Charles or John talked to me about their mother, they all described her in terms which put her beyond criticism, though Clarissa's "She was a *good* woman!" was spoken so fiercely that it may have pointed to complexities in their relationship which Clarissa could not bring herself wholly to acknowledge.

Charles tells a revealing story about Amy in *The Bad Old Days*, when, writing of his childhood and of his time at Copthorne School, he recalls:

> The time finally came for me to sit for a scholarship. Charterhouse, where Robert had won the top scholarship, was selected. I remember nothing about the exam but vividly recall my anxious

> waiting for the result. Term ended and there was no news. My heart sank. After all, there were one hundred and forty candidates for twelve 'schools'. I returned to Wimbledon. As usual the early train enabled me to reach Red Branch House at breakfast time. While I stood in the hall Mother came halfway downstairs in her red dressing gown and said 'Darling, I'm so sorry for you…' I gulped audibly. I had always been told that if I did not get a scholarship I would have to go to some dim, cheap, minor school, and this was my first and last chance. 'Poor darling,' she said, 'we have just heard that you only got the fifth scholarship…' It was the only unkind thing that Mother ever did to me.

Amy had of course been worried that Charles would be disappointed not to have done as well as his brother. And after all, the family was so intelligent ('the clever Graveses' they had been dubbed in their Wimbledon days, when annoyingly they won all the prizes at children's parties) that great success was always expected of them; and in the dining-room of Erinfa, as an inspiration, there hung an oval glass case containing the gold medals won at Trinity College, Dublin by Alfred's father and two of his uncles.

John, the child of Amy's middle-age (she was 45 years old when he was born) utterly adored his mother, whose strong religious faith and extremely moral and righteous approach to life he had fully absorbed. Sadly, his adoration of Amy had unfairly coloured his view of his still more elderly father, of whom he said very little to me except, just once: "Alfred?" A pause while he wrestled with conflicting emotions. "He expected Amy to do as he wanted. And he was too generous with her money."

Robert, like John, was strongly biased in favour of the mother who once, in despair about his behavior, had written of him "I could almost wish he had died in the war"; and equally strongly biased against the father who had worked so tirelessly to facilitate his literary ambitions, hawking his early poems around the London publishers; and who had bailed him out time and again when he faced financial ruin. Of Alfred I heard Robert say slightingly: "He was all right till he gave up drink"; while the deep love he felt for Amy, against whose conventional upbringing he had rebelled so fiercely, survived his own utterly unconventional religious beliefs to be sublimated in his magnificent *The White Goddess*, in part a celebration or even a deification of the feminine principle.

While we were staying at Erinfa, Simon and I enjoyed spending far more time than usual in Daddy's company. One day he found a ball of string and unwound enough of it to rope us in around the chest as though he was harnessing a pair of horses, and the three of us galloped up and down on the terrace outside the front door with Simon and I neighing and whinnying and Daddy shouting instructions.

Harlech Castle dominated the village, and I longed to visit it, but I said nothing and had to be content with glimpses of its walls and towers as we drove past it on our way down the steep road which led to the flat-lands beneath Harlech. At the bottom of the hill we turned right and drove over the railway line and just past the station before turning sharp left towards the sea.

There were almost no houses down here on the Morfa; to the left of us was the Royal St. David's Golf Club where my father had often played; and to the right of us, nothing but flat farmland; and after about a quarter-of-a-mile sand-hills seeming as tall as houses loomed up ahead of us and the road ended beside a grassy space which served as a car park. From here we had to walk, and there was a rough path which led through the sandhills to a broad beach beyond which waves pounded in from the Irish Sea.

On one of our visits, to my great delight, for I loved her so much, and this was a special adventure just for her and for me, Gabriele took my hand, and led me secretly southward through the sandhills just out-of-sight of the beach. "We're going to surprise the others!" she said. So, we scrambled up and down these great hills of sand until we found another opening which led towards the beach. Then we ran out calling "Hello! Hello!" and Mummy, Daddy, Simon and Grandmother smiled to see us arrive from such an unexpected quarter.

It was normally a lovely beach, wide and sandy and made especially interesting because it contained so many shells of all descriptions, from cockles and mussels and whelks and otter shells to large king and queen scallops and long double-sided razor-bills. But on one visit it was far from lovely, because it was covered as far as I could see in all directions with hundreds and thousands of jelly-fish: disgusting flabby creatures looking like round pink blancmanges, about a foot across, which had been washed up and left high-and-dry. Daddy told me not to tread on them, because they could sting, and I remember being amazed at the complete madness of some holidaymakers who were still bathing in the sea. Didn't they realize that at any moment one of these horrible jelly-fish might bump into them, and sting them to death?

On another visit, it was a hot day and we had been having a picnic. Then Daddy, who had been swimming and wore not the modern trunks but an old-fashioned dark-red swimsuit, perhaps dating from the 1920s that also covered his upper body and looped over his shoulders, decided that he and I should set off on an expedition.

So, he kneels down and I climb onto his shoulders and, leaving Mummy and Simon behind us, we set off happily together along the beach towards the south. He was strong and fit in those days, and he carries me for what seemed a huge distance (about a mile-and-a-half) until we can see in the distance a round harbor by the sea full of sailing-boats. Just beyond it is the stretch of land known as Shell Island, though I don't know this at the time; and when Daddy mentions it another day, I notice that a few yards out to sea there is a stretch of yellow sand still rising mysteriously out of the blue water, and I decide that must be the Shell Island of which he speaks. In my imagination it becomes a place of enchantment, and many years later it will be the image which springs into my mind when I first read Shakespeare's 'Come unto these yellow sands'.

One last glimpse of our days on Harlech beach is of Daddy floating on his back in the sea while I am sitting on his stomach dangling my legs in the water. How safe and secure I feel.

All that marred these visits to the beach was the car journey back to Erinfa, because the hill which led up to the centre of Harlech was so desperately steep in places that I was always secretly afraid that EPF 223 would topple over backwards and crash all the way down to the bottom again. The result was that when our holiday came to an end and we returned to White Hazel, alongside many happy memories I brought back with me a recurrent nightmare. In this I am walking along a pavement beside a road which becomes steeper and steeper, and eventually so steep that I am about to fall over backwards and I only just wake up in time.

On the whole it has been a wonderful holiday; but great changes are now in the air, changes that will shortly lead to our leaving suburban Croydon and a large circle of friends and acquaintances and moving to a lonely and remote place in the depths of the English countryside. However, before we say goodbye to 3 Moreton Road, I should record that one event had already taken place there when I was much too young to remember it, a few months old at most, an event which in retrospect could be seen as being one of the most momentous of my entire life, though no-one could have predicted this at the time.

CHAPTER NINE

Robert Graves and Astrological Theory

To put this significant event in context I must mention that there had always been a strong psychic link between my father John and his eldest full brother, my uncle Robert. When Robert was a 13-year-old schoolboy at Copthorne, a moment had come when without any warning he was suddenly overwhelmed by the feeling that something terrible had happened to his six-year-old youngest brother Johnny, and he sat down immediately to write an anxious letter to their mother Amy, beginning "Dearest Mother, Is Johnny all right?"

At that exact moment, hundreds of miles away, my father was crossing the road outside Erinfa. A car suddenly appeared, being driven round the corner much too fast. Amy, realising that her youngest son was about to be knocked down and killed, shouted out: 'Johnny! Lie down!', and he obediently threw himself onto the road, with the result that he had an almost miraculous escape: the speeding car passed right over him without touching him. When Robert's letter arrived the next day, it was clear to my family that he had received from Johnnie a kind of telepathic communication.

When my father himself told me this story, which he did many times over the years, it was partly to explain how Amy had saved his life; partly, perhaps (though I may be teasing him here), to impress upon me the good effects of unquestioning obedience; and partly I believe in the spirit of Hamlet when he tells Horatio so memorably:

> There are more things in heaven and Earth, Horatio,
> Than are dreamt of in your philosophy.

Given both Robert's interest in the supernatural, and his difficult and complex relationship with many members of his family, I thought this an illuminating story which I should include in my first volume of Robert's biography. Sadly, my Publishers thought otherwise, telling me in no uncertain term that no-one could possibly take my work seriously if I included such obvious rubbish.

In any case, although Robert, as we know, had not been not invited to John's wedding, he had continued, on the whole, to take a kindly interest in his youngest brother's life. So, he was aware of my existence from the first; and when in March 1946 he learned of my early and severe illness, he had written to John from his Devonshire retreat (where he was working on *The White Goddess*, that magical book which will endure as long as romantic poetry continues to be written), to tell him:

> My astrological theory is that a child born on the day before the winter solstice who makes a poor start will make a marked recovery at the spring solstice and be in perfect trim by midsummer.

Within a few days I was indeed making a marked recovery; and two months later, when Robert and Beryl and their children were up in London for a few days en route for Majorca, Robert came out to Croydon to visit me. Looking down at me lying peaceably in my cot, and no doubt pleased to see how accurate his prediction had been, he had said with his usual dramatic emphasis when making a pronouncement of this kind: '**He's** all right', meaning that despite being a member of his family (not normally a recommendation in Robert's eyes by this time), he had decided with a flash of insight that I was the right kind of person, one of the élite whose lives would count for something.

I am told that as he spoke, Robert leaned down and patted me very gently on the head. This was an act of unknown spiritual power, a blessing of the kind that he had been given as a boy and which gives me personally a link through only four people with a monarch who had lived three centuries before me. This was Queen Anne, who had touched the young Dr. Johnson in an attempt to cure his scrofula, then known as 'the King's evil'; Johnson as an old man had patted Walter Savage Landor on the head; Landor as a very old man had given a poetic blessing to the young Algernon Charles Swinburne; and in his old age Swinburne, who had a great affection for small children, would stop Robert's perambulator on Wimbledon Common to pat him on the head and kiss him. And now Robert had given me his blessing, for which I have always been grateful.

Robert's decisions in matters of this kind were exactly like the decisions taken by George Armstrong Custer, that is, they were never to be reversed except in the most extreme circumstances; and this happy prejudice in my favour, conceived when I was four months old and lying in my cot, would have consequences.

Robert came out to Croydon to see me once again on 4 July 1948 during a visit to London to see his ailing mother; and again, I have no memory of the event, though it would have been the first time I met not only Beryl, who would later become his second wife and later still a good friend of mine; but also their young children William, Lucia and Juan. This 1948 meeting was the second in a long and tangled chain of events some of which will be outlined in later chapters of this memoir, a chain of events that will eventually lead to my seeing Robert for the last time when by a strange closing of a circle it is my turn to stand over his cot: not a cot of youth and hope, but a cot of old age in Beryl's study in Canellun; and to my writing a formal farewell when in my comfortable book-lined Shrewsbury study I type these words resigning my pen as Robert Graves's biographer after a labour of ten years, with the words:

> farewell for the last time (unless, as I hope, we meet again beyond that narrow but oppressive sea of which he wrote) both to Robert and to many others whom I love. Farewell, Robert. Farewell, dear Father. Farewell, Rosaleen, Clarissa, Charles and Peggy. And farewell also to that magical Deya of my youth.

BOOK TWO

WHITE HAZEL
1949–1951

CHAPTER ONE

Reaching White Hazel

The lives of those about whom I have written are so deeply intertwined with my own life that I am sometimes uncertain whether I am thinking my thoughts or theirs. And when I remember my two years at White Hazel, these years are so clearly the Golden Age of my childhood, and therefore the time from which I remain in perpetual exile, that inevitably some lines by A.E. Housman come to mind. He writes them contrasting his lonely life in London with the beautiful Worcestershire countryside from which he himself feels in exile:

Far in a western brookland
  That bred me long ago
The poplars stand and tremble
  By pools I used to know.

There, in the windless night-time,
  The wanderer, marvelling why,
Halts on the bridge to hearken
  How soft the poplars sigh.

He hears: no more remembered
  In fields where I was known,
Here I lie down in London
  And turn to rest alone.

There, by the starlit fences,
  The wanderer halts and hears
My soul that lingers sighing
  About the glimmering weirs.

There are other places where my own soul may linger sighing: perhaps that shingle shore along the Sussex coast, where it can revisit the crunching sound of my feet on those ancient pebbles, or where it may pause and watch the waves rising and falling beside Brighton Pier under a somewhat ghostly full moon; perhaps the grounds of Holme Grange where when we were young and happy my brother Simon and I hunted for blackberries and forded streams and spied on strangers and climbed rhododendrons and covered small fires with peat so that we could keep them going by night and by day; perhaps, silent and unseen, it may even haunt a corner of the Hi-B, the Hibernian bar, up a dark and in those days smelly staircase in a building opposite the Post Office in Oliver Plunkett Street in Cork. But the place where my soul is most likely to be found is at White Hazel in the heart of Cranborne Chase.

As I consider this, a confusion of images comes upon me. My mind roams far above that ancient Wiltshire landscape, soaring and hovering and swooping through every season and over every lane and cottage and beneath every grassy hillside. There is the bluebell wood in springtime with its acres of bluebells and its huge piles of empty tin cans. There is the farm in summer, looking from this height with its farm-house and farm-buildings enclosing a large square farm-yard, very like the toy farm we would later acquire. There on the hills I can see a narrow road on which, climbing up towards a remote crossroads, is our black 1930s Ford EPB 223. It comes to a juddering halt. I am inside the car for a few moments, and there in the driving seat is my mother who is learning to drive and finding these steep hills very difficult. "John!" she calls out to my father, "I can't manage it!"

And now I am looking down on a cold January day, snow lying heavily on the ground and on the rooftops, and I see a small four-year-old boy warmly wrapped up coming out of a cottage doorway and, pretending not to be able to see it, striding purposefully and naughtily over the nearest garden bed. I am both the observer and the boy and the cottage is White Hazel and this is our new home: old, beautiful, brick-built, with diamond panes of glass in leadlight windows, and all the doors and window-frames painted white.

But why have we come so far from Croydon to this remote Wiltshire countryside?

The critical factor was that my father had become bored and not a little frustrated with his life in the Ministry of Education. His work there had been important and fully engaging: I mentioned that it was very largely concerned with the implementation of the 1944 Butler Education Act, whose aim was to provide as much equality of opportunity as was possible. After a sound training in the basics such as reading, writing and arithmetic, all children from State Primary Schools now faced Public Examination at the age of 11, after which they were to join the type of school which best suited their abilities: a Grammar School, for the cleverest children who were most likely to benefit from an academic education; or a Secondary Technical School, for children of a more practical bent, who would learn the mechanical, scientific and engineering skills that would lead to jobs in industry and science; or a Secondary Modern School, where children deemed unsuitable for either an academic or a technical curriculum could receive training in basic subjects, such as arithmetic, and could acquire a wide range of simple, practical skills such as woodworking or cookery.

These outcomes weren't set in stone: any late developer could move from a Secondary Technical or a Secondary Modern into a Grammar School after competing successfully in a further set of examinations at the age of 13.

It was this system of education that for more than a generation enabled thousands of clever children to make their way from the humblest backgrounds into such world-class Universities as Oxford or Cambridge. Why, the year I myself went up to Oxford in 1964 there were for the very first time and as a direct result of this system more children from state schools than from private schools. Indeed, Grammar Schools by then were providing such a first-class education that there seemed less and less point in paying for one's children to attend a private school. People had already begun prophesying the downfall of the entire private school system, though it was usually assumed that (even if they were outlawed and had to move to Ireland) a small handful of schools like Eton and Harrow might survive to cater for the sons of the more snobbish members of the upper classes.

Now, the Education Act had provided the framework; but the schools were run by Local Education Authorities in each County, and the role of the Ministry in those days was largely advisory. Eventually this became a little tedious for my father. He was not in any case a natural civil servant, since he wanted everything to work as efficiently as possible, and he therefore had little time for procedures which, however long-established, often appeared to his critical mind to be in need of reform.

Whenever he came across what he thought was bad practice, he would investigate it thoroughly and then compose an extremely long letter to his immediate superior. In it he would analyse the weaknesses of the current bad practice in the most minute detail before proposing an equally detailed set of improvements. However, his proposals were so carefully thought-out and so eminently right and sensible that they utterly infuriated the complacent men to whom he wrote. Reading between the lines of the formal replies of theirs that I found preserved among my father's papers after his death, they clearly wished that he had saved his breath to cool his porridge. Unable to find any logical reason for knocking his ideas on the head, they still put difficulties in his way.

> Dear Graves,
> Many thanks for your interesting thoughts. I am not sure that we have time to pursue them at present, but no doubt we will return to the matter at a more appropriate time. Yours etc.

A reply such as this would have been more than enough to deter a lesser man, but to their horror his superiors found that upon its receipt my father would immediately write them a longer and still more closely argued letter, which threatened to become part of a series to which there would be no end until my father's aims had been achieved. How relieved they must have been when he finally made it clear that he would like to leave the Ministry of Education and run one of the schools that he had been helping to advise.

In practice, and for a very obvious reason, this never happened. Imagine a Church of England Rector advertising for a Curate and finding himself interviewing a senior church official whom he had last met on a visit to Lambeth Palace. The reaction would be much the same as my father received from local education authority men who had met him on their official visits to the Ministry, where he had risen to be head of a Territorial Division in the Schools Branch. They were very polite, but they made it clear that they couldn't understand why he wanted to move from his current position, and they had no intention of offering him work. Their unspoken assumption: "For someone of your standing – too degrading!"

By mid-June 1949, my father had been reduced to making a special journey to Copthorne School, Sussex, the private preparatory school where he had been both pupil and master, 'to see if there were any possibilities for him'. But then, later on in the year, came what seemed to my father like a stroke of luck. H. ff. Ozanne, Headmaster and owner of Sandroyd School in Wiltshire, was looking for someone to fill a most unusual vacancy, and in my father he believed that he had found the very man for whom he was looking.

Sandroyd was then a typical boys' Preparatory School of its day. That is to say it offered a traditional education to boarders of 7 to 13 years of age who came chiefly from middle and upper-class families and whose parents wanted them prepared for one of the Public Schools. Founded in 1888 at a private house in Cobham as a small coaching establishment for boys who were on their way to Eton, Sandroyd was such a success that in 1895 it was moved to purpose-built premises in the same town, and there it remained until 1939. In that year Ozanne, anxious about the potential danger of being so close to London in the event of war, took a lease on Rushmore House, a country house in the heart of Cranborne Chase which was owned by the Pitt-Rivers family but had been vacant for several years.

There was already a distinguished list of Old Sandroydians including King Peter II of Yugoslavia; Prince Ataúlfo of Orleans; Infante Álvaro, Duke of Galliera; and other minor European Royalty. 1948 had even seen the arrival in the school for several terms of the 12-year old King Faisal II of Iraq.

However, a far more prestigious pupil was in prospect. Anxious parents would often need to put their son's name down for a private school not long after his birth in order to be sure of securing a place some seven or eight years later; and at some time back in 1942 or 1943, at any rate not many months after his birth, the then Duke and Duchess of Kent had asked Ozanne to put their third child Prince Michael of Kent down for possible entry in the autumn of 1950 when he would be just over 8 years old. Neither of them came down to see the school, perhaps thinking that when the war was over it would return to its Cobham premises; and by 1949 Ozanne was becoming extremely anxious for them to confirm their choice. After all, it would be the making of his school. The Duke of Kent was a younger brother of King George VI, his wife Marina was the daughter of Prince Nicholas of Greece and Denmark and Grand Duchess Elena Vladimirovna of Russia, and Prince Michael himself at the time of his birth had been seventh in the line of Succession to the British throne.

What on earth could Ozanne do to improve his chances? By this time he had no intention of moving Sandroyd back to Cobham; but he could do something to strengthen his team; and he decided that my father, with his Oxford background, his extensive teaching in prep and public schools, his brilliance on the soccer field and his time as a senior official at the Ministry of Education, was exactly the right man for the job.

He would be taken on as Assistant Headmaster, after which there would be a probationary period, though this seemed hardly necessary in view of the fact that back in 1929 John had taught successfully at Sandroyd during its Cobham days; and he was promised (though not in writing) that if all went well, he could look forward to being officially promoted to Joint Headmaster, with an improved financial interest in the school, in the very near future. Now depending upon whether or not one liked him, Ozanne could be regarded either as extremely prudent, or as a man with very few scruples. He certainly believed in hedging his bets, and while royal approval remained uncertain, he persuaded his new recruit that there were good reasons why the proposed Joint Headmastership should be kept secret from everyone, and especially from other members of the Sandroyd staff.

John couldn't however resist telling Amy, and she was so excited by the news of his great expectations, which reached her in the closing months of 1949, that she immediately wrote about them to many other members of the family, including John's brothers Robert and Charles. John was horrified to hear of this, so Amy quickly wrote another set of letters, begging them all not to give John any special title such as 'Headmaster designate' which might give the game away. In fact, they should not write to him at all at the main school address, but should post their envelopes to John TR Graves Esq., White Hazel, Sandroyd School, Rushmore, Tollard Royal, Salisbury, Wiltshire.

Not long afterwards came the December 1949 morning when, lured on by Ozanne's carefully unwritten promises – but why should one worry, when a gentleman's word was still reputed to be his bond – we all said good-bye to 3 Moreton Road and, climbing into EPB 223, drove down ahead of the removals men to our new home. The journey took us through Salisbury, that prosperous, bustling, lovely city dominated by its tall Cathedral spire, which would soon come to be seen by us (and especially by my mother, who had never been a country girl) as an outpost of civilization.

As the cathedral spire receded behind us, we drove on south-westward, motoring along country roads towards Blandford Forum. Then we turned almost due west along a smaller road sign-posted to Ashmore and Shaftesbury, and soon we were passing through the little village of Sixpenny Handley, which felt more isolated and remote than anything we had yet seen; and indeed, as we drove along these roads, through mile after mile of farmland, fields and woods almost unchanged since Saxon times, we seemed to be driving back into an ancient past. And then at last we turned off to the right into the Rushmore Estate along a narrow lane that led for more than a mile through woods and parkland.

The school buildings had begun looming up in the distance when we turned off to the right down a narrow track leading northward through the grounds of the Estate. After a quarter of a mile we had to stop, because our way was barred by a wide wooden gate. "Minnie, could you?" asked my father. Mummy opened her car door and a great rush of country air blew in, and I was aware that the Croydon smells of tarmac and petrol fumes had completely disappeared and been replaced with the scent of damp grass.

Mummy opened the gate and allowed us to drive through, then closed the gate again and ran after us before getting back into the car. Another quarter of a mile, and a driveway led off through grassland to the right. Through another gate, open this time, and we were in a back yard, with a moderately ramshackle garage to the left of us, and two terraced cottages to our right. This was White Hazel. We came to a halt and Daddy switched off the engine and then for a few moments we were overwhelmed by silence. All the familiar Croydon noises of horns hooting and cars passing and half-heard conversations on the street and trains in the distance, all these were gone. We became aware of birds singing, and the sound of a gentle wind stirring the leafless branches.

"Well Minnie", said my father, breaking the silence in EPB 223, "Welcome home. I think they said we'd find the keys under the mat in the porch."

And then Simon began crying, and soon afterwards the furniture van arrived and the car had to be moved out of the way into the garage. The removals men began bustling to and fro with furniture and packing cases full of books and china and, since everyone was busy, I had time to explore.

CHAPTER TWO

Ricky and Simpkins

To me, the most immediately attractive part of our new home was the garden, which was so much larger than our Croydon garden that it seemed at first to be almost limitless. So instead of following the others into White Hazel, I turned down its western side, and walked across a roughly-lawned area of grass with a nondescript tree at its centre. It seemed of little interest, but when the spring came, I would find, quite near the tree, a patch of small blue flowers of a kind that I had never seen before and to which I took an instant and intense liking. When I asked Daddy about them, they turned out to be forget-me-nots.

"And why are they called forget-me-nots?"

"Because one day, when God was walking in the Garden of Eden, he saw some blue flowers and asked Adam and Eve what they were called, just as you have asked me, but they told him that they had forgotten. So He called them forget-me-nots."

After this explanation, I liked them even more, for which of us wants ever to be forgotten?

To the right of the tree, I could see that the lawn stretched out past a few yards of laurel shrubbery towards a small wicket gate which marked the western edge of the property. Instead of going in that direction, I carried on southward and came to a more formal lawn with, close to White Hazel, a wide flower bed stretched most of the way across it. On my side of the long lawn, which stretched away into the distance, there was an edging of decorative white rocks, then a narrow path, and beyond the path one side of a triangular field, empty but ploughed-up, with its other two sides backed by a rough hedge of trees and shrubs. And half-way along the path, I found a tree with an interesting large hole in its side, about three or four feet from the ground.

When I asked Daddy about what I had seen, he explained that the field was not ours, but belonged to a local farmer; while the tree with the large hole in its side was a hollow tree, so I began hoping that it was the home of a family of owls and I imagined them flying out by moonlight making many ghostly tu-whit tu-woos.

At the foot of the garden, twenty yards further on, I found myself looking over some stout wooden fencing at an enclosure containing a curious structure. It looked like a miniature house but had no windows and only one entrance, from which emanated a rich earthy smell like none that I had ever encountered.

It turned out to be a pigsty; and before long it had become one of the most exciting parts of my week to walk down the garden beside Mummy and Simon on our way to feed the pigs. She would be carrying a bucket of potato-peelings and other food scraps, and when she called out to the pigs, several of them, huge wallowing mounds of pink flesh, would come lumbering across their muddy enclosure, snorting and squealing excitedly and smelling richly of that distinctive slightly decaying smell of fresh pig. When Mummy poured the contents of her bucket over the fence, the pigs settled down to an orgy of snuffling and grunting as they made short work of whatever had been put in front of them, and I watched in a state of fascination so complete that years later I would have a strong fellow-feeling for P.G. Wodehouse's character Lord Emsworth, who likes nothing better than to stand for hours contemplating his prize-winning pig, the Empress of Blandings.

Looking back up the lawn, I could now admire the whole width of White Hazel. Created by knocking together two exceptionally well-constructed semi-detached brick-built farm-labourer's cottages on the Rushmore Estate, it was a handsome building in what was a very remote spot: over to my right, I could see a simple fence and then nothing but a vast expanse of wild woodland.

We would live mainly in what had been the western cottage, so our front door was reached through the little porch on the corner of the house closest to where we had first arrived. Returning to the house and slipping in past the removals men, who were still busy, I found that the inner door led directly into a large square room which covered the entire width of the cottage and would become our main living room.

Immediately to my right was a narrow flight of stairs leading up to a landing before disappearing from view; and beyond that an alcove with a low window-seat built into the wall beneath a small square window, too high up for me to see anything through it apart from the leaves of the tree beneath which I had recently walked. On the far wall ahead of me was a broad mullioned window looking out over the long stretch of garden I had just been exploring; and on my left was a wall with a fireplace with a log fire that was already blazing, and shelved alcoves on each side of it.

I was thirsty now and, as if in answer to my unspoken wish, Mummy called me into the room round to my left. This I saw was our new kitchen: a long narrow old-fashioned room with a huge white enamel sink and a draining board and a wooden kitchen table and chairs and a four-ring cooker and a small larder leading off. I must have been out in the garden longer than I thought, because Mummy had already prepared a high tea of scrambled egg on toast which was waiting for me on the table; and not long afterwards it was time for bed.

Then for the first time I trod that flight of steps which led up from the living-room to a small landing, round the corner, up some more steps and then onto a long narrow passageway from which two doors led off: one of them, to the right, into a small bathroom; and the other, to the left, into a low-ceilinged bedroom with a large double bed which almost filled the room. Mummy explained that this was where she and Daddy would be sleeping, though it was not very private, because to reach my bedroom, and Simon's, we had to walk through another door in the far corner of this room. I rather liked this somewhat primitive arrangement. At 3 Moreton Road I had sometimes felt isolated and vulnerable when I was lying on my bed alone; but here, I believed, I would always feel extremely safe, my doorway guarded by both Mummy and Daddy against all the terrors of the night.

It was my fourth birthday almost immediately, and my favourite presents were a wooden steam-engine painted red and green, which soon found a home in a large toy-box that was kept at the left-hand-side of the fireplace; and a curly-haired golden-brown toy dog with an engaging expression, large floppy ears and short legs and tail, whom I named Shaggy-Woof and who lived upstairs because I loved to cuddle him in my bed at night.

Then came Christmas; and instead of one of the large Christmas trees of our Croydon days, we had a tree small enough to fit on the window-sill in the alcove next to the staircase. Its size was disappointing, but at least it was alive; and when the twelve days of Christmas were over, Daddy placed it out in the garden where he watered it in dry weather so that it would last until the following year.

I was sad at first that Gabriele hadn't come with us. I often thought of her, but she had gone back to Germany from where many years later I found that she had written to my parents in the friendliest manner, asking after me and telling them that she was planning to study psychology at Bonn University. Nor could she be replaced. As my father explained in a letter to Amy, it wouldn't have been fair to ask any other young girl to join us, since we were now living in such an isolated spot that 'She would hardly see anyone but us'. We had also left behind in Croydon the excellent Miss Page, an intelligent woman who had become my mother's friend and companion as much as her servant. She was replaced by a farm-hand's wife called Mrs. Maidment, a hard-working but stolid woman with no artistic leanings whom I remember chiefly working her way through seemingly endless piles of ironing, while listening to popular music on the wireless.

This battery-powered wireless had soon become an important feature of my life at White Hazel. It was sometime in January 1950 that Mummy began switching it on and sitting down in the living-room with Simon and me in time to hear the words, broadcast at exactly 1:45 each weekday afternoon:

> This is the BBC Light Programme for mothers and children at home. Are you ready for the music? When it stops, Daphne Oxenford will be here to speak to you.

This was the start of *Listen with Mother*, a fifteen minute-programme aimed at children under the age of five by which Simon and I (aged two and four) had soon become utterly entranced. We found ourselves singing along not only to the introductory tune, using the invented words 'ming-me-mong, ming-me-mong'; but also to numerous traditional songs and nursery rhymes such as this counting song beginning:

> One two, three four five
> Once I caught a fish alive
> Six, seven, eight nine ten,
> Then I let it go again!

Or the magical:

> I had a little nut tree,
> Nothing would it bear
> But a silver nutmeg
> And a golden pear.
>
> The King of Spain's daughter
> Came to visit me
> And all for the sake
> Of my little nut tree

Or the strange:

> Ride a Cock Horse
> To Banbury Cross
> To see a fine lady
> Upon a White Horse
> Rings on her fingers
> And bells on her toes,
> She shall have music
> Wherever she goes.

Or the rousing:

The Grand old Duke of York,
He had ten thousand men,
And he marched them up to the top of the hill
And he marched them down again.

And when they were up, they were up,
And when they were down, they were down,
And when they were only half way up
They were neither up nor down!

Other favourites of mine included 'Pussy cat, pussy cat, where have you been?'; 'Ring-a-ring of roses, A pocket full of posies'; 'Polly, put the kettle on'; 'Ding done bell, Pussy's in the well' and (although it was a little disconcerting to hear Mummy's name in a nursery rhyme):

"Mary, Mary, Quite contrary
How does your garden grow?"
"With silver bells and cockle shells
And pretty maids all in a row!"

After the singing came a story, prefaced by the memorable words, first ad-libbed by Julia Lang: "Are you sitting comfortably? Then I'll begin." And finally, at the end of every programme, we listened to part of the Berceuse from Gabriel Fauré's Dolly Suite, as lovely an introduction to Classical Music as one could hope for.

But although we were entranced by the wireless for fifteen minutes each weekday, it was largely by books that we were entertained and from books that we learned about the outside world, and our books are kept in the alcove beside the fireplace, on the shelves up above the toybox. Some of these, especially the picture-books, are already years out-of-date. *Farmyard ABC*, for example, a large volume with thick cardboard pages possibly dating from my father's Edwardian childhood, begins:

> A is for Apple and Amy you see
> Has found a nice sweet one
> Just under the tree

Amy wears a frilly white dress and a huge white bonnet and blue buckled shoes and carries apples in a wooden trug; and both this and all the other pictures in the book show an entirely pre-mechanical landscape. Here are horses and carts and milkmaids and water being drawn from a well and a farmyard surrounded by barns and filled with an assortment of cows, lambs, calves, pigs and poultry, all living hugger-mugger, and with no trace anywhere of a tractor or baler or any of the machines which in the real world have already been prominent for at least seventy years. It is only fair to add that another large picture-book does contain one primitive-looking tractor, though it mostly shows pictures of orchards and bluebell woods and meadows full of wild flowers.

Picture books like these are intriguing; but I prefer stories, one of which I have soon made especially my own. From the south-east corner of the living-room, a door leads into a mysteriously elegant sanctum with at its centre the beautiful oval walnut dining-table around whose central pedestal I had pushed toy cars in our Croydon days; and here Daddy will often read to me from Rudyard Kipling's *The Jungle Book*, a thick green volume with a golden elephant on its cover. My favourite story, which I ask for again and again, is the one about the brave mongoose Rikki-tikki-tavi in the chapter which begins:

> This is the story of the great war that Rikki-tikki-tavi fought single-handed, through the bathrooms of the big bungalow in Segowlee cantonment. Darzee, the tailor-bird, helped him, and Chuchundra, the muskrat, who never comes out into the middle of the floor, but always creeps round by the wall, gave him advice; but Rikki-tikki did the real fighting.

Single handed, Rikki saves the lives of an English couple and their small son Teddy, by making their bungalow and garden safe for them. It is in the garden that he first hears:

> A low hiss – a horrid cold sound that made Rikki-tikki jump back two clear feet. Then inch by inch out of the grass rose up the head and spread hood of Nag, the big black cobra, and he was five feet long from tongue to tail. When he had lifted one-third of himself clear of the ground, he stayed balancing to and fro exactly as a dandelion tuft balances in the wind, and he looked at Rikki-tikki with the wicked snake's eyes that never change their expression, whatever the snake may be thinking of.

"I am Nag", he says, "Look and be afraid!" But although Rikki is afraid for a minute, as a mongoose it is impossible for him to stay frightened for any length of time, and in any case he knows that it is his business in life to fight and eat snakes, and he does so – first killing Nag, and then a dusty brown snakeling whose bite is as dangerous as a cobra's, and then Nag's wicked wife Nagaina. In the meantime, he has also found and destroyed Nagaina's twenty-five eggs, each with a whitish skin through which he can see the baby cobras curled up, 'and he knew that the minute they were hatched they could each kill a man or a mongoose'. And the story ends:

> Rikki-tikki had a right to be proud of himself; but he did not grow too proud, and he kept that garden as a mongoose should keep it, with tooth and jump and spring and bite, till never a cobra dared show its head inside the walls.

So strongly do I identify with that brave little mongoose that my mother begins calling me affectionately Rikki-tikki-tavi, or Ricky for short; and after a while my old name Richie has been quite forgotten, and I notice that she only calls me Richard on the rare occasions when she is feeling cross with me and believes that I need to be reproved.

I like the other stories too: particularly the ones about the man's cub Mowgli, the Frog: rescued by Father Wolf and Mother Wolf from being eaten alive by the terrifying tiger Shere Khan; tutored in the Law of the Jungle with many a kindly cuff from the brown bear Baloo; and protected by Bagheera the black panther from Kaa the rock python and from the chattering hordes of monkeys known as the Bandar-Log. In the pages of *The Jungle Book* as read out to me by Daddy I also swim through the oceans of the world with the white seal Kotick in his quest for a quiet beach where the seals can avoid the expeditions of men intent on clubbing them to death; I scramble with Little Toomai on the neck of his elephant Kala Nag up bridle-paths that only an elephant can take; and I experience:

> The dip into the valley below; the glimpses of the wild elephants browsing miles away; the rush of the frightened pig and peacock under Kala Nag's feet; the blinding warm rains, when all the hills and valleys smoked; the beautiful misty mornings when nobody knew where they would camp that night; the steady cautious drive of the wild elephants, and the mad rush and blaze and hullabaloo of the last night's drive, when the elephants poured into the stockade like boulders in a landslide, found that they could not get out, and flung themselves at the heavy posts only to be flung back by yells and flaring torches and volleys of blank cartridges

An important part of my early childhood is spent in this alternative world, a large part of it based on Kipling's experiences in Imperial India, and so well-written that in the forests of my imagination, the great, the terrifying, the wholly un-Disneyfied Shere Khan wanders still.

The selection of children's books on the shelves above the toybox included many of the Beatrix Potter stories, each in a little square volume on whose pages a very few lines of text are beautifully illustrated on the opposite page. These stories led me into another alternative world in which animals could talk, and yet which seemed just as real as the normal world. And if there were occasional words that at first I didn't understand, this contributed to the magical element that appears most strongly in *The Tailor of Gloucester*, with its opening words:

> In the time of swords and periwigs and full-skirted coats with flowered lappets – when gentlemen wore ruffles, and gold-laced waistcoats of paduasoy and taffeta – there lived a tailor in Gloucester.

This story became such a favourite of Simon's that before long Mummy began to call him Simpkin after the tailor's cat. So now we had become Ricky and Simpkin.

My own favourite Beatrix Potter story was *The Tale of Peter Rabbit,* in which Peter naughtily goes off alone on an adventure into the kitchen-garden, with the result that he is almost captured and killed by the ferocious gardener Mr. McGregor:

> Mr. McGregor came up with a sieve, which he intended to pop upon the top of Peter; but Peter wriggled out just in time, leaving his jacket behind him.

Mummy read this to me so often that after a while I knew it by heart; and one morning, when she planned to read it to me again, sitting in the alcove beside a roaring fire, I seized it from her hands just as she was about to begin, and said: "I can do that!" Holding the book in front of me at the correct page, I looked at it while reciting the words:

> Once upon a time there were four little Rabbits, and their names were – Flopsy, Mopsy, Cotton-tail and Peter.

Simpkin looked astonished. Mummy smiled and said to me very kindly: "You're holding the book the wrong way up!" She turned it the right way up, and I began again; and now I could suddenly match what I was reciting to the words on the page, and found that without a single lesson I had learned how to read.

Within a very short time, I had become a bookworm of the most extreme kind, and at first I particularly enjoyed reading from the *Mary Mouse* series by Enid Blyton or from the *Railway Engine* series by the Rev. W. Awdry.

The Mary Mouse books came in a distinctive format: each of their 62 pages was just over two-and-a-half inches tall and six inches wide, and contained two red and black illustrations by Olive Openshaw side-by-side, with up to twenty-five words of text beneath each illustration. The words were simple, the pictures were clear, the stories were intriguing tales of family life (and often ended with a mouthwatering feast), the first of them had been published as recently as 1942, and they very precisely reflected the world in which I was being brought up.

Everyone knows his or her place in the social order, and is happy with it: Mary Mouse herself is an idealized hard-working and loyal servant who happily does all the shopping and cooking and washing and cleaning. She and her husband Whiskers Mouse live with their six little mice children in the cellar of the doll's house belonging to Mummy and Daddy Doll, and their children Melia, Pip and Roundy. Daddy Doll, the pipe-smoking sailor who is at the very top of the hierarchy, understands that it is his duty to look after all those beneath him and to treat them firmly but kindly. As for the children, they are very far from being goody-goodies, and often get into scrapes; but they are well loved and have a very clear idea of what is right and wrong, partly as a result of being proportionately rewarded with chocolate buns when they behave well, and being soundly (but never cruelly) spanked when they behave badly.

The first of Awdry's books, published in 1945, was *The Three Railway Engines*. His stories, set on the fictional island of Sodor, feature numerous railway engines. To begin with, these are all steam engines, each with a face on the front of the boiler, the ability to talk and their own distinctive colour and personality. Henry the Green Engine, for example, is like a very difficult child, and begins by being so disobedient that for a while the Fat Director (later Controller) has him walled up in the tunnel from which he has refused to emerge. James the Red Engine is also badly-behaved and once ruins the Fat Controller's top hat with a shower of steam; but my favourite is Thomas the Tank Engine, a small blue engine who longs to do something more important than shunting coaches round his station yard, and for his good behavior is rewarded by being given a branch line and two carriages of his own. A great attraction of these books is that they are prolifically and powerfully illustrated by Clarence Dalby: personally, I shall never forget his frightening sequence of pictures showing Henry the Green Engine being gradually walled up until he has completely disappeared from view.

CHAPTER THREE
Alarums and Excursions

Inside White Hazel I now had Shaggy-Woof; and outside, very early in the New Year of 1950, we acquired a real family dog called Sandy, so named because he was sandy all over. He was a cheerful and adventurous creature who began to accompany us on all our walks, and Simon and I loved him dearly.

One of my favourite walks began with Mummy opening a gate on the eastern side of the White Hazel yard, just beyond the large vegetable plot that was being created by Daddy digging over the rough grass on that side of the lawn. As we passed through the gate, with me walking and Mummy pushing Simon along in his push-chair, we were immediately in an area of beautiful woodland, consisting mainly of beech trees but with coppices of hazel here and there, and with many ancient pathways leading beneath the trees. Southward, we could make our way along a sunken pathway leading along the edge of the woods. To our left was thick woodland, while to our right was a particularly steep bank, at the top of which trees and tree roots and small shrubs with a long fence behind them, formed what appeared to me an impenetrable barrier.

It seemed to me as we walked along it that it was like an enchanted place from one of the fairy stories which Daddy read to us, where we might meet with strange adventures. And indeed one day, at a point where the path had widened out into a glade, and the bank to the right was steeper than usual, a little old woman in a long dark coat suddenly appeared out of nowhere. I thought for a moment that she was probably a witch, but if so she must have been a white witch, because she was jolly and cheerful and clearly knew Mummy, who addressed her as Mrs. Nanson.

"Where did you come from?" I asked her.

In reply, Mrs. Nanson led me up onto the bank to our right and there just behind the trees and shrubs she showed me a small wicket gate that I had never noticed before. "This is my secret gate," she confided in me. Beyond it was parkland and an avenue of beech trees, with five or six deer not far away. "It's lovely, isn't it!" she said.

Mummy had lifted Simon out of his pushchair, and carried him up the bank, and he pointed excitedly at the deer. "Look!" he said. "White fings!"

Then Mrs. Nanson used a little latch on the far side of the gate to open it, and a moment or two later she was gone. From then on, whenever we walked in that direction I would rush up to the gate in the hope of seeing her again; and although I never did, I was always grateful to her for the excitement of having been allowed to share in the mystery of her secret gate.

To our left, other avenues led through the woods. At the end of one of them, we came across a green field with a caravan in it, which Mummy told me was the home of an old man who lived there all alone; beside another avenue, we found mountains of old tin cans, ten or fifteen feet tall, under the trees. When I asked Mummy about them, she said that they must have been dumped there by soldiers during the war, and since they were hidden in the woods no-one had bothered to clear them away. In the spring, however, these same woods were thickly carpeted with tens of thousands of bluebells. It was the most beautiful sight I had ever seen in my life.

On occasion, we walked all the way through the woods into more open countryside. Somewhere there was a bank of sweet-smelling violets. Occasionally, we reached a house and a shop and a road; and when we turned back, we always stopped at a place where a log and a plank had been made into a seesaw, and I sat at one end, and Mummy helped Simon to sit at the other, and we see-sawed up and down while Mummy sang with us one of the songs we had learned from *Listen with Mother*:

See Saw, Margery Daw,
Johnny shall have a new master,
He shall have but a penny a day
Because he can't work any faster!

Sometimes, we set out in the opposite direction, going out through the gate which lay across the White Hazel drive and turning north-westward. This led us past a nearby farm. Almost exactly like the farm we looked at in one of our picture books, it had a broad gateway beside the road, beyond which was a large square farmyard full of different farmyard animals, with ranges of farm buildings all round it, and the farmhouse in the distance at the back.

Daddy had made the acquaintance of this farmer, who was our nearest neighbour and who owned both the pigsty at the bottom of our garden and the triangular field to one side of it; and when in the spring rabbits began eating the vegetables that Daddy had planted in our new vegetable garden, he telephoned the farmer who arranged for one of his labourers to call on us. He was a man said to be expert at catching rabbits. If true, this would not only help to preserve Daddy's vegetables, but would be a useful addition to our diet at a time when meat was still being rationed.

When he turned up one morning in his rough working clothes, he took off his cap very deferentially and I listened to him tell Mummy that he would gladly set a rabbit snare in our garden. When he had done this, and shown her where it was, he found a large stone and explained to her exactly how she should knock the rabbit on the head to kill it once it had been caught. He and I both noticed that Mummy looked rather sick at the thought of this. "If thee can manage it?" he asked a little doubtfully.

My mother, although a city girl, had far too much pride to relish the thought of being bested by this farm-labourer, and she made it absolutely clear that knocking rabbits on the head was practically second nature to her. He looked relieved, adding before he left: "And then thee'll have wonderful rabbit stew!" Which we did. Once Mummy had steeled herself to being an executioner, she had no trouble with skinning and jointing her victims, and I have never smelled or tasted anything more delicious than our rabbit stews. I still prepare an occasional rabbit stew myself, with carrots and onions and a good deal of sage; and I have often thought that rabbit would be as highly prized as duck or pheasant if only it wasn't so cheap.

Indeed, despite thoroughly enjoying such books as *The Tale of Peter Rabbit* or (later on) such films as *Watership Down*, I am an unashamed carnivore, and I have inherited from my mother a complete lack of sentimental attachment to the rabbits, pigs and other animals that we rear in order to eat. Yes, we should look after them as well as we can while they are alive, and it goes without saying that we should end their lives as humanely as possible: so I refuse to touch any meat that has either been farmed, in my view, too intensively; or that comes from Halal butchers, since I find deeply distasteful their normal practice of zabiha in which, after being blessed, animals have their throats cut without first being stunned. But I would prefer our vast herds of sheep and cattle to continue to have a chance of life rather than to be reduced (as they may be in your day) to small groups living in zoos.

To return to our country walks: these had been much enlivened by Sandy's company, but sadly he was with us for only a short time. Less than three months after his arrival, the day came when we were walking along a nearby lane, and Sandy had run on ahead, when a large lorry, far too large for that narrow lane, thundered past us and ran over Sandy and killed him stone dead. The lorry-driver stopped and was full of apologies as he carried Sandy's limp, dead body to the side of the road and laid it on the bank. Mummy and I appeared to take the death in our stride, but it was a considerable shock to all of us, and poor little Simon was disconsolate. 'Sandy kilt!' he kept saying on the way home with tears running down his cheeks. 'Sandy kilt!' And then, as an afterthought: 'What will Daddy say?'

Not long ago, Amy had sent me a post card with a striking image of two horses standing together, one somehow cradling the other, and she had written that she wanted me always to be as kind to my brother as the elder of the two horses was being to the younger. So I did my best to comfort Simon; and a week or two later, when we were down at Rottingdean for Easter, and Daddy asked me whether I would like to send a message to my Grandmother, I dictated and signed (in very shaky capitals) a letter which told her all about it:

> Darling Granny, It's very nice here and we're kind to each other. We've had a nice dog at White Hazel and we gave him some food and he got killed by a motor-car wheel. And Daddy put some nice primroses in my garden and in Simon's.

Unless she had had some premonition of what would happen years later, Amy need not have troubled to put me under a duty of care: Simon was a good companion to me and I loved him dearly, though he did once get me into trouble. His own hair was straight, without the trace of a curl, and he must have become jealous of the admiring remarks which were constantly being directed at the thick brown curls with which my head was entirely covered. At any rate, one morning I allowed him to use a pair of scissors to cut them all off, and to stuff them into one of the pairs of gumboots which lined the entrance porch. This greatly upset my mother, and was I think the only unkind action of Simon's that I can remember during those halcyon days, though in retrospect he seems to have shrewdly avoided getting involved in any of my more hare-brained schemes.

For example, one morning we had been turned out to play in the garden together while Mummy did some household chores. We could not find anything exciting to do, and I was missing Daddy's company and suddenly began to feel very lonely. Then I had what I thought was a brilliant idea for an adventure. Why not set out with Simon to find him?

Our first task would be to escape from the garden through the small gate on its western side, nearest the road, so I walked over there with my brother and examined it closely. It was fastened by a latch on the outside, but I remembered how Mrs Nanson had worked a similar latch on the secret gate by which she went in and out of the wood, and after several tries I managed to open the gate, and turned triumphantly to Simon and asked him to come with me to find Daddy.

Instead of following me, however, he simply shook his head again and again, his large eyes seeming larger than ever. At length, not wishing to be robbed of my adventure, I shut the gate behind me and set out alone.

I was soon out of sight of Simon and White Hazel, and it was an exciting journey: first along a little grassy path overhung with trees and then down the long road that led towards Sandroyd. The sun was shining and there was no-one to be seen in any direction. After what seemed a long time I came to the wooden gateway that lay across the road, and the gate was firmly shut. But again, I remembered seeing how it had been opened; and although it was hard work I somehow managed to swing it open and then to swing it shut again behind me, for I had already learned that to leave it open was a serious offence.

At length I could see the school in the distance. I had formed no very clear idea about what to do next, but near the back entrance there was a patch of ground with a few trees and a shrubbery, and I hid in the shrubbery expecting that at some stage Daddy would walk past and I would be able to run out and surprise him. After a while a crowd of boys wearing games clothes and football boots came running out, but none of them saw me. Then came a master, who looked in my direction. I ducked further down, but he had spotted me, and came over to haul me out of the shrubbery and ask who I was and what I was doing.

When I told him that I had come to find my Daddy, he smiled slightly, but it was not a very kind smile, and he marched me into the school buildings, down a long corridor which smelt of cabbage and then upstairs and along another corridor until we came to the door of a small room inside which there were five or six other members of staff, standing up and talking and drinking cups of tea. They glanced down in my direction, and one of them took charge, told me to keep quiet and stand to one side of the room, and dispatched someone to find my father. A few minutes later he swept into the room, tall and elegant and very much in command, wearing a dark suit and his long black academic gown, edged with the red of an Oxford Master of Arts, which swept importantly behind him.

Without reproaching me, Daddy began examining me closely on my reasons for my having set out to find him; and when I was unable to provide any satisfactory explanation, he sighed heavily and was soon driving me swiftly home. On the way, he seemed surprised to find the gate shut. "I suppose you must have found that left open when you walked down?"

"No, Daddy", I said.

"Then how on earth..."

When we arrived back at White Hazel, we found Mummy in a state of considerable anxiety over my absence, to which she had only just been alerted. Simon had apparently waited for quite a while by the gate, hoping for my imminent return; and eventually, anxious that I might have disappeared on a permanent basis, he had returned to the house to report to Mummy that I was missing. How he had done this was not however tremendously informative, for he had simply stared at her with his wide-open anxious eyes while repeating mournfully over and over again "Ricky gone – Ricky gone!"

My father must have been a little irritated by the fact that his wife had somehow managed to mislay me; but although he made it clear to me that I was not to repeat the adventure, I sensed that he was quite proud of me for having reached Sandroyd so successfully. 'Though how he managed to open that gate!'

As for my mother, I could see that I had unintentionally given her a tremendous fright, and I never ran away again – at least not from her.

CHAPTER FOUR
Bedtime

Bedtime was a very comforting part of our daily routine. First Simon and I were bathed and dressed in our pajamas and then Mummy would read a story to us. She seemed particularly fond of Beatrix Potter's *The Tale of Mr. Jeremy Fisher*, a very independent-minded frog who lives in:

> ...a little damp house amongst the buttercups at the edge of a pond.
>
> The water was all slippy-sloppy in the larder and in the back passage.
>
> But Mr. Jeremy liked getting his feet wet; nobody ever scolded him, and he never caught a cold!

Then it was time for us to kneel down beside one of our beds (usually mine) to say our prayers, a family ritual which I much enjoyed. First came the Lord's prayer, spoken in a language which attracted me because it was even older and more mysterious than that of Beatrix Potter. "Shall we pray 'in heaven'?" I had enquired eagerly of my mother when I was learning this prayer by heart at the age of three-and-a-half back at 3 Moreton Road; and it runs:

> Our Father which art in heaven, Hallowed be thy Name,

Thy kingdom come, Thy will be done, in earth as it is in heaven. Give us this day our daily bread; And forgive us our trespasses, As we forgive them that trespass against us; And lead us not into temptation, But deliver us from evil; For thine is the kingdom, the power, and the glory, For ever and ever. Amen.

The Lord's prayer lay at the very heart of the Christian culture in which I was being raised. Taken more or less directly from the King James Bible of 1611 (in itself substantially derived from the 1525 translation by William Tyndale), it had been recited in this form for over three hundred and fifty years first by most Englishmen and then, as we spread across the globe, by most of the family of English-speaking peoples. It remains the form of words that I still use, despite whatever version others may be using all around me, not only because the old words are very beautiful, but also because to my mind they convey at least one truth that has been lost by well-meaning revisionists.

God, like the Universe He created, cannot be wholly knowable in human terms. The word 'which' in 'Our Father which art' immediately establishes the idea of God as being far more than human yet, at the time of writing, that truth has been substantially diluted by the near-universal replacement of 'which' by 'who'. Now you may have to do this secretly, my dear reader, because when you read this Christianity may have been temporarily persecuted out of any lawful existence in the place where you live; but should you care to recite this ancient prayer once again exactly as it appears above, then you may take it that I shall be enthusiastically kneeling in spirit by your side and echoing your well-chosen words.

After the Lord's prayer comes our special family prayer, the one certainly used in my father's childhood and possibly invented by Amy or more likely translated by her from a German original of her own youth. This invariably begins:

God bless Mummy, and God Bless Daddy and God Bless Richard and Simon and help us to be good, obedient and truthful children.

Then we are allowed to ask for God's blessing on our family pets. By this time, my father has found us a replacement for Sandy, an affectionate Jack Russell Terrier called Spot, with a loud bark, a constantly wagging tail and a smooth coat that is mostly white but includes the distinctive black spot on his back which gives him his name. So, we continue:

> And God Bless Spot and Sandy and Noony and Solomon.
> [Noony and Solomon, you may remember, being part of my Wickens grandfather's household down in Rottingdean.]

Then we are encouraged to thank God for the day that is ending, as in:

> Richard: And thank you, God, for the lovely walk we had today
> Simon: And for seeing the white fings!
> Richard: And for playing Happy Families!
> Simon: And I won!
> Mummy: Yes you did, darling. And anything else?
> Richard: And for Mummy reading to us!

After which there are hugs and kisses and Simon and I climb into our separate beds and are soon fast asleep.

But now, as if my recurring nightmare about climbing up a steep hill was not enough, I began to suffer from a far worse one, which stemmed from playing one of our most agreeable card games. 'Happy Families' involves a pack of cards whose red backs are decorated with a pattern of tiny cream-coloured rabbit shapes, and whose fronts depict thirteen animal families, each consisting of a mother, a father and their two children, one male and one female. Each animal is dressed up in human clothes, and most of them look reassuringly friendly. How could I not warm (for example) to a family of rabbits dressed up very charmingly as Mr. Bun the Baker, Mrs. Bun the Baker's Wife, Master Bun the Baker's Son and Miss Bun the Baker's Daughter? Not perhaps likely to be friends of ours, though Miss Bun has an engaging smile; but decent, honest, hard-working folk.

However, there is also a family of foxes, and I gradually find something more and more terrifying about Mr. Fox. At first sight, with his elegant top hat and his cane and his green jacket and red waistcoat and tall boots, he looks like something of a dandy. He also has a broad smile. It is the family smile, and looks perfectly wholesome on Mrs. Fox and Master Fox and Miss Fox. But on the face of Mr. Fox, I know instinctively that this smile is utterly false, that he is full of deadly cunning and that he means to do me some terrible harm.

When the cards are dealt and I pick mine up and fan them out in my hand it is always a relief if none of the fox family is to be seen. But sometimes there he is, Mr. Fox, staring at me with his horribly malevolent smile. I discard him as soon as I can, but it is never soon enough.

And then the nightmares begin.

Night after night, I find myself transported to the turfy slope of a very steep dark green hill. It is night-time but a full moon must be shining, because I can clearly see that there are no trees or shrubs on the slope or anywhere else on the hill or on the plain out of which it arises. Then I become aware that other people are standing not far away from me. I don't know who they are, but I can tell that they are anxious and uncertain, and I suddenly realize that, rather like Sarah Connor as she dreams of standing outside a children's playground in *Terminator 2: Judgment Day*, I need to warn them of some terrible approaching danger. But I find myself unable to speak.

Psychologists often say that children as young as four or five have no concept of death, but if my experience is anything to go by, they are completely wrong.

Because I know that at any moment Mr. Fox, wearing his dandified human clothes, is about to come striding over the hill behind us, that his utterly false smile will turn into a deadly snarl and that he will begin killing us all.

Sometimes, mercifully, the nightmare ends there, and I wake up and after a while go back to sleep again and dream no more.

At other times, Mr. Fox himself appears, huge and terrifying and dark with the light of the moon behind him, and we all begin to run screaming down the hill, desperately trying to reach the safety of the small house which has suddenly appeared at the foot of the slope. But Mr. Fox comes on steadily and in the longest version of my nightmare some of us have managed to enter the house, and when we turn to look through the windows we can see Mr. Fox just outside, looming large and licking his lips as he prepares to destroy the house and kill everyone in it, and I wake up full of terror.

CHAPTER FIVE

Medical Matters including one Hospital and an Operation

The title of this chapter is a warning, because I know many people who are quite happy to read about the most frightful nightmares, but who recoil in horror from any mention of hospitals, and can't stand hearing people talk about their operations – and that is exactly what I am about to do. You don't like hearing of such things? Then I should skip the next three or four pages. But before you do, let me put your mind at rest: there was nothing actually wrong with me!

So why on earth was I trundled into an operating theatre at the age of only four years and five months?

As it happens, I was rather old for an operation of this kind, but my parents took it into their heads (perhaps on advice from the local GP) that for hygienic reasons it would be a good plan to have me circumcised. Or, as Mummy and Daddy explained it to me at the time ('Jimmy' being the family word for penis): 'You're going to have your Jimmy turned up, then it'll be easier to keep it clean.'

I had been given a postcard album for Christmas, and they both promised to send me a postcard every day. Mummy even asked me what kind of postcard I would like, so I told her 'one with five rabbits in a wood.' And then, after lunch on Sunday 28 May I found myself being driven by Daddy the eleven miles south to the small market town of Blandford, where I was soon installed in the Children's Ward of the Cottage Hospital. After I had changed into my striped pyjamas and climbed into my bed and said 'Goodbye' to Daddy (who kissed me on the forehead, gave me a jigsaw of some sheep and told me to be brave and to remember to say my prayers) I sat up and looked around.

It was a busy ward with fourteen or fifteen children: some of them (although it was still the middle of the day) lying fast asleep in their beds; other sitting up and playing with their toys, and a few of them actually walking around and looking as though they were almost ready to go home again. Daddy had left me in the care of a proper nurse in a traditional nurses' uniform with an upside-down watch and a starched cap, and she pointed out to me three girls called Vivienne, Lucy and Barbara. All three seemed completely uninterested in me, but I could overhear some of what they said to each other; and from the accents in which they spoke and the language they used I had the strong impression that had we all found ourselves in one of the Mary Mouse stories, in which I clearly belonged with Melia, Pip and Roundy, most of my fellow-patients would have been mice-children.

The very next day I was given a white gown to wear and laid on a trolley and pushed by attendants dressed in white along a white corridor with a white ceiling into the operating theatre, which was also white; and when I was lifted onto the operating table there were three very bright lights above me set in a large silvery disc. At this stage, a kindly doctor began talking to me. He promised me that everything would be all right and then reached out his long arms for a mask attached to a flexible tube, which he began pulling towards me. The mask began at a sensible size but then seemed to grow larger and larger as it approached until quite alarmingly it covered my face completely apart from two eye-holes through which I could still see the bright lights, and just in front of them part of the doctor's head.

And then, as the anaesthetic gas which came through the mask began to work, everything faded away. But instead of falling into a normal sleep, as I had expected, I was conscious of being for a long period of time in some kind of parallel universe in which a strange succession of colours, mainly reds and oranges and yellows, swirled kaleidoscopically about making curious patterns in front of my eyes. Everything else had ceased to exist: I had no body, there was no sound, there were no recognizable shapes and nothing meant anything. I was just beginning to wonder whether perhaps I was dead, and these kaleidoscopic lights would go on forever, when I felt a slight bump, and I was suddenly aware that I was back in my bed in the hospital ward. There at last I fell into a colourless and dreamless sleep.

On waking many hours later, I felt too drowsy to want to move very much, and my Jimmy felt horribly sore and was soon found to be still bleeding and in need of attention. When I finally felt well enough to sit up for some breakfast, brought to me on a tray by another nurse with an upside-down watch and a starched cap, I found that I had picture postcards from both Mummy and Daddy waiting for me. Daddy's, addressed to 'Master Richard P. Graves', read:

> Dear Richard,
> Here is a blackbird:
> you can tell him by
> his yellow beak!
> You must keep it for
> your album.
> Much love from
> xxx Daddy

The blackbird had been painted by Winifred Austin, and over the next few days Daddy sent me more of her work, including a robin and a kingfisher.

Without meaning to do so, I had given Mummy much more trouble. Her first card, 'The Fairy Piper' showed the backs of two rabbits who were looking on at a cheerful scene. A Pixie with long pointed ears sits on a large mushroom and pipes a tune for seven fairies who dance as they fly through the air. 'Darling Richard', she wrote,

> This is the only card
> I could find with rabbits
> although I looked for a long time in
> the shop to find one with five

rabbits in a wood as you had
asked me for. Much love
from Mummie.

I remained in the Cottage Hospital for almost a week. It was a dreary time, because while my Jimmy was still healing I was confined to bed; I continued to be ignored by everyone except the nurses; and it was a little disappointing during the afternoon visiting-hour when I seemed to be the only child without visitors. Fortunately, I never felt entirely abandoned, because every morning brought me three or four more picture postcards: from my Brockhurst relatives came lively paintings by the likes of Molly Brett or Margaret Tempest of pussies fishing, or piglets playing on the beach or mice in a toy-shop; and from home came not only more birds including a bullfinch and a woodpecker, but also several flower-pictures including bright orange marigolds, and deep blue cornflowers.

On my return home on Saturday 1 June Mummy sat on the edge of my bed, to which I remained confined for several days, and asked me how her wounded soldier was feeling? 'Not very well!' was the answer, because my Jimmy was still very sore; and she sighed sympathetically and spent an hour talking with me and helping me to put my postcards into my postcard album.

The very next day, she told me that although I had had no visitors in hospital, I did have a visitor at home; and into my bedroom, much to my surprise and delight, came Mrs. Nanson. This excellent woman had already shared with me the mystery of the secret gate; and now, as a 'get-well' present, she gave me a copy of what immediately became one of my favourite books: Munro Leaf's *Wee Gillis,* which she had rescued from the bookshop where it had been languishing since 1939.

This is the story of a small boy who lives in a lonely cottage in Scotland. His father's relations are all Highlanders, and his mother's are all Lowlanders, and Wee Gillis is uncertain which tradition to follow. So he alternates years in the Lowlands as a cowherd, calling the cows home in the evenings which strengthens his lungs; with years in the Highlands where he stalks stags and learns to hold his breath, which also strengthens his lungs, until the day comes when his Uncle Andrew from the Lowlands and his Uncle Angus from the Highlands take him to a place on a medium-sized hill half-way between the Lowlands and the Highlands, and tell him that it is time for him to choose:

They begin calmly and politely; but then as I turn the page I can see a picture on the right-hand side of Wee Gillis standing quietly between his furiously gesticulating uncles, who are leaping up and down with rage; while on the left-hand side I can read in very large black print about how their quarrel continues to become more and more angry.

There they are joined by a large man in highland dress, a piper who wants to try out some fine new bagpipes that he has just made, but finds that he has made them too big and he doesn't have breath enough to blow them. The uncles, seeing that he is so depressed that he is almost ready to weep, also try and fail; but when Wee Gillis is allowed to try, he has such strong lungs that he is successful.

Wee Gillis has found his vocation: he learns how to make music on the bagpipes; he is a welcome visitor to both the Lowlands and the Highlands; but spends most of his time living in his house between them, and playing the largest bagpipes in Scotland.

As I read and reread this story, I felt that Wee Gillis was very like me: a good obedient child who loves his family and expects them to control him while he is young, but who doesn't want to be always guided by their advice; who secretly yearns for independence. This he finds as a bagpipe player, and this I hoped to find as a writer, for I was already powerfully aware, God knows how, not only that the best part of my life would be intimately connected with the magical world of books, a world which lies at a tangent to everyday reality and yet is more true and real than that reality; but also, that being immersed in this world was the only way for me to learn the hidden secrets which might one day lead to wisdom.

As for my circumcision: it had clearly been such a painful and unpleasant experience for me that Simon was never subjected to a similar ordeal and so, in the schoolboy parlance of the day, we had in the family one roundhead (me) and one cavalier (Simon). This would very much annoy me once I began learning about the English Civil War since, despite being branded a Roundhead by my fellows as a result of my circumcision, I was a natural supporter of King Charles I and the Divine Right of Kings and trying to behave like a gentleman; and dead against the wretched puritanical correctness of Cromwell who first executed the King and then tried to ban Christmas.

CHAPTER SIX

Summer at White Hazel

Spring moved imperceptibly into summer, and our new kitchen garden was now full of a wide variety of vegetables. Earlier in the year, Simon and I had watched as Daddy planted row after row of seeds, marked at the end of each row with an empty seed-packet showing what had been planted there, and skewered into position with a short stick. We ourselves had been encouraged now and then to press a few seeds into the beautifully tilled earth, so I felt a proprietary joy when the seeds germinated and the seedlings began to grow.

Harvesting was even more exciting, and there I am, helping Daddy to pick pea-pods: "Only the ones which are fat enough to have peas inside, remember!" And then, when he judged that we had picked enough and had placed them carefully in his wooden trug, he showed me how to pop open the green pods to find in each a treasure-house of deliciously ripe green peas, sometimes five or six, sometimes as many as nine or ten to the pod. We popped them into a white earthenware bowl, and then Mummy would come out of the house wearing one of her flowery summer dresses to collect them and cook them for lunch.

Peas were good, but runner-beans were better, and I very much admired a long double row of runner-beans climbing up two parallel rows of carefully placed bamboo poles. These were set up in the traditional fashion so that the poles crossed over near the top, and were tied to another long pole which rested on the valley formed by their intersection.

First came the astonishingly rapid growth of the new plants which, once they were established, grew every day by several inches as they twisted themselves round and round and climbed up to the top of the bamboo poles; then came their vivid scarlet flowers, which gleamed in the sun; then (provided that there was enough rain) pods began to set and in the autumn we would enjoy numerous meals of long green beans, sweet and delicious and utterly fresh, having been picked only minutes before being cooked and eaten. They had soon become my favourite vegetable.

From mid-June, the weather had been so warm and sunny that we spent a good deal of time in the garden, and Daddy carried out from the kitchen the long narrow blue-and-white painted wooden table which normally lived there, set it on the lawn beneath the tree at the side of the house, and surrounded it with its accompanying blue-and-white painted wooden chairs. Then he turned his attention to the laurel shrubbery nearby, and cut out of it an entrance and a little room for Simon and me which became our play-house for the remainder of the summer.

From here, one memorable morning, we ventured out to find Daddy relaxing on a deckchair nearby, happily immersed in his copy of *The Times*. We thought that it was a great game to pester him mercilessly with laurel leaves and handfuls of earth, which we explained to him were biscuits and cups of tea. He joined in our game happily enough to begin with, pretending to eat the leaves, and to drink the handfuls of earth, until Simon began protesting more and more crossly: "But you aren't really eating them! Go on! Go on Daddy! Eat them properly! Go on!"

Another time, Daddy produced a copy of a new weekly comic, *Eagle*, whose very first issue had been released back in April. Founded by Marcus Morris, an Anglican vicar who wanted to spread the Christian message more widely, it sported on the top-left corner of each front page a distinctive logo consisting of a large eagle with one wing yellow and one wing black, on a dark red background. The rest of the front page and the whole of the second page (both in full colour) were devoted to an exciting Science Fiction cartoon serial headed: 'DAN DARE – Pilot of the future'.

The drawings by Frank Hampson were amazingly detailed and, when Daddy showed this comic to me, I felt as though I was looking into one small corner of a completely real world. I could see that Dan Dare himself was having a difficult time on some remote planet where, at the end of this week's episode, a tall thin people looking to my eyes rather as though they had been created out of plasticine, are forcing him to walk along a high rope, from which he is in danger of falling to his death. We would have to wait until next week to find out what happened next, and to my sorrow I never did find out, because Daddy never bought that next edition. So we had to be content with the one we had, several pages of which Simon and I hung up like paintings inside our laurel house.

When his own summer holidays began, Daddy had much more time than usual for Simon and me, and in the early evenings there were numerous sessions when he took us into the dining-room and read to us. My new favourite since the spring was Lewis Carroll's 1865 *Alice's Adventures in Wonderland* (commonly *Alice in Wonderland*). One of my dictated letters to Amy had included the words: 'The Alice book is very nice. I don't know why the Queen said 'off with her head' and I don't know why the Gryphon said Will you won't you will you won't you, won't you join the dance.' Daddy read *Alice in Wonderland* to us with such finely-tuned dramatic emphasis, that it was a wholly memorable experience which gave me a life-long taste for the surreal.

Who can ever forget their first glimpse of the White Rabbit as he takes a watch out of his waistcoat pocket before disappearing down the large rabbit-hole under the hedge into which Alice follows him? The magical world into which she falls is one in which eating or drinking can make you larger or smaller, and in which she meets a series of strange beings including a Mouse whose tail inspires her with the intriguing words:

'I'll be
judge, I'll
be jury,'
Said
cunning
old Fury:
'I'll
try the
whole

cause,
and
condemn
you
to
death.'

Then there is the Caterpillar sitting on his mushroom and smoking a long hookah, under whose influence Alice recites some verses beginning:

"You are old, Father William," the young man said,
"And your hair has become very white;
And yet you incessantly stand on your head—
Do you think, at your age, it is right?'

"In my youth," Father William replied to his son,
"I feared it might injure the brain;
But, now that I'm perfectly sure I have none,
Why, I do it again and again."

We also meet a Duchess who holds her child in her arms while singing:

"Speak roughly to your little boy,
And beat him when he sneezes:
He only does it to annoy,
Because he knows it teases."

Then there is a grinning Cheshire Cat which can appear or disappear at will either suddenly or 'quite slowly, beginning with the end of the tail, and ending with the grin, which remained some time after the rest of it had gone'; a mad tea-party, with a March Hare, a Hatter and a sleeping dormouse; a Queen who likes shouting 'Off with his [or her] head!" and a Mock Turtle who sings 'in a voice sometimes choked with sobs':

"Beautiful Soup, so rich and green,

Waiting in a hot tureen!
Who for such dainties would not stoop?
Soup of the evening, beautiful Soup!
Soup of the evening, beautiful Soup!
Beau--ootiful Soo--oop!
Beau--ootiful Soo--oop!
Soo--oop of the e—e—evening,
Beautiful, beauti—FUL SOUP!

Daddy himself loved soup, which he taught us to eat correctly in the nineteenth-century fashion, using the sides of the spoon and *never* the tip, a habit which in polite society was considered to be inexpressibly vulgar and which often, he told us, betrayed someone's plebeian origins. His melancholy and somewhat lugubrious rendition of *Turtle Soup* was unforgettable; and all the lines I have just quoted (along with many others, including Alice's saying that 'A cat may look at a queen') became and have remained an indelible part of the background fabric of my life.

Another of the books from which my father particularly liked to read to us was *The Irish Fairy Book*, consisting of stories and poems by Joseph Sheridan Le Fanu, Eleanor Hull, W.B. Yeats and others which had been selected by my grandfather Alfred Perceval Graves and therefore, as Daddy showed me, had APG's name upon its cover. This was the moment when I first became aware that the name of Graves and the world of literature were inextricably intertwined. Later on, my Uncle Charles Graves would put this connection very memorably, when he said to me with a somewhat rueful smile: "If only the Graves family had never existed, there would be a great many more trees!"

In any case, it was in that inner sanctum of my father's, far more so than during my visits to Erinfa, that APG made himself known to me. Although he had died fourteen years before I was born, so I had never heard for myself his soft Irish brogue, he remained, like many of my ancestors, a living presence within our family circle. I already knew that one of the only things that ever made him angry was if one turned down the corner of a page to mark the place that one had reached in a book; and from a very early age I scrupulously avoided doing so in case he should suddenly stride into the room full of red-haired Irish rage.

In his introduction to *The Irish Fairy Book*, APG tells us that the Gaelic peasant 'is a mystic, and believes not only in this world, and the world to come, but in that other world which is the world of Faery, and which exercises an extraordinary influence upon many actions of his life.' This magical realm, with its mermaids, leprechauns, treasure-guarding cats and wild banshees came to seem utterly real to me; and these stories and poems, which could probably be read to children today only in a heavily sanitized version, were an excellent preparation for the adult world for a sensitive and imaginative child such as me, since within the safe context of a family reading I was able to learn about horror as well as delight; hatred as well as love; evil as well as good and extreme danger as well as security.

I would learn much later that APG in his childhood had been just as sensitive and just as much of a bookworm as me. When he was only five years old, searching for fresh reading material, he was in the habit of stealing into his father's study where the opening lines of Spenser's *The Faerie Queen* had immediately captured his interest:

> A gentle Knight was pricking on the plaine,
> Ycladd in mightie armes and silver shielde,
> Whereon old dints of deepe woundes did remaine,
> The cruell markes of many' a bloody fielde;
> Yet armes till that time did he never wield.

Over many secret assignations, despite the difficulties of its Elizabethan English, Alfred had read this great work from cover to cover, with the result that:

> Night after night before I went to sleep I would see the most vivid processions of knights and ladies, giants and dwarfs moving afoot or on horseback across the darkened walls of my nursery. These visions were not always pleasant ones. Often the light on the point of a spear or the jewel in a queen's crown would suddenly expand into a hideous face, which even my tightly closed eyes could not shut out.

In our own daily life, the most magical feature of Cranborne Chase was its herds of deer. I mentioned seeing them from the secret gate at the edge of the bluebell wood, and from time to time we would catch glimpses from the car of Simon's 'White Fings' as he jabbed an excited finger in their direction. And although taking us on walks was normally Mummy's responsibility, one day Daddy decided that he would give us a treat and show Simon and me the 'White Fings' at close quarters.

So, we set out with him on a long walk through a part of the local woods that I had never seen before. Daddy was wearing his gardening clothes – stout shoes and blue shorts and a white shirt. After a while there were trees all round us and little sight of the sky overhead. Then we came to a clearing. "Now wait here boys," said Daddy, "and I'll drive the deer past you. And remember – whatever you do, stay here and don't move!" And away he strode at great speed until within a few moments we had completely lost sight of him.

We waited there, Simon and I, all alone, and time passed.

As you know, we prayed every night to be 'good, obedient and truthful children', and we certainly wanted to be obedient, but when more time passed and there was still no sign of Daddy we both began to feel frightened. Simon whimpered a little and I put my arms round him partly to comfort him and partly to comfort myself. And then I began to think: 'Suppose the deer are driven past us, what's to stop them from trampling us to death? And in any case, how can Daddy be sure of ever finding us again in the middle of this endless wood?'

More time passed. There was no sound apart from a combination of Simon's whimpering and the light rustling of the leaves, and then, alarmingly, the story of the Babes in the Wood flashed into my mind. You don't know it? It's a traditional so-called children's story in which a wicked uncle hires two murderers, and it ends with the two small children they have been hired to kill, being left alone in a wood and dying of hunger; and for a moment I imagined Simon and me lying dead under the leaves. We were clearly in a very dangerous place and, without mentioning my fears to him, I began leading Simon away from the clearing in the direction from which I hoped we had come. Eventually we came through the wood and out onto an open, grassy place which I did not recognize but where I felt much safer.

Sometime later we heard Daddy frantically calling out for us and we called back and when he turned up he seemed very relieved to have found us. "But why on earth did you leave the place where I left you?" I explained that we had been frightened – and although he was clearly disappointed that all his efforts to show us the 'White Fings' had been in vain, he wasn't at all cross with us. I think perhaps he had been a little frightened himself by our disappearance, and he may also have begun to wonder how he would have explained to his wife, who had once mislaid their eldest son, that having reproved her for this carelessness he himself had managed to lose their entire family.

During the summer, there were also occasional excursions to Shaftesbury, our nearest town. A small and sleepy place by Croydon standards, so that it did little to alleviate my mother's increasing sense of isolation, I thought of it chiefly as the place where I was taken to visit the dentist. How I hated and mistrusted him. His front door could only be reached by climbing up the side of a building using a long flight of steps with an iron handrail, which seemed to me to be suspicious enough. And then, after poking around inside my mouth, he decided that I had too many teeth, and that it would be a good idea to remove four of them. Once again I had to be anaesthetized and was taken out of time to the same disagreeably disembodied place I had last visited in Blandford Hospital, and for some indeterminate period I once again watched those seemingly endless patterns of red and yellow light.

At least I could enjoy our journeys to Shaftesbury and back.

On the way there, Daddy drove us along a road high up on a ridge of land, with broad views on each side of it over the Wiltshire countryside; and then we crossed the border into Dorset, and the view vanished and it became much darker as a canopy of trees covered us over, and we began plunging down a road so steep and with so many hairpin bends that it seemed to be a dangerously dramatic journey. I sat in the back turning the end of a window winding handle which rotated on its axis, and imagined that I was steering the car, desperately trying to save as from disaster, as we careered round bend after bend down onto the plain below.

The return journey was less exciting, though sometimes EPB 223 was clearly finding the hill so hard to climb that we slowed almost to a walking-pace, and I had to concentrate all my energy on willing it to reach the top. Fortunately, I was always successful; and once, after a particularly difficult climb, we mysteriously stopped to pick fruit in a roadside garden. This visit was never properly explained to me, and for ages I wondered whether the people who lived there were friends of ours, and, if not, why they kindly gave away their fruit.

In August, Grandad and Aunt Joan came to visit us. It was too hot in the garden for Grandad's jacket, which he had removed; but he wore his habitual waistcoat and gold watch-and-chain and his peaked cap. He had just entered his 70s and was still reasonably fit; and on one occasion he somehow lured or provoked Simon into chasing him round the tree beside White Hazel with a rake, so that he was able to shout out: "Help! Mary! The little monsters! They're killing me!" I remember thinking that this was a little unfair of him, because I had had nothing to do with it; but many years later my mother told me that she thought that whenever Grandad looked at me and Simon, it transported him back to his own childhood, and his close friendship with his brother Harry whom he adored and with whom he was habitually up to all kinds of mischief.

I wonder now whether it was Grandad who, as his visit neared its end, put it into our heads to begin digging to Australia? At any rate, we embarked on this task with great enthusiasm, and had succeeded in digging a substantial hole in the lawn not far from our laurel house before Daddy discovered what we were doing. He was not best pleased, but distracted us by taking us down to the foot of the garden, not far from the pigsty, where he had been scything back some of the long grass in that area so as to provide us with a kind of spiral maze.

I had become more hospitable to visitors than in my Moreton Road days; and when one day two grown-ups arrived unexpectedly with a small boy in tow, I offered to show them the garden. There I am, running happily over a corner of the lawn and heading for the hollow tree, hoping that the small boy will be as interested in it as I am. But then I turn as I run, hoping to give our visitors an encouraging word, and lose my footing. I fall heavily to the ground and as I fall my forehead smashes into one of the white rocks that lines the path which leads to the tree. I am stunned and blood begins pouring everywhere and I can hear one of the visitors screaming.

The next few minutes are rather hazy, though I remember thinking that this accident seems like a very unfair return for my kindness. There is a strong smell of disinfectant as my head is bandaged up. People's voices come from very far away. Telephone calls are made. The visitors fade away and are replaced by Daddy, who looks very grim. Apparently, the visitors were prospective parents and their child, and I heard later that my father was furious with them for having turned up to see him at White Hazel instead of at the school as he had arranged. Now I am being wrapped up warmly and placed in the back of EPB 223 beside Mummy, while Daddy drives us as fast as he can to the nearest doctor's surgery. We are seen as soon as we arrive. The doctor removes the bandaging and examines my forehead carefully.

"I'm not sure what to do for the best. It's a very deep cut. Stitches on their own might be enough, but perhaps we should think of a small operation—"

Mummy breaks in desperately, interrupting him in mid-sentence: "What would you do *if he were your own child?*" It seems strange to me that she is so very anxious, since although I am still a little dazed, I no longer feel in much pain.

"He's certainly had a very nasty blow – he'll be scarred for life. But there's nothing broken. Concussion can be dangerous, of course. I could send him to the cottage hospital and have him kept under observation – but he'd probably be happier at home. Keep a careful eye on him, and don't let him go to sleep for a few hours. If there's any change, let me know at once."

After the doctor had put in a few stitches, we drove home again, more slowly this time; and for several days there were regular applications of a strong-smelling thick yellow ointment. Fortunately, the wound did not go septic. In the short-term, all the white stones were removed from the edge of the path; and the only long-term consequence, just as the doctor had predicted, was that I still bear the scars of that fall, faded a little but still clearly visible in the centre of my forehead.

Not long after this accident, Daddy had to represent Sandroyd at a Conference of the Incorporated Association of Preparatory Schools (IAPS), and first he drove Mummy and Simon and me down to

Rottingdean. Petrol rationing had finally been ended in the spring, and since then there had been much talk of my mother learning to drive so that she could be more independent and feel a little less isolated at White Hazel. While we were staying at Braemar she began to be taken out for regular driving lessons by her cousin Edgar Hilder who lived a little further down Steyning Road with his enchanting wife Jean, a good-looking woman who had the most wonderfully husky voice. On our return to White Hazel, Mummy began having more formal lessons; and since she would need as much practice as possible before taking her driving test, L-plates with a large red L on a white background had soon been attached by Daddy to the front and rear of EPB 223.

At first, Mummy was an extremely nervous driver, and there was one place which gave her particular trouble, a crossroads where four roads meet in open moorland at the top of a steep hill. It is a remote and lonely place, especially on a misty day when visibility is reduced to just a few yards. Here Mummy had to stop on the brow of the hill, and when she tried to move forward again the gears clashed horribly. "I can't do it, John! I just can't do it!" she called out. Once or twice, Daddy had to change places with her and complete the journey himself, but fortunately he was a patient instructor, and indeed he often said that he felt very sorry for Mummy having to take a test at all. "When I first bought EPB 223", he explained to us, "There was no need for a test. The salesman simply drove me round a field for twenty minutes or so, teaching me how to drive, and before long I was off on the open road! Of course", he added, perhaps for Mummy's benefit, "there weren't so many cars on the roads in those days."

By now, Daddy had already begun spending much of his day down at the school preparing for the coming term; but he did not have to set out very early, and one morning after breakfast he wandered down the garden with Simon and me. For some reason (perhaps he had heard that they were about to be harvested) he decided to talk to us about the cabbages that had been growing all summer in the triangular field. We were standing with the hollow tree at our back when he told us how the cabbages had to be picked and then stored carefully until they were needed for eating. Having given us this practical lesson in farming, he was about to set off when he noticed the hollow tree and made some casual comment about it, which we didn't quite understand.

Simon and I puzzled over what Daddy had meant for some time, and eventually I decided that the cabbages needed to be picked by the farmer and then pushed for storage into the hollow tree. Simon sensibly intimated to me with his somewhat limited vocabulary that Daddy might have meant near the tree rather than into the tree, but by this time I had made up my mind and I was adamant.

I wanted to please Daddy so much, and I realized that fate had given me the perfect way of doing so. Simon by this time had lost interest and wandered off, but I began picking some of the cabbages with the intention of pushing them into the broad opening in the hollow tree. It did give me a moment's anxiety when the first cabbage that I treated in this way dropped right down into the darkness where I couldn't even see it, let alone retrieve it. But who was I to question what a grown-up had told me? I worked hard until there were cabbages all the way up to the opening, only stopping because there was no more room. Then I went back into White Hazel to tell Mummy all about what I had done, and how pleased Daddy would be with me.

She sounded very surprised and came out into the garden with me to have a look. "Ricky, are you sure Daddy told you to push them into the tree?"

"Yes, he did!"

When Daddy returned home later that day, he could hardly believe what had happened. The whole story was to him so utterly fantastic that he too needed to walk with me down to the hollow tree to see for himself. He looked inside it and saw the cabbages and groaned and a despairing look settled on his face. It was the look of one who cannot believe that during the comparatively short time he has been away something like this has been allowed to happen. No doubt he was also wondering what the farmer would say when he realized that some of his prize cabbages, which were now well out-of-reach, would not after all be shortly available for sale. Possibly he also felt relieved to think that it was only a short while before I would be spending most of my days a long way away from the cabbages at my first school.

CHAPTER SEVEN

Ashmore School

Mummy was still having driving lessons, so it was Daddy who drove me the five miles to Ashmore School each morning. As we turned right out of Rushmore Park, there was a long stretch of tree-lined road with iron railings on each side, which was famous for being the place where we had once seen a fox running across the road in front of us – happily looking small and harmless and nothing like the fox of my nightmares.

Before long, we passed through the small Wiltshire village of Tollard Royal, whose name gave us our postal address; and then a mile or two later, instead of continuing on our way to Shaftesbury, we turned off westward in the direction of Ashmore. This is another small village of stone cottages and farms, many with thatched roofs. It rests high up on the chalk hills of Cranborne Chase just over the county border in Dorset, and its principal feature is the huge round pond which lies at its centre.

Parking on the grass verge as close as we can get to the north-east corner of the pond, Daddy opens the car door for me, and we walk over the lane and climb up two or three steps to an open gateway. To the left and the right of us there are strong iron railings and ahead of us are the buildings of Ashmore School, on the other side of a broad asphalt playground on which thirty or thirty-five pupils are already milling around.

Daddy hands me over to a woman teacher, and she leads me through an open door beneath the triangular slated roof of the entrance-porch, into what seems to me to be an enormous main schoolroom. Almost everything happens in this room. Here we are lined up to sing at morning assembly, after which we sit behind wooden desks, with several different classes being taught in different corners of the room. We eat here as well, and then after lunch the youngest of us climb onto our wooden desks for an afternoon nap.

Most of the windows are too high up and far away for me to see out of them, but at the far end of the room there are some French windows through which I stare longingly at the grass and trees outside. It is a red-letter day for me when, in the heat of an Indian summer, my class is taken out through those French windows for an outdoor lesson sitting on the grass.

I feel particularly proud of myself for having found a nice little mound to sit on. Unfortunately, this turns out to be an ant-hill and before long the ants, rightly indignant at being sat upon, are angrily crawling all over my bottom and biting me. This is just as painful as they no doubt intend, and my teacher has to pick me up bodily and carry me back into the schoolroom, where my clothes are unceremoniously removed and I am successfully de-anted.

During our outdoor break-times, not yet knowing anyone in my class, and slightly alarmed and intimidated by the packs of swaggering boys who seem to dominate the playground, I tend to gravitate to the woman teacher in charge. She can usually be found sitting on one of the wooden seats that line the inside of the entrance porch, and one morning I tell her all about the pack of cards with which we play Snap at home, and I am delighted when she says how much she would like to see them.

How bitterly I feel her rejection the following day when, having brought the cards in and begun to show them to her, she makes it clear that her interest has been entirely feigned. All she can bring herself to do is to comment "Very nice, dear" before pushing both them and me away.

The lessons themselves are dull but methodical. We learn to chant our ABC and we count up to 10 and do some very simple arithmetic. My class teacher seems surprised that I can read, and that I can already spell my name out in very untidy capitals; and whenever she has time to give me any individual attention, she concentrates on encouraging me to write more clearly.

More interesting things are happening at home, where towards the end of October Amy comes to stay with us for a week. It seems odd to see my Grandmother so far away from her proper place in Harlech, but here she is, very much herself, and radiating the most profound love despite being dressed all in black. What I don't know is that this is the last time that I will ever see this remarkable woman, since the cancer diagnosed before the war is on the march, and Amy is on her way home after staying in Devon with my Aunt Rosaleen while having radiation treatments at an Exeter hospital. Before she leaves us, she kisses my forehead while reminding me once again always to be kind to my brother.

One evening not long after Amy's departure, Daddy announced that as a great treat he was going to drive us all to Sandroyd School to watch a puppet play. It had been a very cold, foggy day and it was a cold, foggy evening and Simon and I had to wrap up warmly before we left the house and clambered into the back of EPB 223. The fog made it seem like a great adventure, with our headlights shining only just far enough ahead for us to be able to see where we were going. When we reached Sandroyd, Daddy led us into the school and we took our seats very near the front of the school Hall. Just ahead of us was the stage, on which a large puppet theatre had been erected, with its curtains closed.

And then the lights in the Hall went down, and the curtains opened, and what followed seemed extraordinary. Remember that I had never been inside a theatre or a cinema, and that like most families in England we had no television set. Why would we? Until very recently, when the Midlands had begun to be served by a television transmitter at Sutton Coldfield, broadcasts had been confined to the London area. So this was my very first experience of watching any kind of theatrical performance.

I found myself looking in upon a strange and entrancing world full of small people dressed in an astonishing variety of costumes quite unlike those worn by anyone in the ordinary world. Other members of the audience may have seen puppets, but I knew immediately that these creatures were completely real and alive. The play was loosely based upon Hans Christian Andersen's *The Tinder-box Soldier*, and the little people were caught up in a dramatic story which involved a soldier returning from the wars, a terrifying witch with a broomstick, secret treasure, a dog with huge eyes, a beautiful princess and a magical tinderbox.

Watching them and listening to them speak as they moved through a succession of realistic interiors was a completely entrancing experience. One of the most memorable scenes involved a small servants' room in which two of the little people were arguing; and at the start of another, the curtains opened on a large gloomy hall lit by a single chandelier with a broad staircase to one side of it down which the beautiful princess was walking. When the play came to an end, and the lights in the Hall went up, I knew that even if I never saw it again, as I never did, behind the final curtain that mysterious world still existed, and would always exist.

Afterwards, we walked out into the cold night air, and found that as well as being completely dark, it was foggier than ever. EPB 223 wouldn't start, the battery being too low; and Mummy had to sit in the driving seat with her foot on the clutch while Daddy grasped the starting crank, and went round to the front of the car with it. Here, as we had often seen him do before, he inserted the crank into a special hole in the middle of the radiator grille. When it was properly engaged, he gave the handle a quick upward pull. This needed a good deal of strength, and fortunately on this occasion it worked on the third or fourth attempt and the engine sprang into life. Daddy got back into the car accompanied by a strong smell of petrol and revved up the engine for a while before switching on the headlights and beginning the drive home. My head was so full of what I had just seen, and it was so exciting to be out in the cold and the dark, that I had nothing to say but kept quiet and snuggled down in a corner of the back of the car, while looking out through the windows as the headlights searched out our path through the encircling night.

Our second Christmas at White Hazel approaches; and at Ashmore School we are visited by the Vicar of St. Nicholas, the local Anglican church a five-minute walk away up the High Street on the other side of the village pond. A youngish man wearing a traditional long-sleeved black clerical shirt and a dog-collar, the vicar stands up in front of us all, and delivers an impassioned speech. "My dear children," he begins,

I wonder whether you realise how very fortunate you are?

Christmas is approaching, the day when we celebrate the birth of our Lord Jesus Christ, and I expect that you will all be having a happy time with your families around you and plenty of good food to eat and heaps of presents to unwrap. That's right, isn't it?

But there are many other children who will have very little to eat, even on Christmas Day and, unless we can help them, no presents at all. So please, tomorrow morning, will each of you bring into school something that we can give away to these poor unfortunate children.

He pauses for effect before continuing.

Now, my dear children, listen carefully. This is very important. I know you may be thinking of giving away something you don't like very much and would be glad to get rid of. But what Jesus wants you to choose is *one of your favourite things*. If you choose one of your favourite things to give away, Jesus will be very pleased with you, because this will be *a real sacrifice* on your part. You will be showing Him how much you care. You will be showing Him that you don't think that because you're so lucky it makes you better than anyone else who isn't so lucky.

Jesus loves us all, and we must do our best to pass on that love not only to our own families, but to everyone else who needs it. My dear children, it is now up to you. You know in your hearts what is right.

And then, after he has led us all in the Lord's Prayer, he sends us home with the words of a traditional blessing ringing in our ears:

The peace of God, which passeth all understanding, keep your hearts and minds in the knowledge and love of God, and of his son Jesus Christ our Lord: And the blessing of God Almighty, the Father, the Son, and the Holy Ghost, be amongst you and remain with you always. Amen.

The vicar's speech had made a tremendous impression upon me. That evening I told Mummy and Daddy all about it, and I added that I knew exactly what I should take with me into school the next morning. It had been for a while by far my most prized possession, a beautiful annual-sized story-book about the adventures of some magical elf, with numerous wonderfully-drawn small pictures with text beneath them on each page.

They asked me a number of times if I was absolutely sure that this was what I wanted to give away – it must have been a special present, perhaps from my Grandmother – but I was adamant, and in the end they allowed me to take it. I have never regretted giving it away, but in recent years I have occasionally searched for it on the Internet, hoping against hope to rediscover its perfection.

By this time, my journeys to Ashmore School had been made more interesting by the fact that I never knew from day to day whether or not we would be stopping to pick up a well-spoken girl called Penelope. She was a year or two older than me, so she was never in my class, but she too was a pupil at Ashmore School, and my parents had met and approved of hers. She lived in a large detached house with a huge garden on the very edge of the road not far from the turning out of the Rushmore Estate, and I loved it when we parked by the side of the road and she ran out with her satchel and joined me in the back of the car. She was just as talkative as me, and we discussed everything under the sun. Once we had a particularly ferocious discussion about whether it was better to be a boy or a girl. I had heard only recently that Mummy was expecting another baby, and that it would be hard work for her, and so I clinched the argument with Penelope, at least to my own satisfaction, by crying out triumphantly: "Well, at least boys don't have to have babies!"

A few days later, Penelope and I were both present at a Christmas party arranged by the school in another large building in the centre of Ashmore. Dozens of us sat on long benches and were wide-eyed with excitement to see down the centre of the table in front of us a mouth-watering selection of large plates laden with sandwiches and jellies and biscuits and every kind of home-made cake, some of them with icing on them. Wide-eyed, because although the war had been over for five years, food rationing for quite basic commodities such as butter, meat and sugar was still in force, when mealtimes came round we were usually ravenous, and feasts like this one were very much appreciated. A by-product of this austerity, which we didn't appreciate at the time, was that we were all much healthier. Even a moderately plump child was a great rarity, and seriously overweight children like the fictional Billy Bunter were hardly to be found in real life.

Sadly, Daddy collected me before it was all over. But although he had chosen this little village school for me to attend, and although it contained a number of really well-brought up children like Penelope, whom I liked very much, I have the feeling that it may have contained too high a proportion of rough-and-ready labourers' children for him to be entirely happy with his choice. I certainly don't recall any other children being invited round to celebrate my fifth birthday on 21 December that year.

What I can see very clearly is White Hazel after the first heavy snowfall of the winter. When I woke up there was a peculiar light behind the curtains; and when I opened my window and looked out, I could see that the sky was full of low-lying clouds which were white with a touch of yellow; and beneath them the whole world was soft and silent and blanketed with thick white snow.

As soon as I could put on my coat and gumboots I did so and then, opening the door from our living-room I ran out across the garden, where each step I took left a deep impression in the snow. Without meaning to, I found that I had run right over the large flower-bed that stretched across the garden near the house. This was exciting because I knew that it was strictly forbidden to step into any flower-bed, but the snow had given me a perfect excuse, so I ran across the flower-bed again and again until Daddy spotted what I was doing and told me to stop.

Fortunately, he was enjoying the snow almost as much as me. By now, Simon had followed me out, and Daddy showed Simon and me how to play snowballs, picking up some snow and shaping it into a round ball before throwing it at another member of the family. I thought this was great fun, but Simon didn't like it at all when one of my snowballs hit him in the chest. He burst into tears and then ran indoors calling out his usual cry when unhappy of "See what it dooz! See what it dooz!"

"You must be careful with your brother!" said Daddy reprovingly; and then he spent most of the rest of the morning making not just an ordinary snowman, but a snow-woman.

"This is Queen Victoria", he told us all when she had been completed and photographed; and years later, when I looked at his photographs, I realised that he had created a very passable likeness of the Queen Empress in her later life, a short plump creature with a generous bosom. My father, though an Edwardian, had been raised in an essentially Victorian family, and his Snow Queen was no doubt a happy reminiscence of carefree days long, long ago at Red Branch House.

It was at about this time that a new element began to be added to our daily family routine. While Mrs. Maidment was doing the ironing in the mornings she had started listening to a new wireless programme, 'The Archers – an everyday story of country folk', which from January 1951 was broadcast each weekday morning at 11:45. Instantly recognizable from its catchy theme tune, 'Barwick Green', it moved after a while to 6:45 each evening. First Mummy and then Daddy started listening to it every day, and it would gradually become a family institution.

But then came two sets of events, one of them involving birth and one of them involving death, which changed everything in our lives forever. Historically, the death came first: it was that of my beloved Grandmother Amy Graves who died on 3 February 1951. What made far more impact on me at the time was the birth almost exactly three months later, on 8 May 1951, of my sisters Elizabeth and Rosemary.

CHAPTER EIGHT
Kerry House

It was towards the end of April that year, that Simon and I were sat down by Mummy and Daddy on the sofa in the living-room and told that we needed to stay with relatives for a few weeks because Mummy, who was now extremely large, was shortly going to have twins. Simon, just over two-and-a-half years old, was to be taken to Rottingdean to stay with Grandad and Aunt Joan at Braemar, while I was to join my Aunt Betty's family at Kerry House, Alexandra Road, Farnborough.

I had little or no idea what to expect at Kerry House, but I looked forward to the journey, since I was told that, at the age of five years and four months, I was quite old enough to be travelling the final stretch of my journey alone. That is to say, Daddy drove me as far as a convenient railway station, paid for my ticket and put it into my purse into which he had also placed a single half-crown. Then, when my train came in, its railway engine puffing along the platform until it came to a stop with a massive exhalation of steam, he walked me alongside one of the railway carriages until we came to a compartment which clearly had a few spaces inside. Opening the door, he asked in an authoritative tone: "Who's going to Farnborough?" A kindly-looking middle-aged woman volunteered that she was, and he added: "Please could you keep an eye on my son Richard? He's going to be met by his Aunt Brockhurst." Feeling annoyed that Daddy had felt it necessary to ask someone to look after me, I climbed up into the carriage clutching my purse in one hand and a small suitcase in the other, the door was slammed shut behind me with a loud thwack, and almost at once the steam-engine began pulling the train forward and my adventure began.

I call it an adventure because by now I had long overcome my Croydon fear of steam-engines, and for a child who loved the Engine books any railway journey was full of excitement. Here I was in a proper railway carriage, with its two long seats facing each other, its central mirrors above the seats on each side, flanked by framed advertisements for exotic seaside towns, and above them its racks for luggage, into one of which my unwanted protectress had kindly lifted my suitcase.

Looking out through the windows, it seemed that the telegraph wires that ran alongside the track were constantly trying to escape up into the sky, before being pulled sharply down by the next telegraph pole. All the time smoke streamed past, on occasion in bursts so thick that even with the windows closed I was likely to reach the end of my journey considerably blackened and smelling of soot. I watched fascinated as trees and fields and forests and unknown villages and towns sped past, and people waved from back-gardens or from the other side of level crossing gates; while all the time through the floor beneath my feet I could hear the wheels of the carriage singing out their constant refrain, di-di-DUM, di-di-DUM as they passed eagerly from one stretch of rail to the next.

When I first began revisiting these events I was as surprised as you may be by the sight of my being left to travel virtually alone at such a young age. Surely, this journey must have happened on some later occasion? But birth certificates don't usually lie, and I have no reason to doubt either that I was born on 21 December 1945, or that my sisters were born on 7 May 1951, and my memory of arriving alone at Farnborough Station is crystal-clear. Nowadays (I am talking of the 2020s) this incident, if reported to the proper authorities, would have almost certainly led to my being taken into care and to my parents being prosecuted for child neglect and probably sent to prison.

But we lived then in a more robust world, as you may do when you read this, though probably not if you are reading it at any time in the 21st century, since at present the western world appears to be heading in quite the opposite direction with its snowflakes and its safe spaces and its cancel culture and its ghastly mental cancer of political correctness.

Remember that back in 1951 it was only twelve years since hundreds of thousands of young children had been evacuated from war-time London and other cities, separated from their weeping parents and packed onto trains knowing nothing about where they would be going, with whom they would be staying, how long they might be away, or even whether their houses would still be standing or their parents would still be alive when they returned – and I knew all those things (or thought I did) except precisely how long I would be away. And in any case, having spent time in hospital I felt that I was an old hand at being away from home, and this was bound to be much better than lying in a hospital ward with a sore Jimmy watching other children playing and not being able to join in.

At length we reached Farnborough Station, where my protectress, who had after all had her uses, kindly passed down my case, opened the heavy door and encouraged me to alight. I handed over my ticket to the ticket-collector, walked to the station exit, and stood there looking out for some time over a deserted forecourt. The waiting was boring, but it was better than what followed.

I had been naturally been expecting my relatives to arrive by car; but when after a while they hove into view they were walking! I was appalled. I had been shown photographs of them, and that was clearly my Aunt Betty in a floral frock and neatly permed shortish hair and sunglasses, walking along the pavement beside my Uncle Geoffrey who wore trousers and a sports jacket and a kind of neckerchief. Just behind them came my two cousins: 15-year-old Rowan, tall and thin, wearing long trousers and an open-necked shirt; and 9-year-old Judith, short-haired and pretty like her mother, wearing a plain jersey over tomboyish shorts. They greeted me kindly, but all I could bring myself to say in reply to them was: "Are we walking?" And then, with a heartfelt mixture of sorrow and accusation: "*We* have a car!"

My Aunt Betty very kindly kept her temper, though many years later she told me how cross she had felt that I was boasting about what I thought of as my beloved EPB 223, but what she thought of as a horrid old wreck of a pre-war car through whose floor (as I have already observed) the road was clearly visible. In the event all she said in her rich, warm and slightly throaty voice was: "Walking is good for you!"

To me, wretched little snob that I was, this came as a severe let-down. I could hardly bring myself to believe that my parents had been so remiss as to send me to live even for a few days among relatives who were so impoverished that they couldn't even afford a car. As we set out along built-up roads with at first not even a trace of countryside, nothing but houses and more houses, I wondered gloomily what on earth I would find when we reached our destination, and whether indeed (knowing the distance between my own home and the nearest station) we would reach it before nightfall.

Then we passed a park, which looked as though it might be a good place to explore, and such indeed it would turn out to be. This was a little more encouraging; and when only a few minutes later we reached my relatives' home, I had to admit to myself that it was much better than I had feared. Kerry House turned out to be a large detached solidly-built red-brick 1930s family home with gabled windows and three stories and an imposing glassed-in porch appropriate to my Uncle Geoffrey's status both as a prominent Freemason and as a respected local Manager with the Midland Bank.

It stood a little way back from the road in its own substantial grounds, with red brick walls along its boundaries, and its own driveway which ran past tall laurels straight down the left-hand side of the garden and then turned sharply right to a range of outbuildings standing just this side of the far wall. The back garden was mostly lawned, with a long oblong lawn, to the right of which a vegetable garden lay under the shadow not just of its own red-brick wall, but of the windowless tall side of the huge and dominating Post-Office building which stood immediately next-door.

Everything about Kerry House was safe, secure, comfortable and middle-class. There was a sitting-room (not a drawing-room) just inside the door on the right, a large comfortable room more Edwardian than Georgian, with a thick carpet with a floral pattern on it, a solid fireplace and a good deal of furniture including a sofa and side-tables and glass cabinets and bookcases and several comfortable easy chairs with white lacy anti-macassars (which I had never seen before) over the top of each chair to protect them from greasy hair-oil. This room seemed to be largely reserved for Geoffrey's use when he come home in the evenings, and Betty would join him there when she had finished washing-up his supper.

There was also a dog: not I thought a proper dog like Spot or the late lamented Sandy, but a tiny little creature with long hair, a Pekingese called Cella (pronounced Sella) who lived in a cubby-hole with its own window just to one side of the stairs. Cella was affectionate to her own family, and sometimes she was held up for me so that I could stroke her behind the ear and feel her silky fur with the warm delicate skin beneath; but she yapped rather than barked and seemed to do so incessantly whenever I was anywhere in the offing, so I ended up rather disliking her.

At the back of the hallway was a large solid staircase and, leading off the hallway down a long corridor to the left, there were two other comfortable downstairs rooms. One of them, to the right, was a kind of family workroom, with a desk under the window where Aunt Betty wrote her letters; the other, to the left, was a smart formal dining-room. But I never saw this in use, because the main life of the family took place at the very end of the corridor, in a long room (with a kitchen leading off) where there was a smart red-tiled floor and a sideboard and a large table at which we ate all our meals.

To me the great distinction of this room was that it contained, in a metal cage on the top of a tall wooden pole, a green and yellow budgerigar with black markings and a long tail. I already knew robins and blackbirds and thrushes from the garden at White Hazel, and other less common birds such as woodpeckers and swifts from my picture-postcard album; but I had never seen such a thing as this exotic caged bird, which chirruped happily whenever Betty came into view.

My Aunt Brockhurst (as Daddy had called her) was not as demonstrative as her sisters – I remember few hugs or kisses – but she was kindly and efficient and a model housewife of the pre-war variety, someone who was at the heart of her family and devoted her whole life to loving them and caring for them. While Geoffrey went out to work all week, she stayed at home and cooked and cleaned and shopped and looked after their two children (of whom Rowan was their biological child while Judith was adopted), and did it all extremely well. It was a large house to keep clean and tidy, even with the help of a daily maid; but Betty was a perfectionist who must have taken to heart the saying that cleanliness is next to Godliness, because my most vivid memory is of her scrubbing and mopping and mopping and scrubbing that red-tiled floor at the back of the house to within an inch of its life.

She was also a very good cook. Mealtimes were an absolute pleasure and, provided that I had finished my main course, she allowed me second helpings of puddings: one in particular, a gorgeous confection with jelly and cake and cream, I remember finishing off one supper-time. "Oh dear", said Betty, as she smiled at me in a conspiratorial manner, "Your uncle was hoping to have some of that when he came home!" Geoffrey, whom I didn't often see, happened to come home earlier than usual that very evening, and just as Betty expected he asked after the trifle he had enjoyed so much the night before, and looked very ruefully at me when he was told that it had all been eaten. "Really? All of it? Oh well, never mind!" But he looked genuinely disappointed, and I'm sorry to say that I couldn't help feeling a little triumphant, as though we had been playing a kind of game which I had won; and at the same time the words of a rhyme from one of my favourite picture-books came unbidden into my head:

> Down, down, down the red lane!
> We won't see old Tom Tomato again!

From then on it became something of a joke between uncle and nephew that whenever Geoffrey arrived home early from the Bank, he would come into the room where I was eating, and exclaim in mock horror: "What! Are you eating my supper *again*? Dear oh dear!" Although he always had a twinkle in his eye when he said this, I was glad to feel that I had Betty's protection, because although Geoffrey was usually the most genial of men, and as time went on he stood out as the most generous of my relatives, almost never leaving me after even the shortest visit without slipping a half-crown into my hands, there was always something a little sudden and unpredictable about him, and at times there was a slightly bitter edge to his sense of humour.

This was not surprising. Despite being an intelligent man who was normally a shrewd judge of character, there had been just one occasion on which, as the Manager of his local Branch, he had made a lending decision that had gone badly wrong; and so although within Freemasonry he rose to one of our very highest ranks, that of a Provincial Grand Master, in the Bank his career had become permanently becalmed.

During the first part of my stay at Kerry House, I saw almost nothing of Rowan, an enigmatic and to me utterly remote figure who I began to think must have no interest in me at all. I only learned many years later that the reason for this apparent neglect was that he was not in the house at all for large parts of my visit, but was away at boarding school. And when I did see him at Kerry House, I feared quite unreasonably that he might be jealous of the attention lavished upon me by his sister, who was normally his most devoted acolyte. I certainly spent a great deal of time with Judith, who was clever, resourceful, unfailingly cheerful and I thought very good-looking.

Fortunately, just like my Uncle Robert, she had a predisposition in my favour. Having first seen me in Croydon when she was three-and-a half years old, and I had only just been born, she had turned to her mother and said very forcefully: "I want one of those!" As for me: I secretly decided during this visit that one day I would marry Judith; and although that was a wedding that never took place, I loved her dearly for the rest of my life.

One of Judith's great attractions was that just like me she was a voracious reader, so when she invited me to visit her in her bedroom, which was just over the way from mine, I found that it was full of exciting reading matter. In particular she had a substantial collection of old Rupert Bear Annuals.

We didn't take *The Daily Express* at home, so this was my first introduction to the strip-cartoon stories of that adventurous bear in his red sweater and bright yellow checked trousers with matching scarf. The stories were told in picture form, with four picture panels to the page in each Rupert Annual, and underneath each picture what was happening would be explained both in a two-line verse and, beneath the verse, in a chunk of prose. This meant a double pleasure: on a first reading I could skim through the story, simply looking at the pictures and reading the verses, and then I could go back to the beginning and read the more elaborate version of the story set out in the lengthier prose sections.

The stories were highly imaginative, and introduced me to a magical world in which Rupert would leave his Nutwood home, meet some of his pals who included his best friend Bill Badger, Edward Trunk the elephant, Algy Pug the Pekingese and Bingo the Brainy Pup, and set off on magical adventures, often inspired by the Professor in his castle or by a Chinese girl called Tiger-Lily and her mysterious father, the Conjurer. I was allowed to borrow the albums one or two at a time and take them into my bedroom which had its own bedside table and reading light, and there were two stories that I particularly enjoyed.

In one of them, the adventure takes place in a world of snow and mountains and fast sledge rides; and in another, Rupert and Algy find themselves in a wood, which becomes thicker and thicker until it is impossible to go on. Then they climb up, and find that the forest is so dense that they can walk across the tree-tops as though they are walking over a slightly bumpy green carpet; and they discover a mare's nest – the abode of a winged horse like Pegasus. After each adventure, Rupert and his pals always return safely home to Nutwood: it is a world that is delightful, intriguing and exciting but never actually frightening; a wonderful place in which for a young mind to roam.

Having become used to country living, my first impression of the enclosed Kerry House garden had been moderately negative, but Judith had soon opened my eyes to a number of its possibilities. One day, for example, she encouraged me to climb up into the laurels at the side of the drive until we could sit with one leg on each side of the brick wall, looking down into the mysterious, unknown world of her next-door neighbours. On another day, she took me down to the bottom of the garden, where someone must once have kept a horse, because the range of buildings there included a stable, in which Judith showed me how to climb up the wooden rungs of a ladder into the loft. I felt very privileged to be there because she made it clear that this was her special domain.

But our greatest adventure was in the house itself. It was one afternoon when Aunt Betty was busy with her household routine, perhaps giving her red-tiled floor its daily mop, perhaps preparing the vegetables for supper, or perhaps taking a well-earned break to listen contentedly to her own favourite serial on the wireless: *Mrs. Dale's Diary*. This had already been running for just over three years, had millions of listeners, and featured a doctor's wife who lived just the same kind of respectable middle-class life as the Brockhursts.

In any case, on this memorable afternoon, Judith and I left the secure part of the house behind us, and climbed all the way up the stairs to the normally deserted attic floor right at the top of the house. Here she pushed open the creaking door of an ill-lit room that was piled high, almost to the ceiling it seemed, with old iron beds and bedding and mattresses. It looked extremely sinister to me. Who knew what might be hiding in those dark corners? But Judith bravely led the way in and I followed her.

Somehow or other we climbed right to the top of the mattresses, and then we mountaineered across them until after an epic of exploration we finally reached the un-curtained window at the far end of the room, and looked out of it at the ground far below with a sense of triumph. Then we had to climb all the way back again, finally escaping with our lives as we shut the door behind us and emerged safely onto the landing at the top of the stairs. This had been by far the most exciting part of my stay at Kerry House, and I was only sad that it was never repeated.

We did however pay one further and equally memorable visit to the attic floor. Rowan told Judith and me one weekend that as a great treat we could come and look at his electric model railway. On opening one of the doors leading into a small box-room, it was impossible to walk straight in, because Rowan's layout, set on boards resting on several tables, filled almost the whole of the available space. And what a lay-out! There were railway lines and stations and bridges and little passengers and a stationmaster and trees and shrubs and a lake made of glass and all in all I thought it was one of the most magnificent things I had ever seen.

My respect for Rowan, which had already leapt up very considerably at the mere sight of his railway, headed into the stratosphere when he invited Judith and me to duck down under the table nearest the door and to join him in the central area from where he operated his trains and points and signals. Switches were switched on, levers were pulled, and soon several trains were running safely round the various interlinking tracks under Rowan's expert guidance. I watched spellbound until, finally, I was allowed to operate one of the trains myself for a few minutes. What an experience!

What bliss! I can only add that after this, my own clockwork Hornby-Dublo set at home, dating as it did from my Croydon days, seemed so utterly insignificant and second-rate that I never bothered to play with it again.

Talking of home, nearly every day the postman would bring me a picture-post-card from either Mummy or Daddy. How pleased I was to receive these cards, which I hoarded carefully so that in due course I could add them to my album. Daddy sent me some interesting photographs of Salisbury, where Mummy had been installed at the Crane Street Nursing Home; while Mummy herself sent me birds and beasts and illustrations from children's books, and her messages were very carefully printed out. I knew that this was meant kindly, so I forgave her for it, but when I first saw this, it made me feel quite cross. Didn't she realise that I was perfectly capable of reading cursive script?

The first messages from home were positive. I learned that Mummy had given birth (how she had done this I had no idea) and that I now had two sisters, Rosemary and Elizabeth, whom I immediately added to the family prayer that I said every night. But it soon became clear that Rosemary was not at all well.

Meanwhile Simon, down at Braemar, was having a lovely time with his Aunt Joan, establishing a bond that would remain strong until the very end of her long life. He too was being sent postcards from home every day. The example I have in front of me has on one side a cheerful picture by Margaret Tarrant of five squirrels playing leapfrog along the branch of a pine tree. On the other side is an orange 2d stamp showing the crowned head of King George VI, and a message sent on 17 May from The Nursing Home, Crane Street, Salisbury as follows:

> Darling Simon,
>
> The sun is shining here to-day & I hope it is at Rottingdean & then perhaps you will get to the beach. Elizabeth is a very good girl and has gained 3 ozs in weight. Rosemary is still not very well. Be a good boy and help Aunt Joan. Please give Grandad my love. Lots to you poppet
>
> XXX from Mummie XXX

The twins had been born on 7 May, so when my mother wrote this postcard telling Simon that Rosemary was 'still not very well', they were both ten days old; and that same day I myself received a very anxious post card from my father asking me 'to say a special prayer to ask God to make Rosemary well again'.

I said my prayer, but tragically within a few days Rosemary was dead. On 22 May, my father attended a funeral service, and wrote to me on the back of a postcard of Trafalgar Square: 'I said goodbye to Rosemary for you all today & gave her some of your nice yellow tulips. Much love from your loving Daddy. xxxxxxxxx'

And now if you look very carefully you can see my mother in her Nursing Home, lying in bed and holding Elizabeth in her arms but unable to stop weeping over Rosemary's death. "Why are you crying?" asks an unsympathetic nurse. "You've got one lovely baby. Isn't that enough?"

As for me: I feel very sad at this death of a sister whom I have never seen. It is explained to me that she has gone to Heaven where Jesus will be looking after her, but I cannot help selfishly wishing that she had been allowed to stay on earth a little while longer.

There is better news of Elizabeth, who continues to put on weight; and eventually she and Mummy are allowed home, where on returning to White Hazel Simon and I meet for the first time this dear little baby with her tiny hands and feet. A good deal of baby-worship follows, which cheers us all up, though Mummy continues to feel Rosemary's loss very keenly, and for several years we continue to remember her each night in our family prayers:

> God bless Mummy and Daddy, and God bless Richard and Simon, and Elizabeth and Rosemary, and make them good, obedient and truthful children. And God bless Spot and Sandy and Noony and Solomon.

But Rosemary is not present and, more mysteriously, neither is Spot. Many years later, I learned that he had killed some small animals and developed a taste for blood, so it was feared that he would be a real danger to a young baby, and it was decided to have him put down before my mother returned with Elizabeth from her nursing home. However, no-one said anything about this to me at the time, and I was left with the vague notion that he had somehow escaped from the garden, and wandered off alone.

How my heart ached for the loss of this friendly companion with his large black spot, who had joined us on so many family walks and who was always so pleased to see me that he would rush up and lick me vigorously all over my face. How I hoped that he hadn't met the same fate as Sandy, and been run over by a lorry. Or perhaps he had got lost and was now searching for his way home? Every morning I woke up hoping that this would be the day of his return, and every day I was disappointed.

In other ways, everything at White Hazel appeared to run on smoothly, the main event that summer being a visit from Aunt Joan. Whenever the weather was good enough, we continued to go on long walks through the grounds and parkland by which we were surrounded, with Simon in his push chair and me walking beside him. These walks were always highly sociable affairs. Pushchairs in those days were designed so that the child who was being pushed along always looked back at whoever was doing the pushing, so there was constant communication between the two of them and each journey, as well as being one of exploration, was a continuation and a development of a loving family relationship. This suited Simon very well. A somewhat nervous child, he loved looking back at his mother and communicating with her as she pushed him along. When anything went even slightly wrong in his daily life, he would still call out anxiously "See what it dooz! See what it dooz!" But on these long walks, with his mother so close at hand, nothing could frighten or alarm him.

I am now considered to be too old for my lovely green tricycle, but fortunately Judith has passed on to me a small blue two-wheeler bicycle that she has outgrown. Occasionally I try riding it with Mummy holding on to the saddle while Aunt Joan pushes Simon's pushchair; but I never manage more than a few feet without falling off, and I begin to fear that I will never learn to ride the wretched thing.

Now, I said that things *appeared* to run on smoothly, and so they did on the surface, but in fact we were on the verge of a momentous change, one that stemmed very largely from Grandmother Amy's death earlier in the year.

CHAPTER NINE
Moving On

It was early in 1948 that there had been a recurrence of the symptoms which had led Amy to be diagnosed with breast cancer some years before the war. In May 1948 she had begun the radiation treatments arranged by her doctor daughter, Dr. Rosaleen Cooper, my Aunt Rosaleen, of whom more later. But although these fifteen treatments down in Exeter had been remarkably successful, the cancer had flared up again in 1950. The next set of treatments had been less successful, and it was on the way back from Devon in October 1950 that Amy had called in for the short holiday at White Hazel that we have already noted. By this time the cancer had begun spreading through the rest of her body, and she must have known or at least suspected that she was dying and that this would be her farewell visit.

My own final letter to Amy, dictated on 21 January 1951 when she was already desperately ill, had been mainly about Spot, and how fast he could run, and included two dreadfully bad drawings of him. 'Goodbye, Granny darling!' it ended, followed by a sturdy capital-letter signature which showed that Ashmore School had been improving my handwriting even if it had been unable to teach me how to draw.

The sad story of Amy's final months, overshadowed as they were by severe family worries, I have written about at length elsewhere. It is a story which features my Aunt Rosaleen as the heroine. She it was who came to her mother's rescue when Clarissa had completely lost the plot; she it was who gave Amy enough sedatives to allow her to die peacefully on 3

February 1951 without another bout of the frightful convulsions which (the cancer having reached her brain) had been such a distressing feature of her final illness.

Nor do I intend to repeat my tragical/comical account of the family gathering which took place in Erinfa at the time of Amy's funeral, though I note that my father was present and that my cousin Jenny, Robert's daughter, commented that 'Uncle John came out best', and was 'all the time quiet, good-natured and sensible', despite 'wearing a frightful false bear coat, the matching half of which had been patched by Grandmother with black velvet.' How well I remember that coat, which always seemed to me to be utterly splendid, with its black fur and its black velvet lining, and which he must have worn for at least another five years.

After the funeral came the traditional reading of the Will. My Aunt Susan's husband Kenneth Macaulay and my father John Graves had been appointed Amy's co-executors, and it was Kenneth who read out the Will, sitting on the drawing-room window-sill and holding it to the light with a magnifying glass, because his sight was failing.

John himself had been left a 1/7th share of Amy's Estate, which amounted to the then considerable sum of £2,000, worth in 2024 terms (depending on how you measure it) somewhere between £90,000 and £230,000. The critical thing was that this gave him just enough capital to be able to extricate himself from Sandroyd School, with which he had become increasingly disillusioned, by resigning and taking out a mortgage on a school of his own.

In later life, both my parents retained unpleasant memories of Mr. and Mrs. Ozanne who had promised them so much, while it suited their purposes to do so. Initially, everything had looked so promising. When the first issue of the school magazine following their arrival was published, they could see that Ozanne had penned a very friendly welcoming message, in which he had much looked forward to the future with Mr. Graves as his Assistant Headmaster.

There was certainly no doubt that, since his arrival, my father had wholeheartedly thrown himself into the life of the school. Not only had he maintained high standards in the classroom and on the games field, as expected, but also he had volunteered to take a leading part in all kinds of school entertainments, often giving humorous recitations of his own devising, or singing songs while accompanying himself on his guitar.

But then had come the day when Princess Marina had been driven down to inspect Sandroyd for herself and in particular to interview Ozanne and to come to a final decision about her son Prince Michael's future. Ozanne was almost beside himself with excitement, and wanted all the glory of this visit to himself. To my father's disgust, he was told that it would be premature for him to meet Princess Marina, so he was excluded from the critical interview. Later he and my mother would be relieved, because it meant that they could not be blamed for the outcome of the interview, which had gone as badly as it possibly could.

Princess Marina, who had stayed overnight in Salisbury, was already horrified to find it was intended that Sandroyd should remain in this utterly remote part of the world and, more important perhaps, she did not take to Ozanne personally. So Prince Michael's name was withdrawn – he went instead to Sunningdale School not far from London – and once the possibility of acquiring this important royal pupil had been knocked on the head, the Ozannes were no longer seriously interested in turning their Assistant Headmaster into a Joint Headmaster. This was less of a disappointment to my father than might have been expected. By this time he had found Ozanne extremely self-centred and difficult to work with, only really interested in those among his pupils with distinguished parents and, just like my father's former superiors at the Department of Education, most unwilling to change any established procedures.

There was another factor in their decision to move on. My mother was, as I have mentioned several times, a City girl at heart; and what to me was a delightful rural idyll was to her a period of being virtually buried alive in an isolated stretch of ancient, almost sinister countryside, very far from family and friends, in a cottage so primitive that drinking water still had to be pumped up by hand from the well beneath. Yes, some family had visited; but only one of her close friends Mira, wife of the celebrated concert pianist Denis Matthews, had ventured to this remote place. Yes, she had made a few acquaintances among the other schoolmasters' wives; but she was unable to be as frank and open with these new acquaintances as she would have liked.

Seeing one or two of these women very occasionally was in any case no substitute for the kind of strong friendships she had made in the previous schools to which she had been attached. Years later she told me that by the time we left White Hazel her sisters (especially the practical and down-to earth Ruth) were becoming quite anxious about her state of mind, and she herself had begun to wonder 'whether I would have gone off my head if I had had to live much longer in that strange place.'

I noticed very little of the strain Mummy was under, though I do recall one very odd incident. Somewhere behind one of the laurel bushes near the garage there was a rubbish dump, and one morning I was poking around there on my own when I discovered to my astonishment that several of my toy cars, despite being in perfectly good condition, had simply been thrown away. I left them there, but told my mother what I had found. When she gave me no explanation, but simply agreed that some of my toys had been thrown out, I had no idea how to take the conversation forward. So it lapsed and those toys were inexplicably and permanently lost.

In any case, during the Easter holidays of 1951, not long before Elizabeth and Rosemary were born, my father had taken considerable pleasure in giving Ozanne a term's notice, and had immediately begun looking out for a suitable school of his own. It would be difficult, even with his new inheritance, to find anywhere even half-decent that he could afford; but he was confident that he could make a success of any school provided it was in the right place geographically, that the buildings were sound, and that there was enough room for decent-sized playing-fields.

These three requirements appeared to be met by Holme Grange School. This was a small and impoverished establishment housed in a beautiful Norman Shaw mansion in the heart of the Berkshire countryside, only a mile and a half by road from the market-town of Wokingham, and only an hour by train from London.

So, one morning at the beginning of June, Daddy told Simon and me that Mrs. Maidment would be looking after us for the day, because he and Mummy would be away looking over a school where he might become the new Headmaster. Mrs. Maidment then took over and Mummy and Daddy disappeared and as the day wore on, I somehow got it into my head that they had bicycled off together and were even now in some leafy lane where the boughs met overhead just as they did along the narrow road below Erinfa.

They both liked Holme Grange and sometime in July, when negotiations had been successfully concluded, Daddy drove us over to have a look. I remember a long drive leading up to the school with, half-way along it, a scruffy-looking caravan parked under some trees over to the right; a middle-aged man with a check jacket and a booming voice who greeted us warmly; and parents and boys wandering here and there on what must have been a Speech Day. But what made the greatest impact upon me were the tempting glimpses I had of the seven acres of grounds which I was told would soon be mine to explore.

The result of seeing these grounds was that I was now delighted by everything to do with the move, apart from the fact that Spot had never reappeared and so wouldn't be able to come with us. "What about Spot?" I asked anxiously as we clambered into EPB 223 on the morning of our final departure from White Hazel. "Don't worry about him, said Mummy. "He'll be all right". And then we were driving away in EPB 223 without him, and I looked out across the Rushmore Parkland to which we were saying good-bye, hoping against hope that Spot had found a new home with a kindly family among one of the houses or farms that could be still be seen in the distance. And then we were on the main road and were gradually leaving Cranborne Chase and White Hazel far behind us.

So ends the Golden Age of my childhood, during which I have acquired a passion for reading, and my soul has taken permanent root in a magical landscape part real part mythical of bluebell woods and running deer and ancient hills over which giants might still roam and beautiful princesses wait in tall towers to be rescued by brave princes. I am also fortunate that my five and a half years first at 3a Moreton Road and then at White Hazel have been long enough to give me that solid foundation of psychological security without which I could hardly have survived what was to come.

If only the same had been true for my poor brother Simon, whose fourth birthday is now imminent. On our arrival at Holme Grange, I am hugely excited, but he has been horrified to learn that we will never be returning to White Hazel. 'Lickly' is how he pronounces the word 'quickly' and, travelling back in time to the very moment of our arrival, I can see his anguished tear-stained face as he looks up at Mummy (who has been doing her best to reassure him), and begins repeating over and over again: "Home lickly! Home lickly!"

BOOK THREE

MY WHITE HOUSE YEAR 1951-1952

CHAPTER ONE

Arrival at Holme Grange

We catch a few glimpses of Wokingham as we drive through it: a sleepy little market town, very pleasant apart from a monstrously ugly red-brick Victorian Town Hall at its centre. We see a few shoppers going about their business and a handful of cars parked here and there. Then we are travelling south-east along the Easthampstead Road. Very soon there are open fields to our left, and then we have to slow down and stop as we reach a level crossing on a slight rise in the ground. Here the large white double-gates have only just swung shut, bringing together at their centre the two halves of a large red circle.

After what seems like a long wait, but is probably no more than a couple of minutes, a modern electric train with light green carriages whirrs steamlessly past on its way to London. Looking up towards the wooden signal-box on its brick base on the far side of the road, we can see the elderly crossing-keeper who gives us a friendly wave before turning the huge wheel in front of him. As he does so, the two halves of the red circle begin to separate, the gates swing open, and we drive through them into real countryside.

Down a long slope we go, and up the other side, past a large farm on our left, and then a handful of farm-worker's cottages on our right. Just beyond these cottages, we take a right fork past a public house marked by the sign of a White Horse swinging from a tall pole. Almost immediately, the road swings sharply round to the left, and two hundred yards further on we turn left again into the rough gravel driveway, with numerous potholes in it, that will lead us up to Holme Grange.

To our left, a brief glimpse of a somewhat gloomy lake, its banks neglected and overgrown. Only twenty years ago, Holme Grange had been at the centre of a very considerable estate, of which more later, and it would have been better looked after. To our right is a brick house that had once been the Lodge, but is now separately owned and occupied; and the first part of the driveway is shared.

After about a hundred yards we reach a substantial horse chestnut tree at the centre of a place where four drives meet. The long one to the left still belongs to Holme Grange and leads down to the further end of the lake and a large cricket field; the short one diagonally opposite leads to another private house, this one almost completely hidden from view by a dense growth of trees and shrubs; and this dense growth continues up the left-hand-side of the main drive which we follow round to the right through land which is wholly owned by Holme Grange.

As the drive straightens up a little, I notice with pleasure that the decrepit old caravan that I had seen on our last visit had been removed from the grassy space beneath trees on the right-hand side. Then the drive veers gently round to the right, past a mass of rhododendrons, until suddenly it opens onto a large roundabout with an elaborate formal garden at its centre and, on its far side, the northern façade of our imposing and beautiful new home. With its great gables, its mullioned and transom windows decorated with leaded lights, its large brick chimneys with fluted shafts, and its red-brick walls (the second storey hung with red-brick tiles) Holme Grange, as it bursts upon our view, is a magnificent sight.

Once Daddy has driven us around the roundabout and we have stepped out of EPB 223 and Simon has begun wailing most bitterly for us to return to White Hazel, we walk towards a truly massive porch, and climb the two steps onto its red-brick floor above which a substantial cornice is ready to protect us from the rain. The porch walls are covered with large white tiles; at the back of the porch we can see on the left a narrow high-up oblong window above the tiles, and on the right a panelled white door. More than twice the width of our White Hazel front door, it features a large round brass door-handle above an equally large key-hole, and Daddy walks fearlessly up to it and rings the bell.

Before long the door swings easily inward on its massive well-oiled hinges, and a young woman in a black uniform with a white pinafore and a broad Berkshire accent is standing there welcoming us into Holme Grange.

"Hello Sir, Hello Madam!"

And then we go in through that vast front door into the front hall where, despite the previous Headmaster on his departure having stripped the building as bare as possible, we find everything in a surprisingly well-furnished state. Because during the preceding weeks, while Simon and I have been down in Rottingdean and Mummy has been at White Hazel looking after Elizabeth, Daddy has been busily attending sales and organizing removals.

Fortunately for him, the end of July had seen the closing-down sale of a preparatory school in South Ascot, not many miles from Wokingham; and here he had purchased not only a set of goalposts but numerous good-looking chairs and tables, quantities of linen, tableware and textbooks, and other valuable items including a carved walnut sideboard for the Common Room, and a Grand Pianoforte by Steck for the Main Hall.

In addition, after Amy's death she had left behind her in Erinfa a great deal of Victorian, Georgian and even older furniture, not to mention a huge number of family portraits of all shapes and sizes and all the family papers that had survived Clarissa's notorious bonfire on APG's death back in 1931. Daddy, who had become the family historian, was happy to take charge of the papers; and was delighted that no-one else in the family had wanted either the old unfashionable furniture or the family portraits, because as it turned out they suited Holme Grange very well.

So now, as we step into the front hall, we can see on the right-hand side a large and very handsome seventeenth-century oak chest, with ancient and intricately carved wooden chairs on each side of it, while along the top of the chest my father has placed a beautiful set of German stoneware drinking mugs elaborately decorated with a frieze of hunting scenes, and the motto: 'AUF der grunen Heide – Such ich meine Freude' which can be roughly translated as:

On the heathland green,
Hunt I with pleasure keen.[1]

The punchbowl which stands at their centre is similarly decorated, and has a lid five inches across on which a Stag and his deer graze happily in the forest alongside several plump rabbits; and at its centre the lid rises up into a knob disguised as a sheaf of wheat on the top of which a magnificent hound holds a dead fox between its jaws.

On the wall above these bucolic scenes hang two of the larger family portraits. And on the other side of the front hall, over to our left, is a superb round table of Connemara marble. This originally came from the Palace of my great-grandfather Charles Graves, Bishop of Limerick, and is now one of my father's most treasured possessions. Beyond it is a coat-stand, an umbrella rack, and an impressively tall grandfather clock, also from Erinfa and in full working order.

Ahead of us is a wall with a large mirror on the left and, to the right of it, tall wooden double-doors. The left one of these doors is half-open, and through it I catch a glimpse of the huge Hall beyond; but before I can explore further in that direction we have turned left, following our uniformed maid past the grandfather clock to the far corner of the entrance hall. Here she opens a door, the top half of which has two large glazed panels, and ushers us through it into the long narrow corridor which leads from the main body of Holme Grange towards the servants' wing.

The floor of this corridor has an elaborate pattern of red tiles and, over on the left, a series of small iron grilles through which we can see some iron pipe-work, all that remains of a now defunct central heating system. I was thoroughly intrigued by this, and on learning that the Romans had introduced central heating into this country, but that no-one had enjoyed it for hundreds of years, I decided quite wrongly that these pipes must be a Roman relic. They certainly looked old enough to me.

On the wall above the iron grilles there were more family portraits, and I remember being particularly impressed by the framed print of a certain John Graves of Mickleton in Gloucestershire who, despite looking

1 A more literal translation would be: 'On the green heath search I for my joy'.

miserably unhappy, had somehow managed to live to 103 before his death in 1616.

Immediately to our left as we walk down the red-tiled corridor is another doorway, and there are two more further down on the right, the second of which leads into a small glazed area looking at first rather like an indoor greenhouse; but we keep on to the end, where there are yet more doors, both ahead of us and to our left and right. Later on I will discover that the door to the right leads out into a small enclosed garden, and that the door ahead leads into my parents' new drawing-room; but we turn left, through the door, usually kept open, which leads directly into what had once been the servants' quarters. And just beside this door, high up on the wall, are the various bells, still in working order, with names beneath them indicating the individual rooms in which a servant's presence might be immediately required.

As we pass through this doorway, I feel that we have entered a slightly sinister area, because after stepping past a very short corridor leading back in to another unknown room, we come immediately to some railings over which I find myself peering down into the unlit depths of a gloomy-looking cellar. Beyond this, is the narrow foot of the servants' staircase, beyond which one corridor stretches into the distance ahead of us, while another corridor set at right-angles to this one leads past a red baize door to yet another altogether unknown region of the building.

I am glad enough to leave all this behind and to follow the uniformed maid up the narrow staircase and away from that dreadful cellar towards our new living quarters. First comes a long steep ascent, then a sharp turn to the left and a shorter flight of stairs, and then another sharp turn to the left and another short flight of stairs which takes us up to the landing; and all the time I am trying not to look down over the banisters at that huge drop where it seems to me that I could easily fall to my death into the cellar far below; but to look up, where there is a massive boxed skylight through which I can see the sky with a few fluffy white clouds sailing past.

Almost immediately opposite the head of the staircase is a large square room, a little on the dark side, looking out eastward over the kitchen yard. Once upon a time it might have belonged to the Housekeeper or perhaps to the Butler, but now, I am told, it is to be Mummy's and Daddy's bedroom. Next door to it on the right, at the head of another long corridor leading back from the servants' quarters into the main body of the school, is a second large, square room. Leading the way into it, having thanked our maid and temporarily dispensed with her services, Mummy tells Simon and me that this is to be our room. It will be a combination of bedroom, playroom and dining-room, and we are to call it by its designated name: the Nursery.

CHAPTER TWO
Holme Grange History

Dear Reader, should you be one of those for whom the very title of this chapter, including as it does the word 'History', has been more than enough to induce a state of mild revulsion or even (in more extreme cases) hopeless despair, please move on immediately, repressing your shudders and, without a backward glance, go to the start of Chapter Three. There you will find what living in a Nursery meant for me and my dear brother and sister back in those remote but still somewhere existing 1950s.

However, we are going to be spending some time in and around Holme Grange, so even if you skip this chapter now, you may wish to come back to it later on, since it will place our occupation of this mansion within a clear historical context. And if you have decided to stay with me, so much the better.

If we hover above Holme Grange School as it is in 1951, with its 22 acres of landscaped grounds, and then travel back in time as far as the 1870s, the lake is still here, but the buildings and the grounds have vanished away and been altogether replaced by open fields, with a few small and scattered areas of woodland, especially to the south-east.

These fields and woodland form the northerly part of the massive Holme Grange Estate, which stretches as far south as Gardener's Green and includes a number of farms, cottages, and even a public house called The Crooked Billet. If we move forward again in time just a little, it is in 1881 that the then owner of the Estate, one Bartle Goldsmidt, commissions the great architect Richard Norman Shaw, fresh from his triumph at Adcote in Shropshire, to design and build an imposing mansion in the midst of these green fields.

Over the next two years, we can watch as the buildings of Holme Grange rise up from their foundations, a beautiful terrace is created on their southern side, and a roundabout on their northern side forms the start of a driveway. This leads to an exit on the Heathlands Road near a new Lodge, and also diverts to a stable block near the Easthampstead Road. Now that the whole estate has been immeasurably improved by these additions, Goldsmidt immediately sells it on to Arthur Fraser Walter whose family is based not far away at Bearwood; and in 1885 Walter sells it on again, this time to Alexander Anderdon Weston, a successful Barrister and a Justice of the Peace.

Having married into the aristocracy (his wife Isabella, whom he had wed in 1870, was the younger daughter of a Baronet), Alexander Weston has decided that he needs a family seat of his own. Holme Grange is also a fit and proper setting for the magnificent collection of prints, many of them now in the British Museum, that he inherited from his Uncle James back in 1845. Still better, the grounds are a largely blank canvas upon which, as a Fellow of the Royal Geographical Society, he can indulge his enthusiasm for exotic shrubs and trees, starting with the sapling of a Giant Redwood tree or Sequoia that is planted not far from the north-eastern edge of the Lake.

Over the next fifteen years the landscaping continues, and even before Alexander's death in 1901, his son and only child Arthur has taken up his passion, travelling as far as China in search of specimen trees and beautiful shrubs. Arthur, a military man always referred to as 'The Colonel', then moves into Holme Grange with his wife the Hon Margaret Beaufort St John, daughter of the 16th Baron of Bletso, while his mother retreats to the Dower House, a much smaller but still substantial house that has been built opposite the stable block.

When Arthur himself dies in 1937 at the age of only 66, there is no child to succeed him, so Margaret, rather than moving to the Dower House, where Isabella had died back in 1922, remains in the main building. Here tradition tells us that she gradually becomes an eccentric recluse, only venturing out occasionally to be driven in her pony and trap along a circular track which makes its delightful way around the grounds that have so carefully been laid out first by her father-in-law and then by her husband.

Then in 1939 comes the outbreak of the Second World War. Holme Grange is requisitioned by the Army; Margaret retreats to the Dower House and, on her death in 1944, since she leaves behind no son or daughter, the entire Holme Grange Estate is put up for sale. Since it is still wartime, prices are depressed, the Estate is sold off in various lots rather than as a single whole, and a prosperous local market-gardener named J.W. Robbins seizes the opportunity to make a killing. He buys the Norman Shaw mansion together with 39 acres of land; and within less than a year he has already made a huge profit by selling Holme Grange and 22 acres of its grounds to one James Gordon Walker, a 32-year-old schoolmaster with private means who wants it for a new school of which he is to be the first Headmaster.

At first, there seems every reason to suppose that this will be a successful foundation, since Holme Grange School begins life as an offshoot from a London preparatory school situated in the heart of Belgravia which is so well-liked that it is bursting at the seams. With the consent of their parents, it is arranged that forty Eaton House boarders should be immediately transferred from London to Wokingham, where their new school uniform retains the Maltese Cross of the parent foundation, but in blue rather than red: so each navy-blue school cap has sewn onto it a dark blue Maltese Cross on a light blue background, and each navy-blue blazer had the same badge sewn onto the front of its breast-pocket.

It must be evident to Gordon Walker that his chief local competition will be Ludgrove School, less than a mile away from Holme Grange, and one of the more prestigious preparatory schools of its day. It too is a refugee from London, having moved as recently as 1937 to its current premises, where it is evidently flourishing under its single-minded Headmaster Alan Barber.

Holme Grange has the advantage that both its school buildings and its grounds are far more beautiful than those of Ludgrove, and that its first Headmaster has far more of the right kind of social connections. Alan Barber, before exchanging the cricket-field for the classroom, had certainly been a highly successful amateur cricketer, appearing in at least seventy first-class matches; but he has no very distinguished relatives; while by contrast James Gordon Walker can boast of a grandfather, Sir Thomas Gordon Walker, who had once been Lieutenant-Governor of the Punjab; and his second-cousin Patrick Gordon-Walker, after being elected to Parliament at a by-election in 1945, will soon be making a name for himself as one of the rising stars of Clement Attlee's post-war Labour government.

Sadly, however, our Gordon Walker has promoted himself well beyond his level of competence. Through no fault of his own, he completely lacks the charisma, the strength of character and the evident moral purpose which are so essential in a Headmaster, and in his new role he can only be described as a complete failure. Over his first five years, the number of boarders at Holme Grange, far from increasing, actually falls from forty to fifteen.

By this time, Gordon Walker has to some extent offset the massive fall in income which this entails by attracting some twenty day-boys from the Wokingham area, but day-boys are not only considerably less profitable than boarders, but much less prestigious. Indeed, the mere fact of accepting local day-boys among its pupils immediately puts Holme Grange so far out of contention that his near-neighbour Alan Barber will not deign to arrange a single sporting fixture with such a socially inferior competitor.

Nor is Gordon Walker's senior master any help. Indeed, quite the opposite. Named Noble, but utterly devoid of nobility, he is a balding man some twenty years older than Gordon Walker with glasses, a confidential manner, a fat belly and a fondness for whisky. With his confidential manner, Mr. Noble ingratiates himself into his Headmaster's confidence; and with his fondness for whisky, he encourages his Headmaster to accompany him on lengthy drinking expeditions either to The White Horse at one end of the grounds or to The Crooked Billet at the other. In these establishments Gordon Walker gradually drowns both his sorrows and, as he descends into alcoholism, any hope he might once have had of rescuing his failing business venture from ruin. All of which explains why by the spring of 1951 a sale has become inevitable; and why any purchaser without very deep pockets is going to have an uphill struggle to put things right.

CHAPTER THREE

The Nursery

In establishing a Nursery for us, my father had reverted so far as he was able to the traditional arrangements for managing young children under which he and his siblings had been brought up at Red Branch House. Clarissa and Rosaleen and Robert and Charles and he had seen far more of their nurse Emily Dykes than of their parents, who were busily occupied with other duties, although Amy never failed to spend an hour with them each afternoon in the drawing-room.

Now that we children had moved into this room in the south-east corner of the old servants' quarters at Holme Grange, our situation was very similar. It was here in the Nursery that we spent a good deal of the next few years. During the day it was our playroom and dining-room; and at night, once we had said our prayers, it also became our bedroom, and we too were in need of a full-time nurse or nanny, mainly because both our parents were now working full-time and flat-out.

Our father had not only taken on the normal administrative duties of a Headmaster, but when term began he would also be teaching almost a full timetable of Latin and Greek, (with some senior English and Geography) besides acting unofficially as Head of Drama, Football Coach, Gardener and Groundsman. As for our mother, having returned to the teaching career which had been interrupted by the first six-and-a-half years of her marriage, she would not only be giving singing and piano lessons and playing the piano at each morning assembly; but, having never before been in charge (outside her teaching duties) of anything more than a single servant, she had also become Housekeeper with the very considerable responsibility of managing both the kitchens and the domestic indoor staff.

As a room the Nursery was perfectly agreeable. Immediately to the right as we came in was a convenient wash-basin, with a cupboard below and a mirror above; and then almost the whole of the wall beyond was taken up by a long south-facing window with leaded lights through which, on a sunny day, bright light poured in. And beneath this window was a low, broad window-sill, wide enough for us to kneel on while we looked out at the magnificent view.

Below us was a small private garden, enclosed to the south by a long line of yew hedging. This was mostly low, but there were tall rounded sections on each side of the three or four steps that descended onto the elegant graveled terrace. This stretched out both to the left and to the right as far as the eye could see. Beyond the terrace was a wide lawn, on the other side of which there were, to our left, azaleas backed by one magnificent copper-beech together with a mixture of sycamores and silver birch and other nondescript hedge-row trees; just ahead of us, a bank of rhododendrons across which one could look out at a broad landscape of virtually unspoilt countryside; to our right, an imposing circle of extremely tall pine-trees; and, to our far right, more rhododendrons and more azaleas with trees behind them.

There were only one or two houses or farm buildings to be seen in the remote distance and, as time went by, I began to feel like any eighteenth-century owner of a country estate looking out from his great house, that these houses spoilt my view and that I would very much like them to be cleared away. If this sounds arrogant, please remember that, living at Holme Grange as we did for so much of our childhood, my siblings and I would be brought up more like minor aristocrats than ordinary people, and no doubt we unconsciously absorbed, besides a few of their virtues, at least a handful of aristocratic vices.

I mentioned that we ate and slept in the Nursery. Our dining-table, usually covered with a white cloth, was the long blue-and-white kitchen table from White Hazel which, with its accompanying blue-and-white chairs, Daddy had installed just beneath the long window. At night-time, Elizabeth began by sleeping in a cot in a corner of our parents' bedroom next door, but Simon and I both had beds in the Nursery from the first. Mine was just inside the door on the left, with Simon's parallel to mine on the far wall; and sometimes, when we had woken up in the mornings and a subdued light came in along the length of the floral curtains, we would talk happily of this and that as we lay there in our pyjamas until Mummy came in to pull open the curtains and persuade us out of bed.

Then we washed our face and hands with soap and water and a flannel in the hand-basin by the door, and brushed our teeth using Ammident tooth powder. This came in a thin round tin, from which we learned to tip some of the powder onto the centre of our left hand before using our right hand to stir it into a paste with a dampened toothbrush.

After this we dressed, and our Nanny for the time being would bring our breakfast up on a tray from the kitchen downstairs, and we would eat it with her at the table. It was an ordinary table with an ordinary white table-cloth, and our food was served up on ordinary white plates; but the only cutlery we ever used was a combination of ivory or bone-handled knives and silver spoons and forks. There were some pieces of solid silver cutlery dating as far back at the seventeenth century, but most of it was silver-plated; and each item, whatever its date, was stamped on the back of its handle with markings including a rampant lion that showed it was real silver; and on the front with the eagle taken from the Graves family crest, of which more later.

This cutlery was stored in the two middle drawers of a large antique Welsh Georgian oak cupboard with small brass knobs, that stood outside the nursery door in a wide alcove on the left-hand-side of the long corridor. This beautiful item of furniture, whose cupboards both above and below the silver drawers were filled with clean towels and linen and such-like, had recently been purchased by my Aunt Clarissa for only fifteen shillings, and given to my parents as a moving-to-Holme-Grange present. I am glad to be able to tell you that seventy-three years later I have it still.

Nothing else in the Nursery would ever be as precious to us as that silver cutlery. There were several easy chairs on a slightly faded carpet; a toy-cupboard; a small bookcase and a built-in wardrobe in the far corner of the room, with a side-facing cupboard above it that reached to the ceiling and seemed impossibly high-up for any normal person to use. There was also a blocked-up fire-place: no-one wanted to light fires on a regular basis, and there was no central heating at Holme Grange, so when it grew cold, we used a two-bar electric fire to keep warm.

The nannies looked after us during the day, though with very mixed success. Personally, with my sixth birthday approaching, I felt far too old and independent to need a nanny, and under my bad influence Simon, like me, soon grew to regard them as enemies to be outwitted. I certainly never loved a single one of them as I had loved Gabriele, and I don't think any of them ever stayed for long.

This is hardly surprising. The only nanny-related incident I still see very clearly happened on a day when it was pouring with rain, driving in fiercely from the north-west. By this time I had learned that with the wind blowing from that particular quarter there would be a dry foot or so underneath the eaves on the southern side of the building. So having escaped with Simon from our current nanny, a German girl who very much liked to be obeyed, there we are, running very fast down the nursery stairs (while as usual I do my best not to look into the cellar), veering round to the right, slipping out of the door beside the drawing-room, and hiding under the eaves. We can hear the nanny calling more and more loudly for us, first in English and then in what we assume is her native tongue.

Before long my father, who has been trying to work quietly in his study, is aroused by her shouting. I should mention that he has a tremendous, almost superhuman knack, invaluable in a Headmaster, for shimmering up like Jeeves and suddenly appearing in the middle of any trouble-spot; and now he turns up rather crossly asking what on earth is the matter. "It's your children", she sobs. "Elizabeth's a good girl, but I can't find those boys anywhere!"

At least Mummy would usually be back with us in time to supervise our high tea in the Nursery; after which she bathed us every evening before bed.

The bathroom was some distance away from the nursery, reached by turning to the right past the head of the stairs and setting out down a long, windowless and therefore somewhat sinister corridor. Doors on the left opened first into a massive airing cupboard, at least eight feet deep and six feet wide; and then into two large handsome rooms looking out over the roundabout: the first of which would eventually become Elizabeth's, and the second of which was occupied by a long succession of chefs, of whom my father employed the good, the bad and the indifferent. Doors on the right opened into three bedrooms overlooking the kitchen yard: first Mummy's and Daddy's large square bedroom, then two narrow and somewhat disagreeable rooms; and finally, another large and comparatively secluded room which was largely hidden from view from outside by the expanse of shrubs and trees which lay between this end of the servants' wing and a driveway which led off from the roundabout towards the back of the kitchens.

Used at first by two female servants including the young woman who had first answered the door to us, it contained, apart from two individual beds, a large Victorian wardrobe, a large Victorian chest-of- drawers, and a large Victorian marble-topped table on which there stood (for washing purposes) a large Victorian jug standing in a large Victorian bowl. Then at last, right at the end of the corridor, we would reach the bathroom door set uninvitingly in the centre of a blank wall.

Such of course had not been Norman Shaw's intention. He had designed a broad window at the end of this corridor, through which light would have cheerfully streamed in. But at some later stage a bathroom had been built on to the servant's wing and, to avoid blocking the light from the room beneath, which was evidently more highly regarded than the corridor above, it projected from the end of the building resting on four tall iron stilts set in a concrete base on the ground far below. This ugly addition to the original Holme Grange was no more than a square box with a flat roof, though its exterior had been hung with red-brick tiles, presumably in an attempt to make it fit in with the rest of the building.

Whenever I opened the door and stepped down the three short steps into the bathroom – and please notice that this extension had been so badly designed that its floor was not even on the same level as the corridor – I could see a hand-basin under the window to my left, a bath along the wall opposite, beneath a long thin window very high up; and, in the near corner round to the right, an old-fashioned WC with a cistern high up above, from which a chain and chain-pull depended.

I didn't like this bathroom any more than I liked the corridor, mainly because although I knew that it was my moral duty to pull the chain after I had been to the lavatory, I was frightened by the sound of its flushing. I never confided this to anyone, first out of shame and then much later because I could guess what a good Freudian analyst might make of it; but for several years I imagined that as soon as I had pulled the chain and the lavatory had begun to flush, a huge snake was rushing up out of the water to kill me. I knew that the only way I could protect myself was by running as hard as I could, up the steps, through the door and along the corridor – and that if I ran fast enough (which thank goodness I always did, but that didn't mean that the danger had ceased to exist) the snake would be powerless to catch me.

Bath-times, though in the same room as the snake-infested lavatory, were a happier affair. Off came my shoes and socks, then my shorts and pants, and then "Skin-a-rabbit!" Mummy would cry out cheerfully as she pulled jumper, shirt and vest over my head, and then I stepped straight into the bath. My place was always sitting at the west end, which I thought was much safer. I was always a little worried about Simon, sitting at the east end with his back to the taps and dangerously close, as I thought, to the plughole. Suppose the plug was accidentally pulled out while he was still in the bath, and he was gurgled away into nothingness!

As for Mummy: she sat on a stool beside the bath, and helped us to soap ourselves while we chatted amiably together. Our conversation was normally about the events of the day; but ever since Mummy had been the schoolgirl Mary Wickens, she had enjoyed being an excellent mimic, imitating her teachers' mannerisms and eccentricities to deadly effect; and now, on occasion, in order to indulge this passion, she amused herself by pretending that she had to leave the bathroom on some important errand. She would be gone just long enough for us to start calling out to her: "Mummy! Mummy! Where are you?"

And then, imitating the voice of Mary McKendrick, one of the close friends she had made while teaching up in Scotland, she would return in character as 'The Scottish Friend'. "Hello children" she would say in a flawless Scots accent, "What's all this noise about then?"

Simon, anxiously: "Where were you Mummy? We wanted you."

"Mummy? I'm not your Mummy. I'm the Scottish friend. Your Mummy's gone awa' the noo and left me tae tak' care o' ye. What can ye tell me aboot yourselves? I hope you're gude obedient children."

"But you're not the friend!" I would protest "You're not the friend – you're Mummy!"

"No I'm not. I'm the Scottish friend! Your Mummy's gone away!"

The conversation that followed would become increasingly surreal. The stories she told us in her character as the Scottish friend were happy stories reflecting her own life long ago in St. Andrews, a time when she was young and independent, far away from her family and with a new and exciting set of friends. But it was also an elaborate tease, and sometimes Simon found it frightening.

"But you *are* Mummy!" He was suddenly on the verge of tears and shaking his arms oddly. And then, realizing that she had gone on too long, the Scottish Friend would explain, still in her Mary McKendrick accent, that it was time for her to do her messages.

"Messages – what messages?" I was intrigued.

"Do you not know that's the word we use for shopping. Oh dear, you're so ignorant. Puir wee Sassenach. Does your Mummy teach you nothing?"

"But you are Mummy!"

And then she would leave the bathroom and after a while, to our great joy, return as herself.

CHAPTER FOUR
Exploration

If we can go back to a time when the autumn term has not yet begun, those last few weeks of the summer of 1951 were an excellent opportunity for me to explore both inside and out. To begin with, I found that on reaching the foot of the nursery stairs (as the servants' staircase had rapidly been renamed) the corridors led off in so many directions that it was easy to lose my way. Unless I was with a grown-up, I avoided those to the left and opposite for the time being, the ones which led to the staff-room, the kitchens and the changing-rooms, not knowing them well enough. But I soon learned that if I turned right and immediately right again, that took me past a set of stone steps leading unshielded down into the cellar, and on into the pantry.

During the holidays this room was often deserted, so that I could wander round it freely. I saw cupboards on almost every wall, and a large double sink with draining-boards on each side of it underneath a long window through which I could see the roundabout and part of the drive. There were also two tables: a narrow one with two gas rings on it which had been placed in front of a blocked-up fireplace immediately opposite the entrance; and a broad one with chairs round it in the middle of the room. There was also a mysterious door just next to the fireplace which I found was always kept locked.

From the pantry it was an easy walk to the rooms, one at each end of the red-tiled corridor, in which my parents were often to be found: either to the drawing-room by the side door in which Mummy might be writing at her desk or playing on her piano, or to the study just next to the Front Hall where Daddy was busily making plans for his first term as Headmaster.

The Drawing-room (designed by Norman Shaw to be used as a smoking-room) was by far the most elegant of our family rooms at Holme Grange. Directly beneath the Nursery, it too attracted the sunlight, which poured through the small leaded-light panes of a bow window before slanting its way across a large semi-circular windowsill on which my mother had placed her metronome, a beautiful round glass paperweight, several Coronation mugs, and a decorated china bowl that in due course would be filled to the brim with sweet-smelling dried lavender. Passing over these, it lit up the edge of an upright Bechstein piano, my mother's pride and joy, placed at a slight angle to the eastern wall; and, in the centre of the room, it reached a modern if somewhat functional set of sofa and armchairs. Finally, the sunlight came to rest on a handsome fireplace with an alcove on each side of it.

On the wall just outside the drawing-room, as a kind of foretaste of the family pleasures within, my father had hung an oval case containing the Gold Medals won at Trinity College Dublin by Charles Graves, the future Bishop of Limerick, and his brothers John Thomas Graves and Robert Perceval Graves; and now in these alcoves on each side of the fireplace in the drawing-room there were huge framed marble portraits, one of the Bishop and the other of his wife Selina, imposing portraits which, like the marble table in the Front Hall, had once featured in the Bishop's Palace. Their grandeur must have made a powerful impression upon prospective parents, who would always be interviewed in this room, and could learn from it that the Headmaster of Holme Grange had distinguished antecedents.

In the alcove on the right, beneath Selina, was a beautiful antique desk with serpentine legs at which my mother conducted both her official and her private business, preparing for her lessons, drafting menus for the chef or writing letters to family and friends. There were little drawers at the back of the desk, and a secret compartment under the baize table-top in which anything really private could be hidden: though thanks to her own mother's training she was never a great one for hanging on to any mementoes apart from photographs; and once she had read any letters she had received, and dealt with any matters they contained that needed dealing with, they were speedily torn up and discarded.

In the alcove on the left, beneath the Bishop, was a traditional wooden gate-leg table at the back of which stood a wireless set and a black bakelite telephone. This was the table to which my parents had their supper brought to them by one of the servants each evening just before 6:45. It meant that while they were enjoying their first course, almost always a bowl of soup, they could also be listening to the latest episode of *The Archers*. Unless of course the telephone rang, when even that shared pleasure would have to be put to one side, because answering the telephone always came first.

Fewer than one in eight households even owned a telephone in those days. It was a large, solid, important instrument with a large, round silver-coloured metal dial on its front, round the edge of which, going anti-clockwise from top right all the way round and down to the bottom, were ten finger-holes for dialling, at the back of which one could see both the numbers in red running from 1 to 9 and then on to 0, and all the letters of the alphabet in black, in groups of two or three. At its centre of this dial was a round white insert, the top half of which had a notice printed in red stating simply:

EMERGENCY CALLS
FOR
FIRE |
POLICE | DIAL
AMBULANCE | 999

While on the bottom half was printed in larger black letters, our telephone number:

WOKINGHAM
66

Resting in a cradle on its top was a large, solid receiver, waiting to be picked up when the telephone rang, and attached to the main body of the telephone by several interwoven strands of thin cabling; while the telephone itself was also attached by more cabling to a black box with a handle on one side which, when turned, connected it with its fellow just down the red-tiled corridor in my father's study.

It would be almost forty years before the birth of the Internet, so these two large black telephones, fixed immovably to their places in drawing-room and study, were our only means of instant communication with the outside world. This made them critically important. A single missed telephone call might mean that we lost a possible pupil and with him up to five years' worth of valuable income. So one of my father's first responsibilities was to ensure that throughout the year, in term-time or holiday-time, morning, noon and night, either he or some other competent person must always be stationed within earshot of incoming calls. This rapidly became known within our family circle as 'Guarding the Telephone', and was a constant preoccupation.

As for the remainder of the drawing room: built-in book-shelves with cupboards below them ran wherever there was room for them. Beside my mother's desk were her books and music; while the space behind the piano contained a jumble of old violins in their cases, piled up anyhow alongside my father's Cello and the guitar he had used so often in entertainments at Sandroyd.

Daddy had a pleasant baritone voice, and occasionally he would treat us to one of his favourite nursery rhymes, such as 'A frog he would a-wooing go' or 'A carrion crow sat on an oak'. But the more musical part of his life had somehow come to an end with his assumption of new responsibilities at Holme Grange. The guitar I never saw again, though I later heard that he had handed it on to Lizzie when she was thirteen or fourteen; and I only once saw him take that Cello from its huge black case to show it to us children; and even then, he only plucked a few notes on it and told us what a terrible time he had had travelling with it on the London Underground, before packing it away again for ever.

On the near wall, on each side of the door, the shelves were full of my father's books, many of them the result of his subscriptions to various Reprint book clubs, mostly undertaken to supply Amy with fresh reading matter in her Harlech retreat. He still enjoyed reading when he had time for it, and I remember he and my mother gradually working their way through a four-volume set of Somerset Maugham's short stories; but the most magnificent item in their drawing room, hidden away in the cupboards below the books, was Daddy's shell collection.

Conchology must have been one of the consuming passions of my father's red-headed youth, for there were at least fifteen boxes, each with four trays of shells, all carefully laid out and labelled with their Latin names. From time to time, he would bring out one of the boxes and show us the contents, which particularly fascinated my brother Simon; and whenever we shared a seaside holiday, Daddy knew the names of every shell that we brought to him for his inspection.

My father's centre of operations was now his study just down the corridor beside the entrance-hall. First you had to open an outer door and then, after two or three feet of hanging space so crammed with jackets and overcoats that navigating it was a little like passing through the coats at the back of the cupboard which leads into Narnia, an inner-door opened not onto the broad expanse of a wintry forest (as I would sometimes hope), but into his extremely small study.

There was just enough room for a medium-sized desk placed at right-angles to the wall under the window, a couple of chairs, a filing cabinet and one or two glass-fronted cases. Daddy would sit at the left-hand-side of this desk on a fine old wooden chair upholstered in green leather and stamped on its back with the cipher of his grandfather the Bishop from whose Palace it had come. On the desk in front of him was a black typewriter which looked almost equally ancient, and a telephone exactly like the one in the drawing-room.

But although it was a very small room, from one of its corners a door opened into an area lined with shelves which ran along the other side of the wall from the red-tiled corridor until it met the back of that mysteriously locked door in the pantry, so there was plenty of storage space. A much greater advantage was its strategic position. Not only was it placed on the very edge of the main body of the school, with the Hall only a few steps away; but it was also immediately alongside the only route leading from that main block to the north-east wing, with its kitchens, staff-room and changing-rooms. And, most important of all, while sitting at his desk just beside the window, the new Headmaster could look out over the roundabout and the main drive, and keep a close eye upon all the daily comings and goings.

One morning, as the start of term approached, Daddy allowed me to follow him all the way from our Nursery into the main school. Down the red-tiled corridor we went, past that curious glassed-in area, which he now explained to me housed a serving hatch for the dining-room, past his study, through the Entrance Hall, and then left through one half of those tall double-doors into the Main Hall of which I had previously caught no more than a glimpse.

It turned out to be a huge space, several times the size of the hall at Ashmore School, and much more impressive than the one at Sandroyd. The walls were covered from floor to ceiling with large oak panels; and the main light came in through the largest and most dramatic window that I had ever seen. This veritable wall of glass was situated mainly on the east side of the Hall, but turned the corner to a small section on the south side; and was composed of numerous framed sections full of leaded lights, exactly like the ones in the drawing-room. Before reaching that window, one came first to a substantial and elaborately carved Victorian oak bookcase with cupboards at each end which had been brought down from Erinfa.

This was crammed with books, many of them stamped on the spine with the name of one Graves or another, and I soon learned that this was indeed the Graves family bookcase. It is said to have been the only extravagance in the life of my great-great-uncle the Reverend Robert Perceval Graves. Family tradition says that the bookcase was made for him while he was serving as curate-in-charge of Windermere in the Lake District back in the 1840s.

On his death in 1893, by which time he was back in Dublin where he had served both as sub-Dean of the Chapel Royal and as Warden of Alexandra College – he was a great proponent of female education – he bequeathed this bookcase to his favourite nephew Alfred, to whom he had given much literary encouragement. Now that it was in the Hall at Holme Grange School, it still contained several of Robert Perceval's published works, including a number of his sermons, several of his poems, and his magisterial (Wikipedia unkindly prefers the word 'rambling') three volume biography of the celebrated mathematician Sir William Rowan Hamilton. More memorably, it contained our greatest family treasure, a copy of the 1845 edition of *Wordsworth's Poetical Works* inscribed:

To
the Revd. Robert Perceval Graves
as a token of sincere affection
from
the author
Wm. Wordsworth

Rydal Mount
14th March
1846

Between the bookcase and the great East Window, was a doorway which led into the Dining-Room. We won't go into it on this occasion, though it is a splendid room, but it contains still more family history, in the form of a number of large canvases, Georgian and Victorian, which cover its walls. They are generally dark and gloomy, with the gloomiest of all being that of my German great-grandmother Luise von Ranke, a sensitive and unhappy woman who in life was completely dominated by her husband Heinrich, the Kaiser's friend; and in death is now destined for many years to look down somewhat ferociously upon rows of schoolboys eating just beneath her. The only really attractive picture is of Helena Perceval, not only a celebrated beauty and a leader of Dublin Society in the 1820s; but also a distant cousin of the assassinated Prime Minister Spencer Perceval, and with a flawless Perceval pedigree extending back not only to a number of Kings and Queens, but also, as I mentioned earlier, to a grandfather of William the Conqueror. What I heard of her from my father was that she had ruined her husband's chances of promotion through being too pushy – and on another wall there he is: John Crosbie Graves himself in his old age, looking extremely melancholy, as though he has become inured to a succession of great disappointments.

Returning to the School Hall: beneath the great East Window is a wide window-sill, and on the back wall is another real treasure: a small bookcase containing an entire set of the thick-volumed 1911 edition of the Encyclopaedia Britannica, with brilliant essays by all the leading writers of the day. I never progressed much further than looking into the volume of maps, the most modern of which contained numerous countries that no longer existed, and depicted a world much of which appeared to be part of the British Empire.

At the centre of the far end of the Hall stands the two-drawer oak writing table at which my father will sit in an antique oak barley twist armchair while taking Morning Assembly. At his back, a substantial open fire-place, unfortunately marred by the addition of a modern ugly square anthracite stove; and at his left-hand-side, right up against the west wall, is the Steck Grand Piano at which my mother will sit to play the morning hymn.

Other doors lead off to the west, but they need not concern us now. What holds my eye as I turn round while Daddy searches through one of the drawers of the writing-table for some important notes that he has mislaid, is my first view of the north side of the Hall. A great deal of its width is taken up with a broad flight of steps, broader even, I imagined, than the stairs by which I had been impressed in the puppet theatre at Sandroyd, and leading all the way up to a landing beneath another large window.

'Richard', said Daddy, who had found his missing notes and seen where I was looking, 'I'll show you a quicker way back to the Nursery from here!' And he held my hand and we climbed up and up those stairs until we came to the landing. Then we turned right and right again, walking past a doorway set in the far corner of the landing and climbed up a few more steps to another much larger landing. From here, corridors and steps ran off bewilderingly in all directions; but at the end of the long corridor to my left I could see the reassuring sight of the Nursery door with our newly-acquired oak cupboard beside it. And very soon, having said goodbye to Daddy, I had completed my first circuit of the two staircases of Holme Grange.

As for the grounds: everything had been so badly run-down during Gordon Walker's Headmastership, that in her later years my mother would enjoy reminding us that when we first arrived at Holme Grange, it was so wild and there were so many brambles that in the autumn it was possible to pick blackberries from any one of its six exterior doors. For Simon and me, this wildness made the grounds all the more exciting, though we discovered them very gradually, usually taking as our starting-point the large white door beside the drawing-room, which opened immediately onto our small and well-sheltered private garden.

Down its centre ran a broad path of white paving-stones, which stretched from the white door to the steps leading down to the terrace. Immediately to the left of this path came first an irregularly paved area just beneath the drawing-room window, on which deck-chairs were placed in good weather; then two large squares of lawn, with a small shrub at the centre of each; and to the left of this divided lawn a long narrow flower-bed which ran between a much narrower path and a tall yew hedge. To the right of the path was another small paved area just beneath the main window of the school dining-room, and then two more flower-beds: first a small one of irregular shape and then a large square one, in the centre of which Daddy had planted out the Christmas Tree that we had brought with us in its container from White Hazel.

The further of the two shrubs in the squares of lawn, a small camellia, had been grown from a cutting given to Daddy by his mother, and was therefore sacred to her memory; and, following Amy's example back in his childhood at Red Branch House, Daddy allocated to each of us children one of the three flower-beds: the long narrow one by the hedge became known as my garden; the small irregular one was Elizabeth's, and the one with the Christmas Tree became Simon's. I secretly thought at first that this was most unfair, since I had always regarded that Christmas Tree as mine; but it settled in very happily in its new position, and after a while I decided that it would be mean of me to go on being jealous, especially as my flower-bed was close to a much more exciting part of the grounds.

For between the drawing-room window and the start of the long hedge behind my garden was the entrance to a patch of real wilderness, and Daddy had strictly enjoined us never to go through it without him. "Why?" I had asked.

"Come and have a look!" he had replied, before taking me through and showing me a sight which I found still more sinister than the fearsome long drop into the cellar. There in a kind of cavern beneath an undisciplined mass of overhanging trees and shrubs were two sections of loose iron railings laid somewhat haphazardly flat on the ground. Daddy lobbed a stone through the railings, and after a while there was a splashing sound. For beneath those railings lay the huge and hungry mouth of the ancient well which must have been used by Holme Grange before mains running water had been installed. The well-head with its winding-gear and buckets had long ago been removed, but the well had never been properly capped and now lay there, as I thought, ready to lure the unwary to their death.

Back in our more secure area, I resumed playing and running around cheerfully in the sun but then, without meaning to, I committed a terrible crime which was that I stumbled over the camellia and effectively killed it by breaking its main stem. Daddy tried not to show it, but I could tell that he was so terribly upset, and I loved him so much that this filled me with a most unpleasant guilt, only moderated many years later when, with small children of my own, I recognized the folly of planting a sacred shrub in a place where those children are going to be running about. Yet I still see and feel my father's sorrow, and a portion of that guilt remains with me.

In due course, as we became more adventurous, especially when left alone, Simon and I began climbing up onto the yew hedge. Our first pleasure was to discover that it had been trimmed to grow so densely that we could walk along its top; and then, far more exciting, we developed a new game of hurling ourselves at it, rolling over the top, and landing with a bump on the foot or so of grass on the other side that divided it from the terrace. When we stood up again, pleasurably shaken but unhurt, we could look across the terrace at the vast southern lawn stretching the whole length of Holme Grange from east to west, and the shrubs and trees beyond it; and the most memorable event of our first few weeks at Holme Grange was watching the felling of one of the circle of pine trees which stood almost immediately opposite the broad flight of red-brick steps that led down to the lawn from the centre of the terrace. Daddy had decided on this felling not because there was anything wrong with the tree, but because he intended that the area contained by the semi-circle of trees that remained, should become the stage of an out-door theatre for the school productions that he was already planning.

This felling was the first time that I remember seeing our Head Groundsman, Mr. Hills. A short plump man in his forties with a jowly weather-beaten face, round spectacles, dirty dungarees and a flat cap, he arrived on the scene with his assistant in tow carrying a massive two-handed saw. Mr. Hills took one end of this, his assistant took the other and, closely directed by my father, they set to work. First, they cut a V-shape very low down on the trunk of the tree on the side that Daddy wished it to fall, which was towards the terrace but not in the direction of the flight of steps; and then they went round to the further side of the tree and resumed their sawing. After a while there was a tremendous splitting noise, and the top of the tree began moving in our direction. 'Timber!' shouted Mr. Hills somewhat theatrically, and then the whole massive tree crashed down with a mighty thud onto the lawn, its top coming to within inches of the brick wall beneath the terrace. Simon and I ran down onto the lawn full of excitement at being able to walk among the branches which only a few minutes before had been so far out of our reach; and within a few days every last scrap of that felled giant had been cut up for firewood or kindling and safely stored away for the winter.

CHAPTER FIVE

Home Grange Comes to Life

Then suddenly the start of the Autumn term was upon us. There had already been days of bustling preparations. A senior Matron had been safely installed in her bedroom just off the landing on the main staircase and, helped by her assistant-matron, was busily making up beds in the dormitories; while at our end of Holme Grange, the Chef had taken up residence in his room next to the bathroom; and I had made my first venture into the Staff Room on the floor below. This was reached by going down the nursery stairs, turning left and going right along to the end of the corridor. Here on my left was a log basket filled with logs; on my right shelves filled with sets of school text-books; and straight ahead through the open door I could see, kneeling on the floor and wrestling with some leather object, the middle-aged man with a check jacket and a booming voice who had greeted us so warmly on our first visit to Holme Grange.

He appeared to be wearing exactly the same check jacket and grey flannel trousers as on our first encounter, and he certainly had exactly the same large but well-trimmed moustache, and exactly the same hair, with no parting in it, slicked back all the way from his forehead to the back of his head. When he looked up and noticed me, he had exactly the same bushy eyebrows, exactly the same kindly yet authoritative gaze, exactly the same slightly careworn look, and exactly the same air of someone who would stand no nonsense and one had better know it; and when he spoke, or rather called out, his voice was just as booming as I had remembered:

"Come on in, come on in young Graves! You probably won't be able to give me a hand, but you can see what I'm doing!"

Walking into the Staff Room at his invitation, and intrigued by the novelty of being addressed by my surname, I could see that the only other person in the room, sitting in an armchair reading a newspaper in his dark, three-piece suit, was a slightly plump individual with a round clean-shaven face, thinning straight dark hair, and dark eyes which looked at me with an indolent air of total indifference. Saying nothing at all to me, he stood up, revealing himself to be short as well as slightly plump, rolled his newspaper under his arm, said "Hinton, I'll catch you later" and strode from the room, on his way out running his fingers appreciatively over the beautiful antique walnut-veneered oval table that my father had brought from White Hazel.

This superior-looking gentleman was Mr. Noble. His bad influence upon Gordon Walker, the previous Headmaster, was as yet unsuspected; and he had remained in post as Senior Master, where he provided continuity. He was also thought to carry a good deal of social weight in the town, where he lived with his elderly mother in a large house at this end of Murdoch Road, by far the most prestigious street in the whole of Wokingham.

Round that beautiful table so much admired by Mr. Noble, my father had placed a set of handsome dining chairs with carved and rounded wooden backs; but the remainder of the staff room, though still comfortable, was more practical and down-to-earth. On the south wall, with an armchair on each side of it, was a fireplace in which log fires burned furiously for much of the year. Just beyond the fireplace stood a stationery cupboard, full of neatly-piled supplies for the staff to distribute to their pupils, including pencils, paper, pens, ink, rubbers, paper-clips and (my favourite) sweet-smelling unused exercise-books; and just beyond the stationery cupboard on the west wall was a window which opened over the drive.

On the north wall there was another window, long and narrow and very high up; between the north wall and the east wall was a door which led into the Boiler Room, notable to me not so much for its huge boiler which supplied hot water to the whole school, as for its vast wooden rack on which clothes were dried, and which could be hauled up and down by ropes on pulleys; and on the east wall, to the right as one entered the Staff Room, was a huge floor-to-ceiling cupboard. In the top part of this the teaching staff had their own private shelves; and down below Mr. Hinton, who was in charge of Games as well as being Head of French, kept the school sports equipment, including five or six leather footballs. It was these footballs that he was now preparing for the autumn term, and I watched fascinated at the elaborate procedure this involved: inserting the bladder into the football, which in itself appeared to be hard work; blowing it up with a pump until the ball was hard enough for use, and finally tying up the laces on the outside of the ball to close the gap through which the bladder had been inserted.

News of only one event from the outside world reached me during this time, and that was because Mummy and Daddy disappeared for most of one Saturday and, when they returned, they came into the Nursery bringing presents for us all, and talked very excitedly about the visit they had just made to the South Bank Exhibition in London. This was the centre-piece of the Festival of Britain, a national exhibition and fair that was designed partly to commemorate the centenary of the Great Exhibition of 1851, and partly to be what its Director described as 'a tonic to the nation' after so many years first of war and then of post-war austerity. It had opened back in May while we were still at White Hazel, and had already attracted millions of visitors to events and displays throughout the United Kingdom.

My particular present was a jigsaw showing the whole South Bank Exhibition from above. It included crowds of people, the vast Dome of Discovery and that great symbol of the Festival of Britain, the Skylon, a vertical steel structure suspended in the air 50 feet from the ground, and rising to a height of 300 feet. It all looked so exciting that I was deeply disappointed not to have been present myself. "I wish I could have come with you", I said. "Oh, Ricky, you wouldn't have enjoyed it!" said Mummy. I felt certain that I would have done, but she was now looking so disappointed herself that I had to pretend to be satisfied.

The actual start of term began with the arrival of the Boarders. From the Nursery I could hear the muted sounds of cars arriving and departing, of car doors slamming, of the traffic of feet on the main stairs and of the hum of excited conversations mostly in a treble key, with an occasional louder tenor or baritone voice breaking in. By the time I fell asleep this had all died down; and then in the morning I woke to a new world, from which both Daddy and Mummy had been substantially removed. Daddy's frequent absences for most of the day we had become accustomed to at White Hazel, but Mummy's absence from breakfast to tea-time came as a shock. Simon felt this particularly and clung first to me and then to our nanny for reassurance. As for me, I have already mentioned that at the age of five-and-three-quarters I felt that I was far too old to suffer the indignity of being told what to do by a nanny, so as usual I planned to escape from her for as much of the day as possible.

After breakfast that day, there were more distant noises as the Day-Boys arrived. Simon seemed uninterested, and wanted me to join him in playing one of our favourite indoor games, which was to transform the area under the table into a private house of our own; but having told our nanny that I needed to go to the lavatory, I slipped away downstairs, where I found that the pantry had been transformed into a centre of frenetic activity.

This involved a team of five or six women who cycled into work each morning from their council housing estates, the closest of which was only just over a mile away on the southern edge of Wokingham not far from the level crossing. Berkshire born and bred and with broad accents to match, they all wore pinafores or house-coats over long flowery dresses, and some of them habitually tied up their hair with knotted headscarves. We were lucky to have them, since they were already part of a vanishing breed. Working at an establishment like Holme Grange no longer carried the social cachet it had done in the days of the Westons, and their more enterprising contemporaries were already working for more money in the local factories. At any rate, although they mostly ignored me, they did not seem to mind my coming in to see them, which I did from time to time over the next few days.

It was to the pantry that dirty cutlery and crockery was regularly brought in: on trays from the Nursery or the drawing-room; and on trollies either from the school dining room, where the Boarders had breakfast and high tea and the whole of the school had lunch, or from the staff room where the resident members of the teaching staff dined each evening. The washing-up was done by hand, so I would often find four of the women standing together beside the huge double-sink beneath the window, with one of them stacking, another washing and rinsing, and another drying-up the cutlery or putting the plates into the huge wooden drying-rack attached to the wall. The fourth would be putting away in the pantry cupboards or stacking another trolley in preparation for restocking the glassed-in serving area where a good deal of crockery and cutlery was kept.

Most of the school laundry was sent away by the Matrons to be professionally cleaned, but the sink in the pantry was also used for a certain amount of in-house cleaning, especially of things like dirty football shorts, shirts and socks. First a sufficient quantity of these would be placed in the left-hand sink, hot water would be run over them, washing powder would be added from a large packet, and then one of the women would roll up her sleeves and begin the washing, plunging her arms into the water and rubbing the dirty clothes against each other until they were clean. For particularly stubborn stains, an item of clothing would be held against a washboard and attacked with a large green bar of soap.

By now, a large iron mangle would have been brought out from the corner of the pantry in which it normally stood, and when clothes had been washed in the left-hand sink, and rinsed in the right-hand one, any excess water could be pressed out of them by turning the handle of the mangle while feeding the wet clothes through its rollers. After this process, the clothes would be carried in baskets through the corridor and along the edge of the staff-room into the boiler room. There the rack would be lowered, and the clothes hung out all over it, before it was pulled up to the ceiling again; and within a day they would all be bone-dry and once again ready to be taken down to the changing-rooms for use.

The labour must have seemed virtually unceasing, since whenever there was nothing else to be done, it would be time for the women to go to the Pantry cupboard which housed dusters, brooms, mops, buckets, dustpans and brushes, and to set out into every corner of the school buildings on their regular cleaning expeditions. However, there were several set breaks, so occasionally when I visited the pantry I would find all the women sitting round the central table. Mugs of strong, milky, sugary tea would be cradled in their hands, as they discussed everything from their holiday plans to the state of the weather, and made cheerful complaints about the failings of their husbands or children. And all the time lighted cigarettes, which they called fags, hung precariously out of the corners of their mouths, while the room gradually filled with smoke.

I much enjoyed my secret visits to this alien underworld; but my participation in it was short-lived, since my formal education needed to be continued. And although I could already read, which by now I did rather well, my writing left a great deal to be desired, and in any case I was still much too young to join the junior form at Holme Grange. In those days, Boys' Preparatory Schools normally took children only when they were at least 7 or 8 years old, but Girls' Preparatory Schools often took children from as young as 5 or 6, and boosted their income by admitting boys until they had reached their seventh birthday. I had therefore been enrolled without my knowledge at a local girls' school called The White House, where I would be starting at once, and where I would remain for a complete academic year.

CHAPTER SIX

The White House

The walls of its agreeable timber-framed building had certainly been painted white, but the Wokingham version of The White House had nothing whatever to do with the building that has been the home of every American President since John Adams back in 1800. However, it was much more than just another Girls' Prep School, preparing its pupils, as did Boys' Prep Schools, for Common Entrance or Scholarship examinations at the age of 13. What set it apart was its Headmistress, the formidable Miss Beryl Caudwell, who had taken it over, given it its current name, and moved it to its present site in 1948, only three years before the Graves family had arrived at Holme Grange.

Having met Miss Caudwell, my father thoroughly approved of her, which is not at all surprising, since professionally speaking they were brother and sister under the skin. Both were intelligent, strong-minded, capable administrators and both were good Christians with a strong religious faith who were utterly devoted to the welfare of their pupils.

Mummy had passed her driving test by this time, and it was decided that she should take me to my new school each weekday morning. Simon is to come with us, leaving our Nanny with just Elizabeth to look after, and soon after breakfast the three of us would set out down the nursery stairs, where instead of turning left to the staff-room or right to the pantry or the drawing-room, we walk straight across the corridor into another corridor at right-angles to it. At the start of this corridor a huge red baize door, which in less democratic days had been permanently allowed to swing shut, is now equally permanently pinned back against the wall. Just beyond it on the left is the door to the kitchen, and a little further down on the right, beyond the back wall of the drawing-room, is the door to the main kitchen storeroom. Passing these by, we reach a glass-panelled door like the one by Daddy's study, and go through it and down a step into another long narrow corridor.

The kitchen yard is now visible through more glass panels to our left, while on the wall to our right there is a long row of pegs with shoe-lockers beneath them, together with doors into various changing-rooms and lavatories. At its end, this corridor would have led into the boot-rooms and a footbath area; but we have already opened a door on our left and walked out into the kitchen yard. Immediately opposite us on the other side of the yard is a huge pile of coal contained by a tall semi-circle of red-brick wall; while to our right, leading directly on from this wall, is an archway beneath which we walk out onto the back drive.

This sweeps round to the extreme left on its way to the roundabout, and a little ahead of us and to the right goes down a steep slope just past the stump of a large tree (perhaps another of Mr. Hills's victims) to the ugly, oblong, flat-roofed corrugated iron building which is the woodshed. Between these two driveways is the one we want, which runs along for some thirty or forty yards before it terminates in one of our six Nissen Huts.

This particular Hut had the standard tall semi-circular corrugated-iron roof and concrete base, but instead of the normal central doorway flanked by a window on each side, it has become our garage, and has a large pair of wooden doors beneath a wooden fascia. During the day these doors are left wide open, so one can see that inside the left-hand door there is a row of bicycle racks for those day-boys who cycle to school; that just inside the right-hand door there is a huge tank full of the paraffin that is needed for the portable paraffin heaters used for heating most of Holme Grange; and right in the middle of the Nissen Hut stands the familiar black shape of our beloved EPB 223. Walking up to it, Mummy opens the driver's door and pulls her seat down while Simon and I climb into the back. Then she sits down and switches on the ignition.

My great-great-grandfather John Crosbie Graves of Dublin (1776-1835).

My great-great-grandmother Helena Graves née Perceval (1776-1850); the toast of Dublin.

My great-grandfather Heinrich von Ranke of Munich (1830-1909) who went deer-shooting with the Kaiser.

My great-grandfather Charles Graves Bishop of Limerick (1812-1899).

My Grandad Sidney William Wickens of Portsmouth and Rottingdean as a subaltern in the Hampshire Yeomanry.

My grandmother Ellen Wickens née Hilder as a young woman.

The Graves family on 12 July 1910. Back row l. to r. Rosaleen, Dick, Clarissa; middle row l. to r. Philip, my grandparents Amy and Alfred, Robert, Susan; front row l. to r. Charles, my father John.

My parents John and Mary Graves (née Wickens) on their wedding day 3 February 1945.

My mother Mary holding me on the day of my baptism 13 April 1946.

Here I am looking at the ducks on Rottingdean Pond and waiting for the tide to come in.

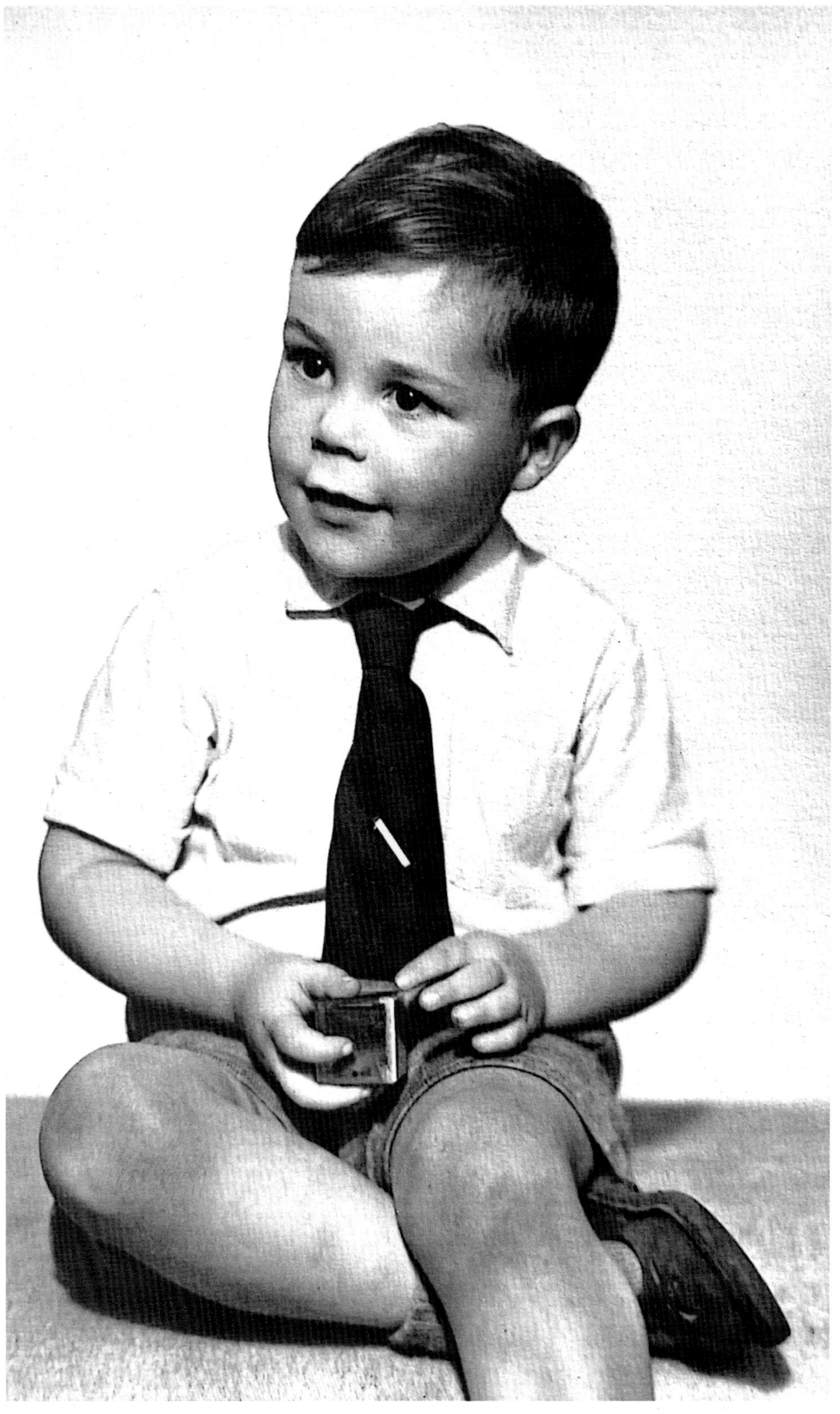

My dear brother Simon William Graves in October 1950 aged 3 years and 1 month.

Daddy with Richard and Simon at White Hazel.

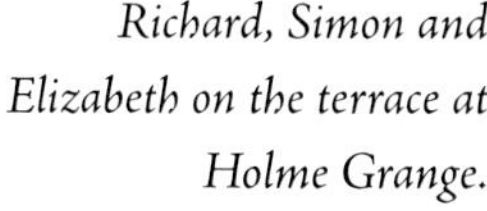

Richard, Simon and Elizabeth on the terrace at Holme Grange.

Holme Grange School from the roundabout.

Holme Grange from the great southern lawn.

Fortunately, starting EPB 223 is not usually a problem, though when the depths of winter arrives and temperatures fall to sub-zero, Daddy has to leave a small oil heater under the engine at night, and cover the bonnet with old rugs, to keep it from freezing-up. Once the engine has turned over a few times, Mummy puts the car into reverse gear and backs us out of the Nissen Hut and up the slight slope towards the kitchen; and then, after changing gear from reverse to first, and from first to second, she follows the drive round until we have reached the roundabout. Turning right when it is safe to do so, we are soon motoring gently down the front drive, past the rhododendrons and the oak tree until we have come to the end of the main drive with the Lodge on our left and the Lake on our right. Pausing for a moment just beyond the gates, there is nothing but farmland ahead of us, and I remember sometimes looking across at the most beautiful wide-open vistas of sky, with perhaps a few clouds whose edges catch the early morning sunlight, and a flock of starlings wheeling past.

Turning right, we follow Heathlands Road as it runs all the way round the edge of the Holme Grange cricket field, with no buildings in sight until we came to the main Easthampstead Road. Here we turn left, past The White Horse and a few farm cottages until, after another hundred yards, we turn sharp left into a narrow unpaved track. This is a private road belonging to Ludgrove School, but using it cuts our journey time in half, and perhaps there is a right-of-way along it, because, so far as I know, no-one ever objects to our motoring along it. In any case it is often in a very poor state of repair, and sometimes so full of pot-holes as to be almost impassable.

Apart from those potholes it is a pleasant enough journey: after passing almost immediately a substantial red-brick house to our right, built somewhat in the Holme Grange style, there is nothing but farmland on each side of us. And while Mummy navigates the potholes, sometimes veering suddenly from one side of the track to the other, Simon and I amuse ourselves by singing invented songs. Our favourite begins "Here we pass, green as grass!" which we think is the funniest and cleverest rhyme ever, so we sing it gleefully again and again, replacing it when appropriate in the depths of winter with "Here we go, white as snow!"

Eventually we come to the entrance to Ludgrove School on our left, and I feel a sense of relief when we have passed it and no-one has leaped out to bar our way. Then after another stretch of farmland Mummy drives us under a bridge carrying the railway line from Wokingham down to the south-east, and from there we soon reach the main Finchampstead Road which, when we have made a left turn, runs in the same direction as the railway. A little further on the road branches off to the right down Evendons Lane, which I mention because it will feature later on in our story; but we carry on along the Finchampstead Road for a short distance further before turning across the traffic into an open gateway. Beside it, a large notice proclaims in bold black letters on a white background that this is

The White House Preparatory School

Beyond this sign there is a range of school buildings; and, as we proceed up the very short drive, we can see to our right a large triangular field, reaching all the way back to the junction with Evendons Lane, and edged by a strip of trees and shrubs so dense that it is all completely private.

The White House itself is an attractive building. It is mostly black-and-white, but all the window-frames and the horizontal timbers between the ground floor and the first floor have been painted the same forget-me-not blue as the dresses worn by the girls who are excitedly milling about. On our first visit, we are met near the front door by Miss Caudwell herself, also in a blue dress. She is a thin, active woman in her forties with piercing eyes and with her long hair done up in a bun, so that she reminds me of my Aunt Clarissa. "Welcome, welcome!" she says, shaking my hand with a fearsome grip which is also like that of my Aunt. "I hope you will be happy here!" And I was.

At first, I was placed in the lowest form of all, which met at one end of the school hall; and here I received some of the most valuable education of my entire childhood. At the very start of my very first day, our form-mistress asked us to leave our desks, and lined us up in three rows just ahead of her at the front of the hall. I had no idea what to expect. "Now then, children", she said, waving her arms as though she was conducting a symphony orchestra, "Let's start from the beginning. Once two is two, Two twos are four, Three twos are six...." I dropped out almost immediately, never having been taught my tables at Ashmore School; and, as we went on, more and more children also fell silent, until by the time we had reached "Three nines are twenty-seven, Four nines are thirty-six" there was almost no-one still chanting.

Our form-mistress didn't appear to mind this at all. "Well done children, very good!" she said. "Take your tables home tonight – they're on the bottom of the back page of your Maths exercise books. Read them over again and again – and we'll have another try tomorrow morning."

She repeated this exercise every single day. I began to look forward to the ritual chanting – it was like a wonderful new game. Before very long, the first five or six tables had become second-nature to me, and I was developing a feeling for many more of them, especially the ten times table which seemed almost ridiculously easy with its ten, twenty, thirty, forty and so on, all the way up to 'Nine tens are ninety'; though it became a little more difficult from then on, and I was still some distance away from the climactic "Twelve twelves are a hundred and forty-four!" At this stage, I had no real understanding about the point of it all, but it was great fun, and this knowledge, so easily acquired, would be invaluable to me for the rest of my life.

Miss Caudwell suddenly descended upon us one morning in the middle of our chanting, removed me from the lowest form with hardly a word, and took me up to the form above, which was known as Transition. I found myself placed in a desk near the back of a large classroom, presided over by Miss Redgrove, a motherly but extremely firm school-mistress who insisted on good discipline and hard work and was rewarded by both. I recall one incident in particular from my time in her form. She had given me a work-book in a series called 'Think-and-Do', which I had been encouraged to take home, where I showed it to my mother. As she read the title a teasing glint came into her eye.

"Oh Ricky", she said. "Think-and-Do? For you? I'm going to call it "Do-and-Think!" Which she did from then on, in the light of my tendency (as she saw it) to act first, often very suddenly, and to think afterwards.

At any rate, each page of the workbook contains line-drawings, with questions attached. You can see me sitting there one morning looking at a line-drawing of a fierce-looking tiger, with the question below reading: "What would you do if you met a tiger?" This is followed by a printed line along which I must dutifully record my answer. After a while, Miss Redgrove asks us, one by one, to read our answers out loud for the rest of the class to hear. Most of my class-mates have decided on: "I would run away". One of them, more ingeniously, has chosen to climb up a tree. And when it comes to my turn, I boldly read out: "I would shoot him!". This seems a perfectly natural answer to me but, much to my surprise and pleasure, it brings the house down, and Miss Redgrove is very complimentary.

Our other glimpses of The White House are equally episodic, and several of them include my Headmistress.

For example, climbing up a narrow winding staircase with the rest of my form, into a class room which smells of disinfected floors and well-washed bodies, which has many of the oldest girls in the school who look at us as if we are unwelcome intruders, and where Miss Caudwell reads a story to us all.

For example, being in the school hall at a dancing class for the whole school. The senior girls know exactly what to do when the piano-playing begins, couple up, and begin waltzing round the room. Miss Caudwell, who is in charge and is clearly enjoying herself, joins in; and I watch awe-struck as she shouts out instructions while energetically whirling one partner after another round the dance-floor. When it is my turn to be seized and dragged by her into the thick of things, I have no idea at all where to put my feet and I am very relieved when she moves on to her next victim.

And there I am one lunchtime, sitting with six or eight others on a wooden bench at a wooden table. The boy sitting just opposite me has odd yellow hair and is going down with chicken-pox. The smell of gravy and cabbage hangs in the air as I stare with disgust at the unpleasant red marks which have begun to appear on his face and on the backs of his hands. Instead of being immediately whisked away and sent home, he is allowed to stay with us for another hour or two, perhaps because we children are not at all discouraged from acquiring many of the standard diseases of childhood: mumps, measles, German measles, whooping cough, chickenpox and scarlet fever. Best for us to have them and get them over with: especially mumps, which is normally only mild in children, but can be excruciatingly painful for grown-ups, with women suffering from a swelling of the ovaries, and men from a swelling of the testicles.

I didn't bring chicken-pox home with me on this occasion. What I did bring home was a note which my musical mother found deeply shocking when I handed it to her in the nursery. Signed by Miss Redgrove, it explained that I had been asked NOT to sing in the school entertainment scheduled for the end of the term. Mummy hurried me downstairs to her Bechstein piano in the drawing-room, opened it up, played a few notes for me to sing – and realised for the first time that her eldest son had no talent as a singer. Personally, I didn't mind at all. I might not be able to hold a note, but I had a good sense of rhythm; and while the rest of my class was on stage singing 'Three Blind Mice', I was allowed to stand beside them vigorously bashing at a triangle, which I thought was far more fun.

And look, do you see that girl with a sensual face, large brown eyes and long brown plaits with ribbons? We're all outside on an asphalt playground on one of our mid-morning breaks when I first notice her. I have just turned away from a group of boys who are playing what I think is a very stupid game, and there she is in the far corner of the playground, looking in my direction, and I immediately realise that there is something about her that I really like. Perhaps she reminds me of my favourite cousin. Just like Judith, she is a year or two older than me, and when I wander over and began talking with her, I learn that her name is Jancis. I find her utterly entrancing, even if the game of 'Mothers and Fathers' that she induces me to play seems almost as silly as the one I have just avoided.

After school that evening, I tell Mummy about my encounter, and how much I am looking forward to seeing Jancis again: which of course I do, most days. Jancis turns out to be the strong-minded leader of a small pack of girls, and because she tolerates me, so do they. Once I am even invited to have tea with her after school, and Mummy drives me straight from The White House to her highly-respectable middle-class home somewhere a little further along the Finchampstead Road. Sadly, this is not a success. Her parents seem surprised to find me so young, they don't seem to get on particularly well with my mother – they may be a little in awe of her as the chatelaine of Holme Grange – we are discouraged from making a return invitation, and Jancis and I never have tea together again.

But we still meet quite often at school, where we talk a good deal on every subject under the sun, and Jancis continues to accept my devotion very kindly. When the summer comes, we are encouraged on dry mornings to play on the lawns at the back of the school and sometimes Jancis allows me to sit next to her on the grass with her friends, looking in my direction from time to time with a slightly amused smile and once in a while, to my great joy, rubbing me gently on the back as though I am some highly-favoured pet. She even overlooks my blunders. One day, for example, feeling confident enough to initiate a new game, I call out: "Let's run from this log!"

"Do you call that a log?" asks one of Jancis's friends in the most withering tone of voice she can manage. "A log? Huh! A log? It's only a stick!" Which it was.

But then comes the end of the summer term. It's time for me to leave The White House before joining the junior class at Holme Grange that autumn, and although I am often told that 'Never is a long day', it becomes clear to me that I will never, ever see Jancis again. However, as I have mentioned before, true love, unselfish love, love of the right kind, never completely dies; and after all these years, foolish as this may sound to you, I love Jancis still because for a brief period of my childhood she made me so extremely happy.

CHAPTER SEVEN

Evenings at Holme Grange

My own evenings after returning from The White House were mostly spent with Simon and Elizabeth in the Nursery; but between high tea and bedtime there was a magical hour when, once I had done my homework, I was more or less my own master. This coincided with a time when the Boarders too had an hour to themselves, and (leaving my brother and sister behind) I would sometimes join them downstairs, where they had the freedom of the Hall and the two rooms beyond it.

In the good old days of Colonel Weston, the nearest of these rooms, entered through a single door in the north-western corner of the Hall, had been the billiard-room. Now it was the VI-form classroom, and also the school Library, so it had several rows of individual pupils' desks, facing a master's desk and his blackboard over on the right; and its walls were lined with bookcases.

Further along the western wall of the Hall, most of the way towards the Grand Piano, came the impressive double-doors with round brass handles which had once led into Colonel Weston's long drawing-room. In his day, it must have been a truly magnificent room, with its elaborately-patterned plaster ceiling; its huge stone fireplace over to the right; and, halfway down the room on the left, a large south-facing bay window from which one could look out across the yew hedge and the terrace to the lawn beyond; with, at the far end of the room, another large window looking out across the western terrace and over a sunken garden with steps leading down to it left and right, full of flowerbeds and surrounded by elegant yew hedging. In addition, should the weather be fine, one could immediately become part of that enticing landscape by walking through a door in the south-east corner of the drawing-room, which opened onto a path and a small flight of steps exactly like the one in our private garden, leading down between yew hedging onto the southern terrace.

As a room it was no longer quite so splendid, since the fireplace had been boarded up long ago and, on arriving at Holme Grange, one of my father's first projects had been to turn it from one classroom into two, by partitioning the room just the other side of the bay window with a wall that was entirely blank apart from a nondescript door over on the far right. Beyond this partition, at the sunken garden end, was the new IV form room; while on this side of the partition, at the Hall end, the new space became both the Vth form and a centre for the handful of Boarders who were left behind at Holme Grange once the Dayboys had departed each evening to their homes.

It was just inside the door on the right that the Boarders had a special corner around three sides of which racks had been installed for them. Here they kept their so-called tuck-boxes, small wooden boxes filled not with 'tuck' such as sweets or biscuits; but with precious items from home such as letters, books, toys and games. It was from one of these tuck-boxes that I remember a boy called Knight bringing out an ingeniously-jointed clown puppet on strings and entertaining us all by making it dance.

Despite being the Headmaster's son, I was made welcome here; and there was, indeed, a happy, family-like atmosphere. This may have been partly because there were so few boarders, at least to begin with; and in the early winter evenings, with a gentle electric light leaving dark corners both in the Vth-form room and in the Hall into which they occasionally strayed, it was a friendly, slightly mysterious place for children.

In the spring, when the evenings grew lighter, the Boarders were allowed to go out to the sunken garden. This no longer had flower-beds, but had become their outdoor playground; and here I would sometimes watch from the terrace while they played all kinds of exciting-looking games including Prisoner's Base (a gentlemanly game of which my father approved) and Kick-the-Can (a vulgar game of which he most certainly did not).

Sometimes entertainments were laid on especially for the Boarders, and you can see me late one evening, lying in bed in the Nursery on the verge of sleep, when suddenly the light is switched on again and people come into the room. I sit up in my pyjamas blinking in the bright light and find myself being introduced by Daddy to the entertainer for that evening. This was John, usually known as J.C. Pickstone, a senior and most distinguished figure in 'The Magician's Club' who had just given a display of magic to the Boarders.

The reason he had been brought up to see me was that he was also the father of my Godfather Nigel Pickstone, and had never met me before. Nigel himself, as I mentioned, had been one of my father's pupils at Malvern College and was now living out in Hong Kong where he had become a highly successful businessman. At this time I knew almost nothing about him, except that my mother always spoke very warmly of him, and although he was never in any kind of regular touch with me, occasionally he would send me an extremely expensive present. His father J.C., who seemed to me to be a most amiable gentleman, performed a few brilliant and completely baffling magic tricks specially for me, and assured me that my Uncle Nigel was in excellent health before leaving for his taxi and his train.

Magic may well lead on to still more mysterious matters, and on another of these evenings as I lay in my bed in the Nursery after dark, there was a most weird and unexplained incident, the recounting of which would undoubtedly frighten any Publisher far more than the story of my Uncle Robert's telepathic powers. To distance myself from it just a little, I offer for your perusal and without any prefatory comment (except to say that it seems a trifle over-written), this entirely accurate description of my feelings and sensations, as recorded by me many years ago.

> Night-time. Holme Grange, a huge ship making its mysterious way through time and space, with its cargo of memories and its crew of sleeping souls. Only my father the captain still awake, working late into the night. I myself lie asleep in my bed in the nursery, but

> my spirit is stirring, and after a feeling as though first my heart and then the whole physical part of me has acquired the consistency of cheese, I am aware of my real self detaching itself quite easily and painlessly from my material body, and floating upwards in spirit. I find with interest and without fear that I can will myself to travel in any direction and, unbound by the normal constraints of the flesh I pass through the wall into the corridor, where a single light burns at the head of the stairs. Passing down the stairs, floating above them, I veer to the right, and enter the long corridor leading towards my father's study. But then I hear a light being switched off and a door closing, and there is Daddy walking towards me. Somehow, he is aware that I am there, and though his lips do not move he is telling me that I should not be there. He is both angry and afraid. Travelling through the world out of one's body is wrong, utterly wrong, and I must never indulge in it again. I turn and flee from his anger and his fear and rush very fast all the way back into the safety of my sleeping body, and soon I am fast asleep too.

Very wisely, you may feel, I have never discussed with anyone that strange meeting, in a corridor lined with portraits of our ancestors, between Daddy's awareness and my questing spirit. Probably my father dismissed it in his own mind as a kind of waking dream, brought on by working too late. But I knew at the time that it was real; and when years later I read of out-of-the-body travel, for example by people close to death on the operating table, I am happy to believe their stories, for at least once I have been such a traveller myself.

After this supernatural horror, ordinary everyday horror may come almost as light relief, but the incident I am about to share with you was very alarming to me at the time.

My parents were out, and in their absence and that of our nanny, Simon and I were being put to bed in the nursery by Suzanne, a young assistant matron with an attractive warm-hearted smile, and a white uniform, tightly belted at the waist, that somehow managed to emphasize rather than to conceal the shapely beauty that lay beneath. I had already admired her from a distance, and when I heard that she would be looking after us, I could only secretly wish that Mummy and Daddy could be out for the evening far more often.

And now here Suzanne was, deliciously and infatuatingly close to me as Simon and she and I knelt by the side of my bed. She joined in while we recited the Lord's Prayer and listened patiently as Simon and I moved on to our special family prayer: 'God bless Mummy, and God bless Daddy, and God Bless Richard and Simon and Elizabeth and make them good, obedient and truthful children' – and then for some unknown reason I looked down towards the black electricity plug at the foot of the wall beside the head of my bed, and saw to my horror that it had been left switched on.

This was the start of one of the most terrifying experiences of my life. I had somehow got it into my head that electricity was a kind of vapour and that when the plug was left switched on, it would immediately begin escaping. I also believed that it was as lethal as town gas still was in those days. So I knew that Death was only seconds away. Holding my breath, I got to my feet and without saying a word I ran from the room, and fled all the way down the long dark corridor ahead of me at top speed, knowing that my only chance was to put as much distance as possible between me and the deadly cloud close behind.

Any mistake at this point would be fatal, and I managed not to trip over the couple of steps at the end of the corridor, veered round to the right and plunged down the main school staircase. All the time I could feel the cloud of electricity coming closer and closer. At the foot of the staircase I turned right, opened the door into the Library, slammed it behind me, rushed to the far end, flung open a window, and began gulping long deep breaths of fresh air.

I was safe, but this was not the end of the horror. I knew that I had only just managed to escape – and that Simon, my dear friend and brother, was undoubtedly dead, that the lovely Suzanne was also dead, and that by now there were almost certainly other dead bodies scattered throughout the school buildings.

Several minutes later Suzanne found me there, still at the open window, and still frightened out of my wits. She tried to persuade me to come back to the nursery, but for a long time, although I could see that

Suzanne herself was amazingly enough still alive, and indeed looking more attractive than ever, I was very reluctant to leave the safety of the open window and the fresh, uncontaminated air. Not knowing what to do, she enlisted the help of the master, Mr. Rushton, who had been left in charge of the Boarders that evening. Mr. Rushton, a decisive young man, immediately took charge. My parents had soon been telephoned and were hurrying home; and not far behind them came Dr. Hargrove, our Wokingham GP.

A slimly-built, clean-shaven, smartly-suited man in his forties with well-polished shoes, a receding hairline, and glasses behind which keenly intelligent and somewhat disillusioned eyes surveyed the world, Dr. Hargrove set himself the very high standards that he demanded of others. Brusque and occasionally intimidating whenever he had to deal with routine matters, or when he suspected that his patients were perfectly well and were simply wasting his time, Dr. Hargrove had the proverbial heart of gold, and was the most sympathetic man imaginable when he believed that any one was in real trouble.

On this occasion, he alone appeared to understand the depths of the horror through which I had passed and, after a private and most sympathetic talk with me, he wisely advised my parents that instead of being compelled to remain for even one more night in the nursery, I should immediately be placed, if at all possible, in a room of my own. As it happened, the long narrow room just the other side of my parents' bedroom was unoccupied. It was not a very agreeable room, and its one window had a somewhat bleak outlook over the cobbles of the kitchen yard; yet it had the great virtue that no electric plug of any kind was anywhere visible; and once a bed had been made up for me, I settled into it very comfortably and slept soundly for the rest of the night.

This would normally be the case in future, though I was still subject to occasional nightmares. If these were really bad, I would sometimes get out of bed, walk along the corridor until I was outside Mummy's and Daddy's room, and listen at their door. I didn't want to wake them up and disturb them, but I found it reassuring to know that they were only just a few feet away from me. Occasionally, I could hear them talking. I could never make out what they were saying, but just knowing that they were both alive and well made me feel better, and after a while I would return to my bed and go to sleep again. Only once was the nightmare so bad that I knocked on their door.

As it happened, it was time for them to get up, and they allowed me to come into their room and stand at the foot of the bed while they got dressed. I watched while Daddy, on his side of the bed near the window put on his shirt and busied himself with his collar-studs and his tie. Mummy, on her side of the bed, stood facing away from me towards her body-length dressing mirror, and removed first her dressing-gown and then her nightgown until she was almost naked. Daddy would later delight in advising me that I should never propose to a woman until I had had the opportunity of seeing how she looked in a bathing costume; and I was now very much aware of at least one of the reasons why he had chosen to marry Mummy. She was very shapely and very beautiful in the flesh; and when I had grown much older I would associate this brief revelation of her physical beauty with the work of Pierre-Auguste Renoir in such paintings as *Dance at Bougival* or *Study, Nude in Sunlight*.

By the way, a coda to my earlier tale is that Suzanne and Mr. Rushton, having been thrown together in such dramatic circumstances, had soon fallen in love with each other. It would however be at least a year and a half before I heard from my parents about their engagement and imminent departure from Holme Grange. I now hope that they enjoyed a long and happy life together; but I am afraid to say that at the time, I felt only jealous of Mr. Rushton, and angry with him for removing the lovely Suzanne, because by this time, despite not having exchanged a single word with her since that memorable evening, I had foolishly begun hoping and imagining that she might wait for me until I was older. But at least my temporary descent into madness had now come to be viewed by my parents through the prism of what they affectionately described as my successful matchmaking efforts.

CHAPTER EIGHT
Enlarging our World

After less than a year at Holme Grange, there were still areas of its interior of which Simon and I knew little or nothing, so it was intriguing when one day just before Easter, while the chef was away on holiday, Mummy promised to show us the kitchen for the first time. It was reached by going down the nursery stairs, crossing into the corridor which led past the red baize door, and opening the first door on the left. At the centre of the room in which we found ourselves was a large well-scrubbed kitchen table made of pine; to our left, a row of white wooden cupboards with white shelves above them filled to bursting with jugs and gravy-boats and herbs and spices and all kinds of kitchen paraphernalia; immediately to our right, the largest refrigerator I had ever seen and then a long window looking out over the kitchen yard; and on the far wall, in a wide alcove, the massive gas cooker with rings above and ovens beneath on which or in which all our Holme Grange meals were boiled, simmered, fried, stewed or baked.

None of this interested me very much apart from the long window. I had noticed that the only openable sections had tall vertical bars in front of them, but that these bars were not set very close together. Pressing myself between two of them, I was just beginning to squeeze through, with a view to seeing whether I could step down onto whatever it was that covered the three or four feet of a raised section before the yard proper began, when Mummy noticed what I was doing.

"Ricky! Don't be so silly! The bars are there for a purpose. Come and look over here instead."

Extricating myself a little crossly from the bars, I followed her into the first of several doorways just to the right of the cooker. This one led into what Mummy told us was the Scullery: a small narrow room with a sink beneath the window at the far end. Here the scullery maid would spend her day cleaning all the kitchen pots and pans and other cooking utensils as fast as the chef could dirty them. Then came a larger room, also with a sink, where another maid prepared the vegetables; and Mummy showed us, on a table-top, an exciting cylindrical machine which, when filled up with water, could somehow peel large quantities of potatoes quite effortlessly.

In another corner of this room were two or three of the boxes in which our vegetables would regularly arrive from A.J. Robbins Ltd, known simply as 'Robbins', the 65-acre market garden owned by the family that had sold Holme Grange to Gordon Walker and still owned the Lodge and much nearby land, including the fields on which the Holme Grange boys played football. I recognized the boxes because it was a great treat to be allowed to accompany Daddy to Robbins when he had decided to drive there in EPB 223 to make a personal selection.

Robbins was about half-a-mile to our southwest, and reached by turning left out of the Holme Grange drive onto the Heathlands Road, first going down into the dip where the Emm Brook runs beneath the road, on its way to the Loddon and then the Thames, and then up the other side where the entrance to the long Robbins driveway was clearly signed over to the right. After passing through open fields full of vegetables on each side, we would park at the centre of two vast hangars beneath which were stacked piles and piles of boxes containing a wealth of every kind of fruit and vegetable that was currently in season within the United Kingdom.

With no freezers, and so little being imported, what we ate was almost entirely seasonal. Some vegetables such as carrots and potatoes could be safely stored by our farmers for several months, and so were available throughout the year; but there were no lettuces or fresh green beans or fresh tomatoes or fresh strawberries in mid-winter; and even someone completely locked away from the outside world could easily have observed the passing of the seasons simply by looking at the food that was on his plate.

It was now that Mummy told us that she had our lunch to cook, and that Simon and I should go outside to play, so she directed us back into the kitchen and then out again through a third door in that corner of the room, which led into a narrow corridor and yet another doorway, this one leading to the outside. We wandered through the kitchen yard, and stood for a while beneath its entrance archway, trying to decide which direction to take.

So far as we were concerned, playing outside meant exploring, and whenever we were able to do so we resumed our exploration of the grounds, through which we would journey for many months like two intrepid nineteenth-century travellers making their way further and further into the unknown interior of Africa.

Our very first expedition had begun from the place beside the southern lawn where the stump of the felled pine-tree was still fresh and raw. After examining it closely in case there were any fresh secrets for it to reveal (there were none, though the fall of the great tree remained a stirring memory) we had bravely set out southward through the semi-circle of trees that remained, into what was for us terra incognita. Our way was clear right up to the iron railings that marked the southern edge of our property, at which point there were thick masses of rhododendrons both to left and right. The ones to our left appeared to be virtually impenetrable; but to the right we were able to push our way through the outer branches of the rhododendrons onto a dark and gloomy path, virtually roofed over and with its floor covered by a thick layer of peat. It seemed a haunted place, and when I came to know it better, I could almost see the ghostly apparition of the widowed Mrs. Weston on one of her lonely carriage rides along this track that had now almost ceased to exist, and which after a short distance petered out completely.

At this point Simon would have liked to return home by the way we had come, but: "Come on, Simon" I said enthusiastically, "Just follow me! It'll be an adventure!" So we continued into the rhododendrons and somehow or other I pioneered a passageway through them, climbing over some of the thick boughs and squeezing my way between others, until at last, having gradually veered round to the right, I was able to lead the way out into the light. From here, we could look back across the lawn at the awe-inspiring sight of the whole southern frontage of Holme Grange.

"Look", said Simon, pointing. "There's Daddy!" And there he was in his gardening clothes at the very western end of the long garden bed that ran on each side of the steps just beneath the terrace. He had already planted roses all the way along, and now he was busily adding other perennial plants, including clumps of lupins, and his favourite montbretias. Because he had read it out to me, he knew that I much enjoyed A.A. Milne's 'The Dormouse and the Doctor', which begins:

> There once was a Dormouse who lived in a bed
> Of delphiniums (blue) and geraniums (red)
> And all the day long he'd a wonderful view
> Of geraniums (red) and delphiniums (blue)

And a few weeks later he asked me to help him to plant out some delphiniums and geraniums.

This combination of old and new planting meant that from the spring onwards, the whole area around the southern lawn looked magnificent. First came the flowering of the azaleas, followed by that of the rhododendrons, all of them carefully chosen specimen plants whose flowers came in a wide variety of colours. Then came the roses and all the other flowers that Daddy had planted including evening primroses, so-called because they produce delicate yellow flowers on tall stalks which achieve perfection on a late summer evening and have already begun to fade by the next morning.

The view from the entrance to the kitchen yard where Simon and I were now standing was far less impressive, but some of it was still intriguing. We knew the way to the garage very well, but, some distance to the left of that particular track was a narrow path bordered by a few trees and shrubs which led to an area between the garage and the main drive that we hadn't yet explored, and so it was in that direction that we decided to set out. However, we had only taken a few steps along this path when we saw

Mr. Hills in the distance emerging from a Nissen Hut, and as he came out we could see that he was carrying a long dangerous-looking scythe and we could hear him roaring out very angrily at the top of his deep bass voice: "Simmy! Simmy! Where are you, Simmy? Simmy!"

This gave both of us a terrible shock, but it was much worse for Simon because it was his name that was being called. He clung on to me shaking with fear, and our first thought was that Mr. Hills had gone mad and was about to hunt Simon down and do him some terrible damage with the scythe. We were about to turn and run for our lives (or rather for Simon's life), when another figure appeared from further away, coming out of yet another Nissen Hut, and calling out in broad Berkshire "Here I be Mr. Hills! Here I be!"

I recognised him immediately as the flat-capped assistant who had helped Mr. Hills with cutting down the Scots Pine by the front lawn. "It's all right, Simpkin", I whispered to my brother. "It's not you he means!"

"Here I be, Mr. Hills" repeated the real Simmy as he shambled forwards in his shabby overalls. "Here I be. I been tidying up in the Tool Shed."

"Never here when I want you, that's your trouble" complained Mr. Hills. "Bring out the sharpener for me – I can't have sparks flying around in there." And then he noticed us. "You'll enjoy this, young sirs!" he said deferentially, before turning and calling out again at the top of his voice "SIMMY!"

It turned out that the Nissen Hut behind him into which Simmy had disappeared was known by everyone as Mr. Hills's shed, and from what I could see of its contents most of the interior was a huge junk-heap. Near the door was a small desk covered with piles of loose papers, then came a large wooden workbench with vices of different sizes attached to its sides and a variety of tools stacked up on it in a completely haphazard fashion. Beyond these was a small clear area of concrete floor with one or two chairs on it and an ancient black paraffin heater; and then the rest of the Nissen Hut contained a jumble of tools, ladders, step-ladders, half-empty cans of paint, abandoned sections of pipework, lengths of wood, and a vast assortment of items in need of repair, from relatively new stacking chairs that needed fresh canvas backs or seats attached, and oil stoves in need of new wicks, to old sofas and antique mowers which looked as though they had been lying there untouched for many years.

From somewhere among all this clutter, Simmy emerged carrying a curious-looking metal contraption about four or five feet tall with a treadle near its base and a round grindstone at its top, and set it down on the flat path just outside Mr. Hills's shed. By pressing one of his feet on the treadle, Mr. Hills made the grindstone revolve on its axle, faster and faster, and then at just the right moment he applied the edge of his scythe to the stone, and as he applied it we heard the high-pitched scream of the grinding and watched fascinated as showers of sparks flew off. From time to time, he paused to examine the edge of the scythe closely. "There. That'll do!" he said eventually. "She wouldn't have cut butter yesterday!" And then he thought for a moment, and asked: "Young sirs, would you like to see where we keeps her?"

We followed him up the path towards a second Nissen Hut, passing on our left a straggling untidy compost heap, at the back of which was a somewhat straggly horse-chestnut or conker tree; and on our right a large clump of damson trees. Then we came to the Nissen Hut known as the Tool Shed, in which we found neat rows of tools in racks on each side, and gleaming mowers of various sizes down the middle. There were also three large garden trolleys, wooden on metal frames, with two central wheels, sides that could be let down, and metal handles across each end, handles broad enough so that if the trolley contained a really heavy load, two boys could push at one end, while two more pulled at the other.

Past the Tool Shed, I could see that the path ran on, with clumps of bamboo to the left and a hedge to the right, and I was all for leaving Mr. Hills to his garden tools and continuing our exploration, when I heard Mummy shouting in the distance: "Ricky – Simkin! Where are you? Lunchtime!" And that brought an end to our expotition for the time being.

The word 'expotition' we had acquired from A.A. Milne, two of whose works were now to be found on our Nursery bookshelves. The first of them, *When We Were Very Young*, is a book of light verse including not only 'The Dormouse and the Doctor', but also 'Disobedience'. I have already given you the first stanza about James James taking great care of his Mother, though he was only three; and here is what happens when she foolishly disobeys her son's instructions:

King John
Put up a notice,
"LOST or STOLEN or STRAYED!
JAMES JAMES MORRISON'S MOTHER
SEEMS TO HAVE BEEN MISLAID.
LAST SEEN
WANDERING VAGUELY:
QUITE OF HER OWN ACCORD,
SHE TRIED TO GET DOWN
TO THE END OF THE TOWN -
FORTY SHILLINGS REWARD!"

The second of them was a thin dark-green volume which Mummy was already reading to us for a second time. From its opening line: 'Here is Edward Bear, coming downstairs now, bump, bump, bump, on the back of his head, behind Christopher Robin', it is utterly enchanting. I immediately identified with Christopher Robin, the boy whose existence is largely untroubled by adults, and who is therefore free to live alone with his front door in the middle of a tree-trunk, in a forest peopled by toys of his that have come to life.

Edward Bear is the most important of these, and the name by which his friends know him becomes the title of the book, *Winnie-the-Pooh*. His principal passion is a love of honey or rather 'Hunny', and his schemes go wrong so often that he is described, but in a kindly way, as a bear 'of very little brain'. The gallery of his friends includes Eeyore, the depressive donkey; Owl, who talks like a very pompous teacher and is generally considered extremely wise, but who spells his name WOL; Rabbit, an exasperating bossy-boots with a seemingly endless supply of friends and relations; Kanga, a kindly kangaroo who gives her small child Roo 'strengthening medicine'; and Pooh's best friend, the timid Piglet, with whom he hunts for large elephants or 'Heffalumps', tracks Woozles, and joins Christopher Robin on an 'expotition' to the North Pole.

Pooh is an inveterate rhymester, and Simon and I were soon enjoying lines like:

Cottleston, Cottleston, Cottleston Pie,
A fly can't bird, but a bird can fly.
Ask me a riddle and I reply:
"Cottleston, Cottleston, Cottleston Pie."

My favourite chapter was the one in which Pooh, visiting Rabbit in his underground home and liking 'a little something' at eleven o'clock in the morning, eats so much honey and condensed milk that he becomes wedged in the doorway on his way out. After which Christopher Robin, on being asked for his advice, says:

"Then there's only one thing to be done," .... "We shall have to wait for you to get thin again."

"How long does getting thin take?" asked Pooh anxiously.

"About a week, I should think."

"But I can't stay here for a *week*!"

"You can *stay* here all right, silly old Bear. It's getting you out which is so difficult."

Over the next few months, Winnie-the-Pooh became so embedded in our family life that Simon and I knew just what Mummy meant if she said: 'Don't be so Eeyoreish!' or 'Don't be such a Heffalump!' Not only had our journeys of exploration became 'expotitions'; but also 'Time for a little something!' was our regular cry at about eleven o'clock in the morning, when it was usually 'elevenses', and we were hoping for a biscuit and a cup of hot chocolate.

One holidays, when it had rained incessantly for days and days and days, you will find Simon and me looking out of an upstairs window through the driving rain over the roundabout and the front drive. The part of the drive that is nearest to us has become a sheet of water; and if I seem rather anxious, it is because I feel as though we have stumbled into the chapter headed 'IN WHICH PIGLET IS ENTIRELY SURROUNDED BY WATER'. Were we too about to be completely marooned, I wondered, and would we have to be rescued by some equivalent of the good ship *Brain of Pooh*?

In the meantime, very little from the wider world had intruded itself into my consciousness apart from the death on 6 February 1952 of King George VI. Although I was only seven years old, I understood that this was a momentous event. It was not just that he had been King for my entire life, but that I had become used to seeing his head on every single British stamp that had ever reached me and on a high proportion of the coins that were in everyday use.

That amazing coinage! It was not only family history that was all around us. As soon as Simon and I started receiving pocket-money, which we did soon after moving to Holme Grange, British history was to be found in our pockets and our purses. Most coins were removed from circulation only when they had become so worn as to be virtually unreadable, so in our change we would find coins not only from the reign of King George VI (1936-1952), but also from that of his father King George V (1910-1936); his grandfather King Edward VII (1901-1910); and his great-grandmother Queen Victoria (1837-1901), whose head appeared on one side of many of our large bronze pennies, together with the inscription:

> VICTORIA DEI GRA BRITT REGINA FID DEF IND IMP

which is short for:

> VICTORIA DEI GRATIA BRITTANIAE REGINA FIDEI DEFENSOR INDIA IMPERATOR

and which means:

> Victoria, by the grace of God Queen of Britain, Defender of the Faith and Empress of India

Very occasionally, we would even come across a penny from as far back as the 1860s, when Victoria was younger and prettier and not yet Empress of India, and had her hair done up in a bun. However, these were few and far between and usually so very badly worn that they were on the verge of being withdrawn.

I had better explain that although its basic unit was One Pound, just as it remains, our currency in those days was far more complex than the one which succeeded it in 1971. The Pound itself came not as a coin but as the £1 banknote that since 1914 had displaced the golden sovereign of my father's childhood. Each pound was divided into twenty shillings, and each shilling was divided into twelve pence; and money was routinely described, not just by Latin scholars but by people of every class, as Lsd (ell-ess-dee) because libra, solidi and denarii were (roughly speaking) the ancient Roman equivalents of pounds, shillings and pence. A sum of, say, one Pound, thirteen shillings and six pence would therefore be written out (with the Pound sign being an ornate capital L) as: £1 – 13s – 6d.

Each Pound could also be divided into four crowns (though in practice these were only minted as commemorative coins), eight half-crowns, ten florins, or forty sixpences; and our everyday currency included ten-shilling notes, three-penny bits, half-pennies, and farthings representing a quarter of a penny. This complexity was the delight of my better mathematics teachers, who were rightly ambitious for the mental development of their pupils: imagine, for example, the intricate workings involved in attempting to divide £145 / 15s / 4¾d by fifteen. And since these notes and coins were such an integral and everyday part of the first twenty-six years of my life, I will describe them very briefly in ascending order. [And if you've heard quite enough about the coinage, you can always skip to the end of this chapter, which I don't much mind, because you'll miss out on a rather pointed contrast between Simon's financial acuity and my own evident greed.]

We shall start with the farthing (¼ d), a small round bronze coin worth one quarter of a penny, with a portrait of the reigning monarch on the obverse side (as had all British coins) and (after 1936) a robin on the reverse. Then came the half-penny (½d) (usually pronounced 'haypenny', or more colloquially 'haydee'). These were slightly larger round bronze coins, on the reverse of which (after 1936) was The Golden Hind, that famous galleon in which Sir Francis Drake had set out in 1577 to circumnavigate the globe. The penny (1d) came next, a large round coin, bronze until 1922 and then copper, with a seated Britannia on the reverse. Britannia, by the way, had been the name given by the ancient Romans to what was now the southern part of Great Britain, and had now become a female warrior carrying a trident, personifying both Great Britain and the British Empire. Then came threepence (3d), known variously as a threpenny- or thrupenny-bit, and the most distinctive coin of all. About the same size as a farthing, but much thicker, it was minted in brass, had various designs on the reverse including a thrift plant and a portcullis and, most important of all, it had twelve sides.

The sixpence (6d) came next, a small round coin roughly the size of a farthing. I valued sixpences hugely because a 6d was the pocket-money coin for which Simon and I waited so eagerly each Saturday morning. How gloomy we would feel and what long faces we would wear later on in the day if our sixpences had been forgotten. We knew that it was terribly bad form ever to ask directly for our pocket-money: that would have been considered a horrible display of greed. So either Mummy had to remind him, or Daddy had to notice our gloomy faces and ask us what on earth was the matter. In due course we were each given a small leather purse in which to keep our money, and 6d in those days was quite enough to go shopping with.

We did not know it of course when we first began receiving them, but these coins had been almost solid silver until 1920. After that year they were increasingly debased until 1946 when, although still silvery in appearance, they began to be made entirely of cupro-nickel. It was Simon, always far cannier than me where money was concerned, who was the first of us to discover this, and he immediately began hoarding up those early silver sixpences whenever he found one in his change.

Simon also collected the early shilling (1/-), a round coin just a little smaller than a halfpenny and worth twelve pence, which had also degenerated by 1946 from silver to cupro-nickel. Then came the florin (2/-), a round silver and then cupro-nickel two-shilling piece only just smaller than a penny. Finally came the half-crown (2/6d), not the most distinctive but by far the most impressive of our coins, larger and thicker than a penny; and although it too was now cupro-nickel, the two shillings and sixpence that it represented seemed like riches to me. The only time one of them came my way in those early days, as I have mentioned before, was as a present from my Uncle Geoffrey, to whose very occasional visits I began to look forward with the utmost greed imaginable. It was only very rarely that this most generous of relatives left without giving me as a 'tip' the equivalent of five weeks' pocket-money in a single coin.

At any rate, the death of King George VI meant that his image was replaced on our stamps by that of his beautiful daughter Queen Elizabeth II, who also began appearing on all freshly-minted coins, and whose Coronation the following year would be such a major and memorable event in all our lives.

CHAPTER NINE
Rottingdean

Not long after the 'Simmy' incident, we set off for our annual seaside holiday in Rottingdean. My father drove us down there, just as I have described in my prologue to this memoir. I left us on Marine Parade, the road leading eastward out of Brighton, with Daddy raising his hat when he reached a point that he felt was more or less opposite the nursing home where I had been born; and as we drove on along the coast road, with the endless sea down to our right, and grass-covered chalk downs above us to the left, Daddy kept up his usual running commentary.

"Look over there! That's Roedean, the famous Girls' School"; and about a quarter of a mile further on, where there was another large building up to the left, and the paths leading to it had handrails beside them: "That's St. Dunstan's, where they look after soldiers who have gone blind!" The buildings were certainly impressive enough, but in all the years that we drove past them, we never once saw what might have really interested me: perhaps a party of Roedean sixth-formers in their swimsuits on their way to the sea; or a line of blind veterans, whom I liked to imagine still in their military uniforms and clinging bravely onto the handrails while they told me stories of their wartime exploits.

What was far more exciting was our first glimpse of the great eight-sided Windmill that stands like some Guardian Angel on Beacon Hill high above the village of Rottingdean. Just as heartily as we had cried out: "Thalassa, Thalassa, the Sea, the Sea!" we now cried out: "The Windmill!

The Windmill!" It hadn't been in working order for more than thirty years, but with its Kentish-style cap and its four huge patent sails it was an impressive and unforgettable sight and, as soon as we saw it, we knew that our holiday had really begun.

Dropping down the steep hill beyond the Windmill into the hollow where the village lies, we paused at the traffic lights. When these lights turned from red to amber to green, most of the cars went straight on up the next hill, past a number of sea-side bungalows, and on towards Newhaven and Eastbourne. But we turned left into the village, along Rottingdean High Street, which was narrow, charming, lined with old-fashioned shops and usually very quiet: though not so quiet, Mummy told us, as it had been in her own childhood, when she and her sisters and their Hilder cousins had been able to walk arm-in-arm down the very centre of the street. After only a couple of hundred yards, we took a right turn up the steep slope of Steyning Road. About half way up this slope, EPB 223 pulled in beside the fourth of a row of six terraced three-storey houses. This was Braemar, a pleasant-looking brick building with large windows, its second storey hung with red-brick tiles beneath its windows, and on the ground floor a closely-cut laurel hedge between it and the pavement.

We climb out of the car, rush to the front door and ring on the bell. The door is opened a moment later by Aunt Ruth, who must have been watching out for us through the net curtains on the front window. She greets me as she always does with a hug and a kiss; and as she holds me for a moment I have a vague recollection of a much earlier visit, when she took me in her arms and sang to me very lovingly:

> My little honeybunch went to the war,
> My little honeybunch came back four!

Joan, an equally warm-hearted but (to me at least) slightly more daunting proposition, is waiting for us a little further down the narrow hallway, at the foot of the long steep stairs. She is already famous in the family for giving us kisses so fierce that they make our cheeks ache, and on this occasion she adds a hug that could almost be called ferocious, pressing me very tightly to her bosom. Next, I look into the entrance to the sitting room on the right, but Grandad is nowhere to be seen, and sadly we have hardly arrived before it is almost time to say goodbye to Daddy. These days, he never stays with us at Braemar even for a night. This is mainly because, as I explained earlier, he needs to be back at Holme Grange guarding the telephone; but also because staying in Rottingdean appears to be bad for his asthma, and it is well-known that asthma is Daddy's Achilles heel.

Indeed, my father had almost died of asthma as long ago as the summer of 1912 when at the age of nine he had been a Boarder at Copthorne School. After suddenly finding it difficult to breathe while on the cricket-field one pollen-filled afternoon, he had been helped indoors by two of his comrades while a third ran ahead to warn the matron. By the time she reached him, he was running out of oxygen and his face was turning blue. With great presence of mind, she thrust her fingers down his throat, which made him sick and somehow or other brought his asthma attack to an end and saved his life.

And now, although in every other respect he appears to be thoroughly fit and well, Daddy has very occasional asthma attacks and never goes anywhere without what he calls his 'Hoofer'. This is a Rybar inhaler[2], a hand-held black plastic atomizer dating from the 1930s. It features a mouthpiece with a tiny screwcap, below which is a cylindrical container for Rybarex, the medicinal inhalant; and below that is the rubber bulb which Daddy has to squeeze fiercely two or three times in order to drive a very fine spray of the inhalant through the mouthpiece and into his lungs, where it normally provides almost instant relief. Unfortunately, it is so small that it is just as easy to lose as a large bunch of keys, and "Has anyone seen my Hoofer?" is a cry that echoes and re-echoes throughout my childhood. Hearing it always fills me with acute anxiety, though should this happen on an occasion when Aunt Clarissa is present, she will call out cheerily and very annoyingly that 'Nothing is lost in the Divine Mind!"

Once Daddy has checked that all our suitcases and other belongings have been unloaded, and has made sure that he has handed over the large box full of vegetables that he has brought down from Robbins as a contribution to the cost of our stay – "Oh, John, you shouldn't have!"

2 Science Museum object 1995-11001

say his sisters-in-law, more or less in unison, but their happy smiles tell of their gratitude – he kisses us all goodbye, climbs back into EPB 223, makes an elegant 3-point- turn in Steyning Road, and gives us a cheerful wave before heading back towards Brighton on his way home.

Once he was out of sight, and we had stopped waving, we went back into Braemar, where Grandad had now appeared from the back of the house. This kindliest of men, with his twinkling eyes, and his lined oval face above which his hair was beginning to turn grey, was as usual wearing jacket, bow-tie, trousers and waistcoat; and in one of his waistcoat pockets he wore as usual his round gold watch, attached to a curious chain, some parts of which were silver and some gold, and which hung loosely across his somewhat portly stomach helping to give him an air of quiet prosperity.

This was a true reflection of his worth, since although Grandad was now in his early seventies and officially retired, he still owned and managed a small portfolio of properties including several houses in Portsmouth and one or two more in Rottingdean, where I believe he also had a part-interest in a butcher's shop on the High Street. He would often don his flat cap, an item of headwear which I could not help comparing unfavourably with Daddy's more elegant bowler hat, and set off down the road either to attend to some business or other, or on occasion to join one or two of the cronies with whom he enjoyed an occasional pint in the Plough Inn hard by the village pond.

On this occasion, after saying hello to us all, he retreated to his current centre of operations. This was the large and ancient roll-top desk which stood in a corner of the front sitting room, on the far wall just opposite the doorway. Once it was unlocked and opened up it was an impressive sight, with its numerous compartments around the writing board chock full of bottles of ink and keys and letters and writing paper and envelopes and stamps, and everything he could possibly need to carry on his business. Nothing ever seemed to be left lying around, the desk was almost always closed and securely locked, and the rest of this room was always kept neat and clean and tidy so that it stood ready should there be at any hour of the day or night a sudden influx of unexpected and important visitors. Principally for the use of these visitors it contained, just inside the door on the right, a large and well-upholstered sofa with thick cushions to sink into, broad armrests at each end, and a comfortable back whose upper reaches were protected from oily hair by two large antimacassars; while opposite there were two equally luxurious matching armchairs.

In the days when it languished virtually unused in the sitting-room at Braemar, I only recall once sitting on the sofa myself. This was when Mummy had gone out with the others for a walk, and for some reason, perhaps because I was thought to be a little under-the-weather, I had been left behind in the sitting-room, my consolation being a vanilla ice-cream to eat and one of Richmal Crompton's *William* books to read. The others had just shut the front-door behind them, and I had only had time to take a preliminary bite of my delicious ice-cream and to open the front page of my book when Grandad, in whose charge I had been left, came into the room, made his way over to his desk, and opened it up as usual. I loved him dearly, and normally I would have been very pleased to spend time with him, but on this occasion I felt only high anxiety as I realized to my consternation that he had no ice-cream of his own.

What was I to do? Strictly speaking, Grandad was of course an adult; but when we talked together, he had not only a child's slightly mischievous sense of humour but also a child's simplicity and directness and I felt instinctively that he had a sensitive heart. It clearly wasn't up to me to protect him; but how could I possibly let Grandad find out that he had been so cruelly forgotten? I felt that it would break his heart, and immediately hid my ice-cream from view.

After only a few minutes of this deception I was faced with another dilemma. My ice-cream had begun to melt. Knowing that my name would be mud if I damaged the sofa with a melting mass of squidgy ice-cream, I managed to smuggle it out of the sitting room and threw it away, virtually untouched, on the coal-heap at the back of the house.

When the others returned, I explained to Mummy what had happened. She was moderately sympathetic, but told me that Grandad wouldn't have minded (which I couldn't really believe) and she clearly thought that it had been a sad waste of a perfectly good ice-cream.

At least I still had my Richmal Crompton book, which I took into the second sitting-room, entered through a doorway near the foot of the stairs, and continued to read. This was my first introduction to eleven-year-old

William Brown and his family and friends and his dog Jumble; and now that the episode of the melting ice-cream was behind me, I was very soon laughing out loud. The very first *William* book had appeared back in the Twenties; and depicts a neo-Edwardian world in which middle-class parents can afford at least a cook and a housemaid and are not surprised to be entertained by a better-off family employing a whole range of servants from a Butler to a 'Boots'. This world had long ago vanished; but in an important sense Richmal Compton's books have never dated, because she is such an acute observer of human nature.

All her characters stay far enough this side of caricature to be fully recognizable as types of real people, from the horribly spoiled Violet Elizabeth Bott, who gets her own way by threatening to 'thcream and thcream until I'm thick', to William's elder brother Robert, who at the age of seventeen falls madly and foolishly in love with every pretty girl he meets. William himself is a strong enough character to be the leader of Ginger, Henry and Douglas, his gang of 'Outlaws'; but he is also, like most of us, trying to make sense of a world he does not fully understand, a more humorous and less tragic version of Housman's 'I, a stranger and afraid/ In a world I never made.' It is the elaborately-plotted consequences of his own misunderstandings which provide much of the humour; and William is also the prism through which we observe, but never unkindly, the frailties common to us all.

This second sitting-room in which I am uproariously laughing out loud is the sitting-room in general use, with its table and easy chairs and shelves filled with books and the upright Piano on which Mummy had practiced during her holidays from the Royal College of Music. In that context, she enjoys telling me how when Betty was being courted by Geoffrey and they had retreated to this room for some privacy, she would come in to do her daily piano practice and occasionally steal sidelong glances at them to see whether or not they were holding hands. There was also a window at the back through which I would sometimes see Noony, the black Braemar cat, prowling about over the coal heap. This was almost the only time that I did see her, for she fled from the house as soon as we arrived, only returning for mealtimes in the kitchen when she thought that the coast was clear.

To reach that kitchen one first of all had to walk past the staircase to the very end of the Hall, where a door opened into the dining-room. This was dominated by a magnificent mahogany linen press, with its cupboard above and its drawers beneath crammed not only with clean sheets and towels and tablecloths, but also with tins of food, tennis balls, scraps of fuse-wire, balls of string and a whole treasure-house of objects that we children were strictly forbidden to touch without permission.

At the back of the dining-room was the door into the kitchen, which had its own much smaller table and chairs, an Aga cooker with four hotplates and two ovens, one usually empty cat-basket for Noony, and one usually full dog-basket for Solomon, a good-natured elderly dachshund with a lugubrious expression and large floppy ears, who didn't run away when he heard us coming, and never yapped at me as Cella had done at Kerry House. "That's what he likes", said Aunt Joan, showing me how to stroke him along the spine from head to tail, which seemed to make him very happy.

There was also a door into the garden, though now that I was becoming used to the Holme Grange grounds I began to find it difficult to see how it could lay claim to being a garden at all. To begin with, a good deal of space was taken up both by the coal heap and by an outside lavatory, which was a curiosity in itself. Why on earth have a lavatory outside, I thought to myself, when there was a perfectly good one next to the bathroom upstairs? There was also a large potting-shed, and then garden beds on each side of a path running down to a back gate. It was this back gate that I liked more than anything else in the Braemar garden, because I soon found I could escape through it into the long narrow path which led both to left and to right and from which I could spy into our neighbours' back gardens.

Almost every day, unless it was actually pouring with rain, a group of us walked all the way down to the sea. Often, we went the back way along the Twitten, a path parallel with the High Street and starting from a little further up Steyning Road. This was a relatively dull walk, with nothing on the western or village side of the path but a tall flint wall; and on the eastern side, laurel shrubberies and occasional glimpses of playing-fields. I much preferred walking through the village, where I still enjoyed stepping on and off the door-steps which, in flights of two or three, led up to most of the shops and private houses along the High Street. And if we went through the village, there was also the chance that on the way there or back we might go into one of the shops.

On our side of the High Street, there was a sweetshop called Lucy Ann's which, not surprisingly, was my favourite; and fortunately for me it was one of my mother's favourites too, because it also sold cigarettes and tobacco. Mummy only rarely smoked at home, and then very discreetly, because of Daddy's asthma; but whenever she got together with her sisters, they all smoked like the proverbial chimneys.

Outside Lucy Ann's, a large bow-window rose above a cobbled area at the side of the brick pavement, and displayed a tempting selection of what lay inside. Just beyond the bow-window, two steps led up to the entrance of this eighteenth-century cottage. Here a door with glass panes in the top half of it opened into an old-fashioned and magical shop of a type I had never seen anywhere else, though something very like it features as Sir John Tenniel's illustration of 'Alice and the sheep in the shop' in Lewis Carroll's *Alice Through the Looking-glass*, of which more later.

As we shut the door behind us, I can see that every square foot of wall space is covered with shelves, and almost every shelf is covered with tall glass jars, and every jar is filled with a different variety of sweet. I am also aware that the air is full of a special scent emanating from those chocolates and sweets that have been laid out on an old wooden counter just inside the door on the right. Behind this counter stands the formidable Lucy Ann herself. She wears glasses and a shawl, her hair is tied up in a bun and to me she seems to be almost as old as the shop itself. I notice that she calls Mummy 'Mary', and speaks to her in a bluff and cheery manner as though they are very old friends, perhaps even relatives. Then, after exchanging a few words with her, and perhaps selling her a packet of cigarettes, she leans over the counter and turns her attention to Simon and me.

"Well boys, how are you?" she asks. And from that moment I am always in an agony of suspense, willing her to do the right thing while preparing not to show any disappointment if she does not. Because once we have answered that we are very well, thank-you, she usually, but not invariably, follows this up by saying: "Would you each like to choose a sweet for yourselves?" In that case, like my new hero William Brown, I will normally choose a Humbug, a Bullseye or a Gob-stopper; though it is an extremely difficult choice, since I have recently become very fond of sherbet-lemons.

Another shop I like very much is on the other side of the road, up three steps rather than two, with another large bay window and an interior that smells deliciously of newly baked bread. This baker's shop is somehow connected with us, but I find it a little confusing because the owner is said to be a cousin of ours yet Mummy and the Aunts call him 'Uncle Harry', and how can a cousin also be an uncle? Uncle Harry himself is a hearty-looking man, who comes in from the back of the shop with a tray of bread balanced on his head, slides it down into its appointed place in a single well-practiced flowing movement, and turns to give us all the warmest of welcomes.

Once we had reached that dangerous crossroads where cars and buses and lorries thunder along the main coast road, our route to the beach was the same whether we had come along the High Street or down from the Twitten; and soon we had reached the broadest part of the under-walk beside the hollowed-out storage area where it was possible to hire deck-chairs (which, much to my disappointment, we never did), and to look out over the low wall at the beaches ten or fifteen feet below.

These Rottingdean beaches, separated from each other by breakwaters which ran out from the Underwalk at intervals of some thirty yards, were not reliably sandy – it all depended on the winter storms, which in some years deposited thousands of tons of sand on the rocky beaches, and in other years stripped them almost bare. Most times, during the years that I was a regular visitor, the best beach was almost immediately below the deckchairs. The steps by which we reached it were so broad and deep that as I scrambled down them, I imagined they must have been built by giants.

Then my feet began to scrunch over the shingle at the top of the beach; then there was a tidemark of strong-smelling slippery green seaweed to negotiate, and then a little further down we would come to stretches of sand. Some of these were too narrow to be worth bothering with, but some were wide enough for Mummy and the Aunts to spread out the rugs they had brought with us, and to settle down while Simon and I built sandcastles or ran about or went paddling and splashing in the sea either with Mummy or one of the Aunts until it was time to go home again.

Occasionally, instead of going down to the sea, we set out in other directions. My favourite inland walk involved turning left out of Braemar, walking a little way up Steyning Road and then turning left again between several large wooden posts onto the narrow asphalt path that was a continuation of the Twitten, and ran between the last of the terraced houses and a small slope of green grass leading up to a flint wall. This wall, too tall for us to see over, formed the eastern edge of that part of Rottingdean: beyond it were only fields.

Continuing northward, we walked past the end of the still narrower path that led down behind Braemar, and then the path began to curve round to the left, past a handsome double-fronted three-storeyed detached house with a large porch at its front and a garage just beyond; and then downhill past a small sloping green with a row of cottages stretched along Vicarage Terrace just below it. Beyond the end cottage lay our route to the Plough Inn, the village pond (where I still enjoy feeding the ducks), and the village green; but instead we turn right onto Whiteway Lane, which runs back eastward. The first twenty yards or so are overhung with laurels even taller than the ones at Kerry House, and just as good for climbing; and then the tarmac gives out and we can see why it is called Whiteway, because beneath our feet is an ancient chalk track which leads across the Downs in the direction of Saltdean.

Within a hundred yards there is nothing but open country in every direction but the one from which we have come. Whiteway winds along beneath a rise of ground to the south. Above it is only farmland; and below it are green fields surrounded by low flint walls. The sloping ground is steep in places, and is crisscrossed with small paths scored white into the chalk beneath, along which Simon and I like running at top speed, backwards and forwards, up and down, this way and that, while the grown-ups stay far below us on Whiteway, pushing Elizabeth along in her pram. From time to time, sheep are released onto this land, so the grass is mostly cropped very close; but there are occasional patches of brambles, and Mummy enjoys telling us how when she was a girl she too had walked these paths with her sisters and picked many pounds of blackberries.

Once we had returned to Braemar and had eaten our high tea, it would soon be time for us to be taken to say goodnight to Grandad, before walking upstairs to be bathed and put to bed. The bathroom was at the head of the stairs on the first floor, and was intriguing to me because it contained Grandad's shaving mirror. This was a round mirror which rotated freely on a green pedestal stand; and although on one side the glass gave me a normal reflection, when I spun it round to the other side, I faced a magnifying glass which powerfully distorted my appearance. But the chief interest of the first floor in my eyes was that on the wall facing the bathroom there was a magnificent antique hand-painted cuckoo clock. Lovingly tended by Grandad, it was in perfect working order, and every hour on the hour a small wooden cuckoo emerged from a door near the top, magically accompanied by a few notes of song.

After our bath, Simon and I had to climb another flight of stairs to the very top of the house, where we made our way to the front bedroom in which we had been allocated twin beds. I was given the one nearest the door, with Simon to my left. As usual Mummy joined us as we knelt down to say our prayers, one sentence of which had now been extended to run: "God bless Spot and Sandy and Noony and Solomon *and Budge*.". This was because on moving into Holme Grange the previous year we had inherited a very ordinary small black cat. He was not nearly as elegant or aristocratic as Noony, but he had a stubborn character that we admired: his very name derived from the fact that when an angry and now departed chef had demanded that he should "Budge, blast you, Budge!" he had refused to do so.

Once we had said our prayers and climbed into bed and been kissed goodnight, we lay back on our pillows facing towards the curtained window. Often when Mummy had left the room Simon and I would talk quietly about what we had done that day and what we were hoping to do the next.

One particular evening, when Simon had drifted off to sleep, I got out of bed, walked over to the windows, pulled back one of the curtains and looked out over the moonlit scene. It was wonderful to be so high up that one could look not just across the street but over the village rooftops to the sea beyond. Mummy had been reading us *Peter and Wendy*, J.M. Barrie's novelization of his 1904 play *Peter Pan; or, the Boy Who Wouldn't Grow Up*. I believed in it completely as a record of what had really happened, and the words in which Peter explains the way to Neverland: 'Second to the right, and straight on till morning' had thrilled me with their mystery and their beauty; but now, as I looked out of the window, it was difficult to be certain where that direction lay.

Climbing back into bed again, I wondered whether it was really possible to fly. And after a while, recalling my out-of-body experience at Holme Grange, I convinced myself that if I had enough faith it *would* be possible. So I lay on top of my eiderdown, shut my eyes and willed myself to begin floating up into the air. Once I had done that, I knew, I would be able to float out through the window, take the second on the right and go straight on till morning, enter the wonderful Neverland and perhaps even meet Peter Pan and Wendy. Nothing happened, and I had to assume that my faith was not strong enough; but it was a hope that haunted me for several nights.

Of another evening in this room at the top of Braemar I have a far less agreeable memory. In our Nursery at Holme Grange, the lights were always turned off and the doors closed when we went to bed, but to allay our fears of the dark we had become used to going to sleep with night-lights, short thick candles which burned for several hours and made the darkness less alarming. Here at Braemar we had no night-lights, but a small light was left on in a corner of the room, and one evening Simon and I stared at it until the image of the filament became somehow imprinted on our retinas; and then, as our eyes relaxed, the image, a kind of half-ring of orange light, appeared to start drifting towards us.

"Look!" said one of us to the other, "Things are coming out of the light!" So we stared even harder, and more and more of these tiny images appeared to come out of the light, until we were menaced by a vast host of half-rings, which would keep advancing until by a mental effort we looked further away, which seemed to throw them back for a while before they once again began their relentless advance. Eventually, when we were both thoroughly scared, having begun to feel that these half-rings of light were some kind of alien creatures bent upon our destruction, I ran downstairs to get help; and Mummy and the Aunts had to come upstairs and explain that if we stared at a light for long enough, our eyes would start playing strange tricks.

At length the day came when Daddy reappeared in EPB 223. We were delighted to see him again, even though it meant that our holiday was over. Our luggage was strapped on to the roof-rack, and then it was time to leave. We looked out for Noony, who had as usual disappeared; we stroked Solomon, kissed Grandad on the forehead, hugged the aunts, received one of Aunt Joan's special kisses, and walked out to the car with aching jaws. Then we set off for Holme Grange again, with me still clutching a piece of white chalk collected on the sea-shore, and remembering for a long time the smell of the seaweed and the cry of the gulls.

BOOK FOUR

HOLME GRANGE: THE CORONATION YEAR 1952–1953

CHAPTER ONE
Autumn with Miss Goad

Soon after our return from Rottingdean in that late summer of 1952, it was time for me to join the junior class at Holme Grange School. This meant that immediately after breakfast each day I had to put on my school uniform with its black indoor shoes with elasticated strips on each side instead of laces, its long grey socks held up by garters, its grey shorts, its white shirt and its navy-blue blazer with a Maltese Cross over the breast-pocket. But before I could put on that blazer, I had to wrestle with a light blue tie with dark blue diagonal stripes. Mummy helped me to tie a knot in this wretched tie – why on earth were ties ever invented, I asked myself – and it was many days of seemingly hopeless struggle before I could manage it on my own.

Then I had to walk down the nursery stairs, along the red-tiled corridor and into the main Hall. By the time I arrived, rows and rows of stacking tubular chairs with canvas backs and seats had been laid out, each with a small green copy of *Songs of Praise* upon it. I found my place among other members of Form 2 in the very front row where, thanks to the presence of some of the Boarders whom I already knew, I felt quite at home. As the Hall filled up, I could see Mr. Noble and Mr. Hinton and Mr. Rushton and several other teachers along the wall to the right of me; and then Mummy came in with her own much larger green copy of *Songs of Praise* and sat herself down at the Grand Piano.

A few moments later, we all hushed and rose to our feet in absolute silence as Daddy strode purposefully into the Hall and made his way to the front wearing his Academic Cap and Gown. After depositing his mortar-board on the desk, he sat down, opened the desk drawer, took out a large mark-book, and began the roll-call; and it felt very odd when he reached my name and intoned 'Graves!' and I had to respond by calling out: 'Sir!'

Then came the Lord's Prayer, which of course I knew very well; and this was followed by a hymn sung by the entire assembly and beautifully accompanied by my mother. It was she who chose the hymns, each of which precisely fitted the mood she was in that morning. Often, she chose Sabine Baring-Gould's optimistic and cheerful *Onward, Christian soldiers,* set to rousing music by Arthur Sullivan of Gilbert and Sullivan fame:

> Onward, Christian soldiers!
> Marching as to war,
> With the Cross of Jesus
> Going on before.
> Christ, the royal Master,
> Leads against the foe;
> Forward into battle,
> See, his banners go!

This matching of hymns to moods spilled over into her private life, and I already knew to watch out for squalls if ever I heard her singing out loud Isaac Watts's famous hymn, the one beginning:

> O God, our help in ages past,
> Our hope for years to come,
> Our shelter from the stormy blast,
> And our eternal home.

This was always a sure sign that she was in an angry and depressed mood. Fortunately, it was a rare occurrence, and in normal circumstances her most extreme expression of displeasure, a relic of wartime endurance, was a deep sigh, accompanied by the words: "What we do for England!"

My own personal favourite in that little green hymn book, and another that we often sang, was John Bunyan's *Who would true valour see*. Since it had been set to music by the great Ralph Vaughan Williams, this had some special significance for both my parents: for my mother because she had often seen an elderly Vaughan Williams walking the corridors of the Royal College of Music, and for my father because he was always extremely loyal to the schools he had attended, and Vaughan Williams was an Old Carthusian.

Who would true valour see,
Let him come hither;
One here will constant be,
Come wind, come weather.
There's no discouragement
shall make him once relent
His first avowed intent
To be a pilgrim.

Whoso beset him round
With dismal stories
Do but themselves confound;
His strength the more is.
No lion can him fright,
He'll with a giant fight,
But he will have a right
To be a pilgrim.

Hobgoblin nor foul fiend
Can daunt his spirit;
He knows he at the end
Shall life inherit.
Then fancies fly away,
He'll fear not what men say,
He'll labour night and day
To be a pilgrim.

Having promised not to be daunted by hobgoblins or foul fiends, we listened to a few announcements, rose to our feet again while our Headmaster and Head of Music left the Hall, and then, one class at a time, ably directed by Mr. Noble, we stacked our chairs and left for our form-rooms.

For those of us in Form 2, this meant walking (no running allowed) up the long flight of steps at the back of the Hall until we had reached the main landing. Looking down the long corridor to our left I could see far-off the door of the nursery where, since Simon had now followed me to The White House, my sister Elizabeth would be alone with our Nanny. The prospect of joining them was not enticing enough for me to cut and run for 'Home', so I followed my class-mates as we climbed up a further flight of only two or three stairs just ahead of us, and then turned to the left and walked along a short corridor. This led past the closed door on our right of the Assistant Matron's room, to an open door directly ahead of us.

Through this we trooped into our classroom and the care of the strangely-dressed Miss Goad. There she was on our right, a curious relic of Victorian days with a careworn survivor's face sitting at her large teacher's desk and waiting impatiently for us to arrive. Her grey hair was tied up in a bun, she wore a shawl over her shoulders; and although her eyes were usually kindly (and on the whole it was a happy classroom) her nose was sharp and something in her manner made it immediately obvious that she would stand no nonsense.

When she stood up, it was also clear that she was very thin. When she walked around the classroom, as she sometimes did, I could see that she had a slight stoop, and that beneath her shawl her clothes, all in muted browns or greys, were extremely well-worn, if not actually threadbare; and, at a time when most women wore skirts which ended just below the knee, hers practically touched the floor. When she spoke, her voice was clear but reedy; and although she was probably only in her fifties she often looked much older.

From where Miss Goad sat at her desk, she faced several rows of the most old-fashioned desks in the school. They had iron frames which looked as though they might have come all the way from Coalbrookdale at the very dawn of the Industrial Revolution. To these frames were attached wooden seats wide enough for two children to sit on side-by-side, wooden backs to lean against and sloping wooden desks on which to write. Near the top of each desk was a long groove in which pens or pencils could be rested, and two round holes for inkwells, though we were considered to be far too young to be entrusted with writing in ink, so to my great disappointment these were never used.

Over to her right, a large window looked out over my garden far down below; but from my desk I could see nothing but the tops of the trees and the sky. There was nothing else in the room of interest apart from a shelf or two of books and a large blackboard. This was attached to a free-standing wooden frame in the shape of an upturned V, with a rope to stop the legs sliding too far apart, and a small shelf immediately beneath the blackboard for a formidable board-rubber made of thick cloth and backed with wood, and for several lengths of round, white chalk.

Miss Goad's great passion was Nature Study. When the weather was fine, she loved to take us on 'Nature walks' through the Holme Grange grounds, so that she could tell us all about the birds and insects and flowers and shrubs and trees that we encountered; and her very first task was to issue each of us with a 'Nature NOTE BOOK', on the front of which I proudly wrote 'Form 2' and just beneath that, in a neat cursive script: 'Richard Graves.' Our Nature books differed from ordinary exercise books in having alternate lined and unlined pages so that information about a particular bird or animal could be entered onto the lined page, and a drawing made on the unlined page opposite. One of my earliest pencilled entries on a lined page reads as follows:

Tawny Hare
Colour, upper parts tummy and chest
underneath white
tips of ears black
Tail white
White underneath.
Babies have their eyes open they have short fur coat they can wakl
Food cabbage lettuce roots carrots

And on the unlined page opposite, there is a drawing of the tawny hare in question.

Beneath my writing, Miss Goad has written in red ink: 'Good' and then as an afterthought has corrected my spelling mistake by adding the word 'walk'. My writing certainly looks perfectly acceptable: it is large and neat, although clearly the only words for which I have learned to write in a cursive script are those of my own name, for every single letter of every other word is individually printed out.

As for the drawing of the hare, this is not just good but excellent. If only it had been my own work! But it was not. It was my mother's. She supervised my homework almost every evening, sitting beside me at the Nursery table; and having realized from my feeble White House efforts that my drawings were completely lacking in any artistic merit, and not wanting me to be publicly shamed, she had begun doing all my drawings for me. Well, almost all. Among many beautifully drawn pictures of (for example) a rat, a squirrel, a magpie, a pied wagtail and a common bat, there is one of a Barn Owl which is clearly by me, since it is so dreadfully bad, nothing much more than a horrid squiggle, that I myself have wisely crossed it out. And if what my mother did sounds a shade dishonest, may I say that it stemmed only from the protective love that she extended to all her children and grandchildren, a love so fierce and so profound that it overcame every obstacle that any of us could ever set in its path.

Sadly for Miss Goad, she could not teach us Nature Study the whole time, and much of her teaching was of a more prosaic nature, involving Reading, English and Maths (the traditional 3 R's of elementary education, Reading, wRiting and aRithmetic), together with some History, some Scripture (which meant stories from the Bible); and a little Art. None of this gave me much trouble: in particular, despite my inability to draw, my painting was said to be 'quite artistic', and my reading was pronounced 'Excellent – reads aloud with great expression.'

Our daily reading lessons involved all of us either in reading out words that Miss Goad had written in white chalk on the blackboard, or in reading out loud to her from specially graded reading books. My classmates appeared to find this extremely difficult, and while they floundered, Miss Goad herself became increasingly frustrated. Thus:

> CHILD (reading from book): "J – an – et, Janet; w -nt, won't"

> MISS GOAD (interrupting): 'No, no No! Can't you see that it's an 'e', not an 'o'! Went – WENT! **WENT!**"

Fortunately for me, once Miss Goad had discovered that I was already an advanced reader, she allowed me to abandon her reading lessons and told me that I could sit at the back of the class reading any book I liked from the school library. Having made my choice, I showed it to her, and she thoroughly approved. It was William Harrison Ainsworth's 1840 novel *The Tower of London*. These days, few books would be thought more unsuitable for a 6-year-old, but Miss Goad turned out to love literature as well as Nature Study, and she had no foolish notions about children reading only books containing the restricted vocabulary and content thought suitable for their particular age.

The Tower of London, in case you haven't read it, tells the tragic history of Lady Jane Grey. Back in July 1553, she had been our Protestant Queen for only nine days, when her stay in the Tower of London, where she was awaiting her coronation, became imprisonment under the Roman Catholic Queen Mary; and she was executed early the following year. It is a dramatic tale, no longer very accessible to modern audiences because its sentences are densely constructed and its vocabulary is somewhat antique.

Fortunately, not knowing any better, I was unaware of these difficulties, and although some of the finer details of the plot may have escaped me, I lived for many weeks in the atmosphere of the Tower itself, with its dark, dank passages, its dungeons, its flaring lights, its strangely clothed and strangely-speaking figures and the occasional alarming appearance of its two resident giants, Gog and Magog. Most dramatic of all, I was there in person when on the final page the executioner swung his axe and the brave sixteen-year-old Lady Jane was beheaded on Tower Hill. 'Jane had placed her head on the block', writes Ainsworth,

> and her last words were, "Lord, into thy hands I commend my spirit!"

> The axe then fell, and one of the fairest and wisest heads that ever graced the human form, fell likewise.
>
> Thus ends the Chronicle of the Tower of London.

A memorable ending from which, like any would-be writer, I learned much. I say 'would-be writer', and writing was already my chosen destiny, if only because I could never find enough of the books that I liked reading, and so I assumed that in the end I would have to write them myself.

In the afternoons, after lunch in the dining-room with the portraits of my ancestors looking down upon me, there were organised games, of which more later; and then another hour-and-a-half with Miss Goad. After that, having said goodbye to my class-mates, I would soon be back with Simon and Elizabeth in the Nursery, where before long Simon and I would be glued to *Children's Hour* on the wireless.

CHAPTER TWO
Imagined Worlds

Children's Hour! That incomparable gateway into imagined worlds. It began at five o'clock each evening just when we were sitting down in the Nursery to our High Tea – perhaps baked beans on toast, or tinned sardines, or a boiled egg, to be eaten alongside a cup of tea and followed by as much bread-and-butter and jam as we wanted. A small portable battery-operated wireless set would be on the table and, once it had been switched on, Simon and I fell completely silent.

Children's Hour normally began with a quarter of an hour for children who had only recently outgrown the 'ming-me-mong! ming me mong!' of *Listen with Mother*. I found this the least exciting part of the programme, but Simon was enchanted by much of it. He particularly liked the *Toytown* stories, in which human characters such as the very pompous Mr. Mayor mingled with animated toy animals such as Larry the Lamb. Larry bleated in perfect received-pronunciation English, and although at first I was only doing my best to like *Toytown* for Simon's sake, I soon discovered that like my mother I had a talent for mimicry. I began amusing Simon by bleating to him like Larry the Lamb: "Oh deaaar Mr Maaayor, Simon saaaays this is a perfectly aaaaawful high teaaaaaa!" and all these years later I can still bleat with the best of them.

What was more to my taste were the dramatized series for older children, which began at around 5:30pm. These included stories by Anthony Buckeridge, a schoolmaster who wrote about the impulsive but resourceful Jennings and his short-sighted friend Darbishire, two schoolboys of 10 or 11 whose boarding-school life, in a prep-school very like Holme Grange, was full of innocent adventure. They never came to any serious harm, their lives presided over by the genial Mr. Carter and his colleague Mr. Wilkins, who disguised a good heart beneath an irascible exterior, occasionally flaring up with his trademark: "I – I – I … Corwumph!" But their stories had an enormous appeal for children like me who would have welcomed much more adventure in their own rather too well-managed lives.

Still more exciting were historical series such as Rosemary Sutcliff's *The Eagle of the Ninth*, set in Roman Britain, or science fiction adventures such as Angus MacVicar's *Return to the Lost Planet*. How true it is that the wireless, or radio as it later became, has the best pictures, because they are the ones created in the mind of the listener. How completely was I transported in my imagination to such places as the thick forests of second century Caledonia, and the rocky wastes of the planet Hesikos; and for many years I was haunted by the vision of a chain of beautiful Caribbean islands that I had 'seen' from a passing sailing-ship.

As well as listening to the wireless, I continued to be a ferocious bookworm. Years later, when I was having some difficulty getting my own three children to bed, my mother, who was visiting, reminded me that at their age I was often reading two books simultaneously at bedtime. "You had one at the head of your bed", she told me, "and one at its foot; and after reading a page of the first, you would move on to a page of the second, and so on, back and forth, and I was lucky if I managed to persuade you to remove a single item of clothing from you each time you passed by!"

Books, or the money to buy them, were now my favourite presents; though I was outraged when my seventh birthday came round in December to be given a book of verses by AA. Milne entitled *Now We Are Six*. "What!" I thought to myself. "*Now We Are Six*! But I'm *Seven*! Don't Mummy and Daddy understand anything?" This did not however put me off AA Milne. As soon as both birthday and Christmas were over and I realised that I had acquired enough money to do so, I bought my very own copy of AA Milne's sequel to *Winnie-the Pooh*.

This was *The House at Pooh Corner*, some of which I read out loud to

Simon, and all of which I also read and reread privately because it gave me such pleasure. It introduced us all to the game of 'Poohsticks', which involves two or more people dropping sticks on the upstream side of any bridge, and then dashing across to the downstream side to see which stick is the first to emerge. It also contains such unforgettable stories as that of the apparently irrepressible Tigger, a newcomer who annoys everyone by his boundless and often misplaced enthusiasm. It is only after they have launched a successful plot to 'unbounce' Tigger, who now becomes utterly dispirited, that Pooh and Piglet and the other denizens of the forest realise that they prefer him as he was, despite his annoying habits, and have to work hard to undo the change for which they are responsible. One can see from this how well AA Milne understands human nature. Think for example of the relatives of a very sick man who find themselves longing for him to resume the annoying habits by which they will be able to recognise that he has been restored to health. There is no reason for Milne to feel sad that the success of his children's stories has come to overshadow what he thinks of as his more important work. There is a sense in which his plays, his novels, his screen writing and his work for *Punch* are no more than a preparation for his children's books, which have become immortal, and which he ends so memorably with the words: "Wherever they go, and whatever happens to them on the way, in that enchanted place on the top of the Forest, a little boy and his Bear will always be playing."

CHAPTER THREE

Friends and Football

Although Simon remained my very best friend, I was gradually spending more and more time with my Holme Grange contemporaries. Among the Day-boys, these included Andrew Cullen, who was bright and cheerful and highly intelligent and almost always seemed to have a rueful smile on his face and some entertaining story to tell. He was already a member of an established Holme Grange family, since his very much older brother Thomas had been one of Gordon Walker's most senior and successful pupils; and, like me, Andrew was being given piano lessons by my mother, but with far more satisfactory results.

I myself had begun learning how to play the piano from a lovely book of elementary pieces called *The Farm*. It had a green-and-white cover, with a picture on the front of a hay-cart being drawn along by a horse. This was a good start, because it reminded me of one of my favourite toys from my White Hazel days, a hay-cart with many detachable pieces that I had been able to hitch up to a little toy horse. Indeed, I mastered the first piece so well that I used to play it as a party trick for at least the next forty years. But by the time I was beginning my third piece, the business of being taught by my mother was beginning to irritate me.

She spoke kindly enough when I made a small mistake and she had to correct me; but when I repeated that mistake, and a note of exasperation crept into her voice, then there was something too deeply personal for it to be endured. Finally, I retaliated by taking her instructions too literally. "Do keep your eyes on the page!" she instructed me one memorable morning. So, ungrateful vermin that I was, I leaned all the way forward until my eyebrows, at least, *were* touching the page. And that brought my piano lessons to an abrupt end! It was just as well because although I love listening to music, I have no musical talent whatever. Her gift, as it often does, skipped a generation: but that's a story for another time.

Andrew Cullen, by contrast, was genuinely musical, so my mother loved teaching him and in retirement she would remember him as one of the small handful of pupils she had taught who could have become truly remarkable pianists. He and his family lived not far away in a house on the Easthampstead Road, where I was several times invited to tea. I hardly met Andrew's father, who was almost always out at work when I visited, but he was clearly a successful businessman who was providing extremely well for his family. Their house was beautiful, the rooms were large and well-furnished, and the gardens were extensive and beautifully maintained. Andrew's mother seemed to me to be a little on the elderly side, and although she was unfailingly friendly towards me, and her teas (or possibly those of her cook) were always good, she appeared to be permanently anxious, and I soon realised that it was a household over which some great shadow had fallen.

The cause was not far to seek. I have already mentioned Andrew's eldest brother, Thomas, who was just as charming and intelligent as Andrew himself; but there was also a middle brother, Stephen, who was mentally impaired as a result of having cerebral palsy. At the age of eleven or twelve he talked and behaved like a child of four or five; he looked odd, with slightly protuberant eyes; his movements were curiously uncoordinated and he was clearly a tremendous burden to his whole family.

Back in 1952, of course, those with cerebral palsy, usually labelled 'Spastics', were officially deemed to be ineducable, and 'Don't be so Spastic!' was a favourite schoolboy insult directed against anyone thought by their comrades to be acting in an extremely feeble or pathetic manner. With hostile public attitudes like these, to have a 'Spastic' in one's family could only be a constant course of embarrassment and even shame, and the Cullen family were positively heroic in the way that they always treated

Stephen with the utmost care and consideration and never ever shut him away from visitors.

Another new friend was David Potter, the eldest son of a Housemaster from Wellington College, the famous Public School that was only a ten-minute drive away to the south of us, not far from the little village of Crowthorne. His mother Fraye Potter was a lively and witty and attractive young woman who, just like my mother, was married to a teacher who was also a considerably older man, and they had soon become very good friends.

Fraye's second son Chris was about the same age as my brother, and Simon and I were once invited over to Wellington College for a memorable party in the Potters' private quarters at one end of the House they managed. At the centre of this huge building there was a staircase which ran up from landing to landing and from floor to floor round the edge of a large central space. There was also a good deal of dark oak panelling, the lighting was poor, passages and rooms led off in all directions, and here in this slightly sinister setting at Fraye's instigation we played games of 'sardines' and 'murder in the dark'. And although this was a private part of the House, occasionally we could see young men who were actually Wellington College schoolboys walking busily through it, which gave me a sense of being just on the edge of a vast institution somewhat like the Tower of London, where everything ran smoothly according to its own internal but to me quite unknown rules.

Three more of my contemporaries come to mind, all of them Boarders: James Blewett, Paul Girling, and David Over.

Blewett was an individual with dark hair who stood out mainly because he was said to suffer from epileptic fits. This made us all very wary of him. I don't think we ever saw him actually having a fit, but we had lengthy discussions about what we should do if he did have one – should we, for example, run to the Pantry to find a wooden spoon to put between his teeth? Or would we be too late and find that he had bitten off his tongue?

Girling was a very good-looking and hugely popular boy, for whom I would vote the following year when he stood in a mock class election as the Communist candidate; and then there was a small thin boy with large eyes in an elfin face called David Over. He shared my zany sense of humour and for a while was a very close friend: I remember once characterizing him, in the midst of same madcap game or other, as 'My vital enemy, Over!'

Some of these boys I first met not within the classroom, but in the boxing ring (of which more later) or on the playing-fields. The whole school played football several afternoons each week during the Autumn and Spring terms. At lunchtime, we would all be told what team we were in, and on what football pitch. Then after lunch I would walk down to the changing-rooms, find my particular numbered peg, about-half-way along the corridor beside the kitchen yard, and change into my games clothes: grey shorts with an elasticated waist, a white or blue shirt depending on which team I was in, and long grey socks held up by garters.

Then I had to exchange my indoor shoes for football boots. These were stout boots with rubber studs that were nailed into the soles and had to be replaced from time to time when they wore down. They also had extremely long laces that could only be tied together in the approved Granny-knot once they had been crossed over, wound underneath the boot and back up to the top, crossed over again, and drawn around the top of the boot by the ankle, with one lace being pulled through an eye-hole at the very back before the final knot was tied.

Our main football field was still leased from J.W. Robbins of the wealthy market-gardening family; and it was reached by crossing the sunken garden, and walking down a narrow path over some rough grassy ground which led between the long, low branches of two magnificent oak trees to the very edge of our Grounds. Here a small iron gate opened onto a large field with a deep hollow where water sometimes collected, two or three large clumps of trees, and room for several football pitches. However, the most junior game, the one to which I was naturally assigned when I started at Holme Grange, used a football pitch established on our own land at the very top of a large field dotted with apple trees which ran down the eastern side of the Grounds.

Here, our football matches were presided over in a somewhat amateurish manner by our Senior Master Mr. Noble, who did not deign to turn up in games clothes, but wore instead a thick black coat and a long scarf and ordinary walking shoes, and carried a whistle and an umbrella. As for me, I showed no particular aptitude for football, but I very much liked the idea of winning, and in one of my very first games I managed to infuriate Mr. Noble by what he considered to be a complete lack of sportsmanship on my part, so that after the game he complained bitterly to my father.

What had happened was this: I was on a side that was evidently going to lose. Twice our opponents had raced down the field and kicked the ball straight past our hopelessly unsuccessful goal-keeper into the back of our net. I felt a sense of mounting humiliation, and I felt it all the more keenly because I was playing at right-back, which meant that I was one of the defenders who should have been keeping the other side at bay. However, on their next triumphant charge down the field they kicked the ball too far ahead of them. I managed to trap it and then, while I was trying to clear it, I was such a poor footballer that I accidentally kicked it over the back line.

"Corner!" shouted Mr. Noble, blowing his whistle loudly and waving his umbrella vigorously, and I now discovered that what I had done was not necessarily a mistake. According to the rules, once the ball had been kicked out of the back of the football field by a defender, the attackers were awarded a free corner kick. This sounded good for them, but meant in practice that their advance was stopped in its tracks, and while they prepared to take a free kick all the way from the very corner of the football field, we defenders were able to regroup and prepare to drive them back to the other end of the field. Having seen this work once, and despite Mr. Noble's repeated instructions that I should stop doing this, for the rest of the game, whenever the ball came anywhere close to our goal, I simply kicked it out over the back line so that our opponents had no chance of an immediate goal but had to take a corner kick instead. Eventually they were so completely demoralized by this tactic that they lost heart and more or less gave up.

"Did he break any rules?" Daddy asked Mr. Noble, who was still seething with rage when he presented me to my Headmaster.

"No, but –"

"Well then!" said Daddy, smiling his sweetest smile and giving a little shrug; though later on he told me privately that I shouldn't make a habit of it; and Mr. Noble had his revenge in my first end-of term Games report, when he wrote: 'Very promising and keen but is at present a bad loser'.

CHAPTER FOUR

Working with Miss Robinson

After a single easy-going term which in retrospect feels as though it was largely spent reading at the back of Miss Goad's classroom, I was promoted in January 1953 to Form 3a. This was situated in another upstairs classroom at the opposite end of Holme Grange, so to reach it my new classmates and I had to turn not left but right at the top of the main stairs. Here a corridor led past a doorway on the right leading into an area that I already knew, filled with washbasins and lavatories and urinals, and then turned sharply left and sharply right again.

There were now three doors from which to choose: the one to the left led into a small square room used as his bedroom by one of the members of staff; the one ahead led into a very large dormitory, which at one time must have been the master bedroom. It was directly above the former drawing-room below, and had magnificent views over the lawn and rhododendrons and azaleas and Scots Pines to the south; and just beyond it, through a doorway on the extreme right, one could descend a couple of steps into the former dressing-room, a narrow peaceful room far removed from the hurly-burly of school life which was now used by the matron and assistant matron for sewing and mending and storing the boarders' clothes. The door we wanted, however, was the one to the right.

This led directly into Miss Robinson's classroom, a large square room with the usual blackboard and teacher's desk facing four rows of desks that were very much more modern than the ones I had become used to with Miss Goad. These were individual children's desks whose sloping tops had hinges at the back and could be lifted up to reveal the storage space beneath in which exercise books and text books and spare pencils and a pencil sharpener could be kept for easy access when needed. There was also a tall cupboard at the back of the classroom full of powder-paints, large sheets of paper and other excitements.

Miss Robinson herself was a brisk, efficient and fair-minded teacher, very much younger than Miss Goad and with a penchant for elegant flowery dresses. Fortunately for her, I had numerous childish illnesses that spring term, so I was often away, which must have made her life a little more agreeable, because I was not the easiest of pupils. For one thing, my spelling and use of capitals had been badly influenced by A.A. Milne, whose attitude to both is somewhat cavalier. And to make matters worse, my handwriting, which had been so neat and careful for Miss Goad, suddenly deteriorated and became disgustingly untidy.

Poor Miss Robinson!

In a largely unsuccessful attempt to improve my handwriting, she insisted on my spending many long hours using old-fashioned copybooks. These dreadful books, against which my whole being rebelled, were about the size of normal exercise books, but turned on their side, and with each page containing printed examples of what was considered to be perfect handwriting in a neat cursive script. Below each line of this perfect script, was a space into which it could be copied; and the pages were very carefully ruled, so that one could see not only the line upon which each letter should stand, but also the imaginary line to which each 'g' or 'j' or 'p' or 'q' or 'y' should drop down, the imaginary line to which each small letter such as an 'a' or an 'e' or the lower part of a 'b' or a 'd', should reach up; and the imaginary line to which capital letters and letters such as 'b' or 'd' or 'h' or 'l' should ascend.

Trying to copy the script accurately was bad enough; but in order to improve our morals as well as our handwriting, the sets of words that were to be copied consisted either of proverbs from the Bible, such as 'Pride goeth before a fall'; or of maxims such as 'Experience makes us wise', 'Justice favours no man' or 'Lost time is never found''. I suppose that copybook writing did teach me how to write cursively, but I didn't enjoy being preached at; it made very little impact upon my untidiness; and whether or not it had any effect upon my morals I must leave others to judge.

Miss Robinson's luck was no better when it came to her history teaching. For this purpose, she issued us all with text-books with soft green covers on the front of which were outlines of the *Niña*, the *Pinta* and the *Santa Maria*. These, she told us, were the famous old sailing ships in which Christopher Columbus and his followers had made their first voyage across the Atlantic back in 1492; and inside the green cover were stories both of this famous voyage of discovery and of the Kings and Queens of England in Tudor times. To my great delight, we began with Lady Jane Grey about whom, having only recently completed *The Tower of London*, I considered myself an expert; and my first History essay for Miss Robinson was on the subject of her successor, the much-maligned Queen Mary, whose life I summed up thus:

> She marryed the King of spain, and she felt nothing stood in her way and she made the parliment make the services in the old way but soon she realized that Her plan was failing and soon after dide.

As I said earlier, poor Miss Robinson! Instead of treating this totally inadequate homework with the scorn that it deserved, she contented herself with adding the very gentlest of reproofs: 'You could mention the burnings.' As time went on, I am glad to say that she gained in courage, and beneath a later piece of work headed 'Prep: The Pilgrim Fathers' she wrote forcefully: 'You can do much better than this; it is very lazy work. Please do it again.' My revised version runs:

> The Pilgrim Fathers were some men who were in holand. But they thought that they had better sail to America becess they dident want their children to be dutch, so they went to America after to England in England they fitted up a ship, the Mayflower they wanted to go to Virginia but they Landed at Cape Cod, on the way back they were often attacked by Red Indians not one man or woman reternd they died from cold and hunger

Oh dear!

A few weeks later, when I had been asked to write a letter from a Gentleman hoping to join King Charles I, and I gave as my only reasons for supporting him that 'I have been turned out of everything else', and that my wife and family were worrying me for money, she commented wearily that this was at least 'Original'; and indeed her only genuine praise for my historical endeavours came when I handed in pencil drawings of a Roundhead and a Cavalier. 'These are very good' she wrote. She was quite correct. Unfortunately, they were not mine. My mother had continued to help me just as she had done when I was in Miss Goad's class, but here her contribution is even more glaringly obvious, because beneath these impeccable drawings is a sketch of my own purporting to show Charles I hiding in a tree while being pursued by the Roundheads.

I myself was perfectly happy with this dreadful piece of work, since it included all the details that I wanted included, and I saw it as it should have been rather than as it was; but as a drawing it is beneath contempt. Yet again, I can only say 'Poor Miss Robinson!' Having approved the earlier drawings, and noted the sudden and terrible deterioration in quality, she must have realized that her earlier praise had been utterly misplaced. But instead of telling me so, she remembers that I am the Headmaster's son, and writes only: "rather small".

This was also the term when I began studying French, making what Mr. Hinton politely described as a 'promising start'; and Mr. Wyndham Roberts, my first specialist teacher of Mathematics, presented each of us with a blue exercise book, each page of which had been lightly printed with almost 1,500 small squares into which numbers could be placed. He then taught us how to improve this lay-out by using a ruler to draw careful margins on each side of the page: a narrow one to the left, so that we could number each individual sum, and a wide one to the right in which to show any relevant workings.

After a rather shaky start, I soon got the hang of simple multiplication and division. Curiously enough, for it has all been comparative simple ever since metric measurements were introduced in 1971, it was addition which was complicated. One of my first exercises for our new maths teacher involved adding three sets of miles, furlongs, chains, yards, feet and inches – for which, obviously, one had to know that there were 12 inches to a foot, 3 feet to a yard, 22 yards to a chain, 10 chains to a furlong and 8 furlongs to a mile.

To be fair, Wyndham Roberts may have been showing off at this point. Chains and furlongs were usually left out of our calculations and, having reached yards, one normally needed to know only that there were 1,760 yards to a mile; though one could always curry a certain amount of favour with sportsmen by knowing that there were exactly 22 yards or 1 chain to a cricket-pitch. By the start of the summer term, we were also studying fractions, so I was soon able to add $3\frac{5}{8}$" to $1\frac{1}{4}$" and come up with the correct result of $4\frac{7}{8}$"; and soon after that we moved on to long division, which I found relatively easy, since it involved nothing more than careful layout and an easy command of one's tables.

I soon began to feel that Mathematics was extremely satisfying, and at some point I was awarded my first silver star. Why did I find it so satisfying? Not simply because of that silver star, though that might have had something to do with it. I think it was because I was becoming tired of the fact that in (say) History, everything seemed to be a matter of opinion, and if my opinion differed from that of my teacher (which it often did) I was automatically found to be in the wrong. With numbers, however, nothing was a matter of opinion. One was either right or wrong, and with care one could almost always be right. Let me add as an after-thought that although much of my subsequent mathematical education has turned out to be almost completely pointless, I have often found it very useful to be able to do long division.

It was while I was in 3a studying under Miss Robinson that I learned another valuable lesson, this time from my father. It came about because from time to time, Miss Robinson would instruct us to learn a poem for our Prep, and the very next day this poem had to be either recited or actually written down from memory. Attempting to learn one of these poems, instead of being any kind of a pleasure, was a terrible torture to me, and no doubt I tortured everyone else in the Nursery with my bitter complaints.

Fortunately, one evening when I was trying unsuccessfully to learn the words of Robert Louis Stevenson's 'Keepsake Mill', from his *A Child's*

Garden of Verses, my father happened to look into the Nursery. Seeing my anguish, he asked me what the matter was. When I told him, he smiled a slightly secretive smile and said: "I used to have the same problem when I was a boy, but *my* father explained exactly what to do. Don't make a conscious effort to learn the lines. Simply read them over several times just before you go to sleep, and when you wake up in the morning you'll find that you know them."

"But how on earth..."

"Don't worry. Your brain will do the work for you while you sleep!"

To my astonishment this turned out to be absolutely true; and the following morning Miss Allen was equally astonished when I was able to recite all 24 lines of *Keepsake Mill* by heart, beginning with:

> Over the borders, a sin without pardon,
> Breaking the branches and crawling below,
> Out through the breach in the wall of the garden,
> Down by the banks of the river, we go.

A few days later, just to give the procedure a further test, I read over another of RLS's verses, the mysterious *Windy Nights* which begins:

> Whenever the moon and stars are set,
> Whenever the wind is high,
> All night long in the dark and wet,
> A man goes riding by.
> Late in the night when the fires are out,
> Why does he gallop and gallop about?

Once again, it was a complete success.

Despite this, whenever I recommend this method of learning to others, they are extremely sceptical; so it was with some pleasure that I read in *Mail Online* back in May 2020 that there are now sound scientific reasons that explain exactly why it works. While we sleep, our brains apparently 'replay the firing patterns our neurons underwent while [we were] awake'; and this process, known as 'offline replay', is said to underly memory consolidation. The main thing is that it works, you have my word for it; and this was just the start of a wonderful process by which over the next six or seven years my mind was stocked with memorable verses that have been a comfort and a pleasure to me for the rest of my life.

CHAPTER FIVE
The Coronation

We had been thinking a great deal about our new Queen ever since the death of George VI back in February 1952. Personally, I had been very struck by the romantic story of Princess Elizabeth having been staying in a tree-house in Africa when she heard the news of her father's death. Then there were the coins with Queen Elizabeth's head on them which began appearing in our pocket-money and in our change; and the stamps with Queen Elizabeth's head on them which were suddenly present on so much of the huge quantity of post that was driven up to Holme Grange in a red Post Office van each morning.

The day of the Queen's Coronation had been fixed for Tuesday 2 June 1953. After years of austerity, it was exciting to have something to celebrate, and the closer that date approached, the more the whole country seemed to be caught up in a kind of Coronation fever. We ourselves had been subscribing to a children's magazine called *Sunny Stories* since not long after moving to Holme Grange; and from 17 March 1953 we were able to start reading a serial account written by Marion Crawford, known affectionately by her charges as 'Crawfie', about the two young Princesses Elizabeth and Margaret when she had been their Governess.

We had soon learned that within her family Princess Elizabeth was usually known as Lilibet; and since my own sister was called Elizabeth, and we often shortened *her* name to Lilibet I could not help feeling that there must be some special unexplained link between our family and the new Queen. I already knew that I must have some link to royalty myself, because my name was Richard, and the previous year my Aunt Clarissa had sent me a post card on which she had written: 'I thought you would like to see this statue of King Richard on his beautiful horse. He is waving his sword!' And there on the other side was a photograph of the statue of King Richard I in Old Palace Yard beside the Houses of Parliament. How I had longed to have my own horse and sword and ride into battle!

It was certainly intriguing for us children to read about how the royal children had behaved and Crawfie, (much to the fury of the Queen Mother who never forgave her former employee for this apparent breach of trust, despite having partly encouraged it in the first place) recounts many incidents in which our new Queen took part as a child. Many of these were perfectly charming, but it is this one, not quite so charming, which made the most impression on me:

> There was a certain Mademoiselle who taught French to Lilibet.
>
> They used to write out endless columns of verbs and during those French lessons I used to play with Princess Margaret next door.
>
> One day I heard very strange noises coming out of the schoolroom, so I went in to see what had happened. I found poor Mademoiselle shaken with horror.
>
> Lilibet, rebelling all of a sudden and goaded by boredom to violent measures, had picked up a big silver ink-pot and placed it without any warning upside down on her head.
>
> There she sat, with ink trickling down her face and slowly dyeing her golden curls blue. I never really found out what had happened. But it was not often that Lilibet was so mischievous.

In a successful move to improve the circulation of *Sunny Stories*, the second part of Crawfie's story was accompanied both by a separate 'Royal Album', and by a sheet of six royal photographs that could be cut out and pasted into the first six of the Album's twenty-four blank spaces. The remaining eighteen photographs were supplied with the next three issues of *Sunny Stories*, and their arrival and subsequent pasting-in immediately became one of the highlights of my week.

At about this time, like a number of my school-fellows, I was also the recipient of a Coronation cut-out model book. This contained pages of thin cardboard, onto which brightly-coloured images had been printed; and when these images were carefully cut out and fitted together with tabs, it was possible to create a three-dimensional model of the magnificent Gold State Coach. This was the enclosed carriage drawn by eight horses in which Queen Elizabeth would be travelling when she processed through the streets of London on the way to her Coronation at Westminster Abbey.

Known as 'Old Rattlebones' because it was so uncomfortable to ride in; and drawn along by no fewer than eight horses simply because it was so heavy, it had been used in every Coronation since that of George IV back in 1821. From examining my uncut pages, I could see that it featured beautifully gilded elaborate carvings of cherubs, dolphins and sea-gods and that its side-panels were covered with wonderful paintings. Admiring it all very much, I worked on my cardboard model with the greatest possible enthusiasm, and when it had been completed, I showed it proudly to Miss Robinson. She made a few vaguely appreciative comments but seemed less excited than I had hoped, possibly because bitter experience had taught her that in artistic matters I could not be entirely trusted to have done all the work myself.

Wokingham was also full of Coronation mania. Most of the shops had at the very least bunting and photographs of the Queen and Prince Philip in their front windows, and all those that could reasonably do so were exhibiting Coronation memorabilia: Coronation spoons, Coronation plates, Coronation cups and saucers, Coronation biscuit tins, Coronation musical boxes, Coronation tea-pot stands, Coronation tea-towels; and Coronation mugs. As *The Wokingham Times* reported:

> Probably the most impressive shop window was one in Peach Street, in which, surrounded by royal purple, was a lifelike image of the Queen in full regalia and holding the orb and sceptre. Quiet dignity was symbolized by the crown in a florist's window containing no less than five-and-a-half thousand heads of Gnaphalium. Another

shopkeeper displayed a collection of souvenir Coronation mugs, dating back to William IV.

It went without saying that my parents were thoroughly loyal to the Crown, not least because they were both devout Protestants, and the Queen was Head of the Church of England. So we had soon acquired a Coronation mug of our own, and this was placed on the windowsill of the Holme Grange drawing-room alongside earlier mugs commemorating the Silver Jubilee of George V and Queen Mary in 1935; the Coronation of King Edward VIII on 12 May 1937, a Coronation which of course never happened because of his Abdication on 11 December 1936; and the Coronation of King George VI and Queen Elizabeth in 1937.

Much of the Coronation service itself dated back for centuries; and over most of those centuries it had been witnessed by only a small and highly select group of the most important people in the land. A change had come in1937, when large parts of the Coronation of King George VI and Queen Elizabeth were broadcast on the radio. This time, we learned, there would be a still greater change: at the Queen's request almost the whole ceremony, (apart from her being anointed with oil), was to be broadcast on television.

News of this change meant that although a television set was still a considerable luxury, there had been a rapid increase during the early part of 1953 in the number of households who owned one. Despite living at Holme Grange, we remained part of the 80% who did not; but on Coronation Day itself Mummy and Daddy took the three of us children to the home of kindly dayboy parents who, although they lived in a very modest house not far from the centre of Wokingham on the Easthampstead Road, were one of the 20% who did.

We were invited into their living-room, which was only just large enough for a modest three-piece suite and a few chairs; and there, perched on its stand in a corner between the window and the fireplace, was a very small black-and-white television set which immediately became the centre of our attention. The screen was tiny, no more than twelve inches wide, and at times the picture was so fuzzy that we appeared to be watching events through a snow-storm; but to me, watching television for the very first time, it was a near-miraculous experience.

Here we are in Wokingham and able to watch, however indistinctly at times, what is going on in central London over thirty miles away *as it actually happens*. There is our beautiful young Queen arriving at Westminster Abbey in her Gold State Coach, even if we can only see it in black-and-white. There she is processing up the Abbey Nave with her long train held by six Maids of Honour; and there is the Archbishop of Canterbury who, after saying "Let us Pray", recites the Collect for Purity. This had been translated from the Latin by Thomas Cranmer back in the sixteenth century as follows:

> Almighty God, unto whom all hearts be open, all desires known and from whom no secrets are hid, cleanse the thoughts of our hearts by the inspiration of thy Holy Spirit, that we may perfectly love thee, and worthily magnify thy holy name through Christ our Lord. Amen.

Prayers like this were already familiar to me from our Sunday visits to All Saints Church, Wokingham, of which more later.

Then comes a prayer specific to the occasion:

> O God who providest for thy people by thy power and rulest over them in love, grant unto this thy servant Elizabeth our Queen the spirit of wisdom and government that being devoted unto thee with her whole heart she may so wisely govern that in her time thy church may be in safety and Christian devotion may continue in peace. That so persevering in good works unto the end she may by thy mercy come to thine everlasting kingdom through Jesus Christ thy son our Lord who liveth and reigneth with thee in the unity of the Holy Ghost one God for ever and ever. Amen.

Later on in the service, we watch as the Queen, having been anointed with holy oil while hidden from view, is publicly invested with a coat of cloth of gold lined with shimmering silk, in which she receives her regalia, including the golden spurs of chivalry, the great sword of State and the golden bracelets of sincerity and wisdom. Then come the orb, the ring, the royal sceptre and the rod of equity and mercy; and the crowning itself.

After which the whole congregation calls out 'God Save the Queen!' three times; there is a magnificent trumpet fanfare; the Archbishop intones a prayer beginning 'God crown you with a crown of glory and righteousness' and the Queen ascends to the throne.

From here she receives the homage first of the Archbishop of Canterbury and then of the other Princes and Peers of the realm, including her husband Prince Philip, the Duke of Edinburgh, who declares in an oath dating back to Norman times:

> I Philip will become your liege man of life and limb and of earthly worship and faith and truth I will bear unto you to live and die against all manner of folks so help me God.

After this homage there is another more elaborate fanfare of trumpets, and the most important part of the service is over.

What had made the greatest impression upon me was not the actual crowning, but the tremendous force of the acclamation given to Her Majesty by the Queen's scholars of Westminster School as she had first entered Westminster Abbey and they sang out:

> Vivat Regina!
> Vivat Regina Elizabetha!
> Vivat! Vivat! Vivat!

The morning of Coronation Day had brought us news of another almost equally exciting event. We took two daily newspapers in those days. One of them, *The Times*, still covered its front page with advertisements as it had done since its birth back in the 1780s. But the front page of the *Daily Mail* for 2 June 1953 was headlined:

THE CROWNING GLORY –
EVEREST CONQUERED

This dramatic story was sub-titled: 'Edmund Hillary plants the Queen's flag on the top of the world', and gave us the news that: 'Everest is conquered. A Union Jack has flown on the 29,002ft. peak carried there by a New Zealand bee-keeper. Nature's greatest prize belongs to the Queen this Coronation morning.'

Despite being great explorers, men drawn from the British Empire and Commonwealth had failed to be the first men to reach either the North Pole in 1909 or the South Pole in 1911. The result was that they were particularly keen to conquer the so-called 'Third Pole' of Mount Everest, and had been attempting to do so since the days of my Uncle Robert's friend George Mallory back in the 1920s.

Eight expeditions had already failed, so the conquest of Everest by Edmund Hillary and Sherpa Tenzing Norgay in this ninth British expedition was a cause of great celebration. Hillary was immediately appointed a Knight Commander of the Order of the British Empire, while John Hunt, the British Army Colonel who had led the expedition, was made a Knight Bachelor. They and their team were showered with numerous other honours; and the Conquest of Everest, just like the Coronation, had also been commemorated on film.

It was indeed only a few days after the Coronation that the whole school was marched down the Easthampstead Road to Wokingham's Ritz Cinema, situated a little way back from the left-hand-side of the road shortly before its T-junction with Peach Street. Here we watched *A Queen Is Crowned*, a documentary film written by the poet and playwright Christopher Fry, and narrated by Sir Laurence Olivier. We were only able to watch it so soon after the Coronation because the whole of the ritual was known before the event, so that Sir Laurence had been able to pre-record his narration back in May. Now we could watch the ceremony in technicolor, and I much enjoyed my view of the Gold State Coach that I had modelled so carefully being drawn through London by eight Windsor Greys wearing their distinctive red Morocco harness. And not much later in the year we would all be trooping down to the Ritz Cinema a second time, to watch *The Conquest of Everest*, an exciting documentary full of magnificent mountain scenes and covering the earlier unsuccessful expeditions before leading up to the triumph of 1953.

These were indeed inspirational times, especially for those of us who were young. I and my schoolfellows had already learned a little about the glories of the first Elizabethan Age, including in particular our defeat of the Spanish Armada and the pioneering exploration of men like Sir Walter Raleigh; and now the success of our mountaineers, coming on the eve of the Coronation, was hailed by many commentators as the portent of a glorious new Elizabethan Age.

CHAPTER SIX
Exploration

Simon and I had become acquainted with the roundabout and the area immediately around it very early on. Looking out from the Holme Grange front-doorstep, to its right there was thick vegetation punctuated only by the large gap made by the back drive and, a very short distance further on, by the much smaller gap where a pathway led directly into an area of shrubs and trees, a pathway that was notable each spring for the beautiful lilac blooms of the tall syringa that overshadowed its entrance. To its left, after the start of the south-western terrace, edged by a tall yew hedge, there was a wilderness fronted by a grassy area just beside the roundabout in which stood four massive fir-trees. Then came a shrubbery, and then, between a narrow, paved path and the exit to the main drive, there was another corrugated iron Nissen Hut. This one had the standard semi-circular shape. It housed two outdoor classrooms and its large, plain, unadorned windows set in a red-brick wall stared back at the main school buildings from the other side of a small square lawn.

Within the roundabout itself, the flower-beds at its centre were encircled and sub-divided by narrow grass paths laid out in a curious pattern. From above they would have looked exactly like the drawing of a keyhole, centred as they were on a narrow paved path which ran from just opposite the front door straight into the middle of the roundabout, where it opened out like the top of any keyhole into a small paved circle.

To make a good first impression on prospective parents, it was important to keep this area looking neat and tidy. So, when he was free from other responsibilities, my father, who had always been a keen gardener, could often be found working in the roundabout flower-beds dressed in his very oldest gardening clothes including dark- blue shorts, an old dark-blue skiing-top with a zipper down its front, and a dark-blue ski-cap.

While he was in this gardening-mode, with a fork in his hands and a wheel-barrow full of weeds by his side, visitors driving up to the school would often mistake him for a groundsman."Excuse me, my good man, I'm sorry to trouble you, but I have an appointment with the Headmaster in fifteen minutes. Can you help?" And then, having graciously accepted the small tip that had been offered, perhaps a six-penny piece, Daddy would touch his ski-cap appreciatively, conduct them into the building, and leave them waiting in the drawing-room at the end of the red-tiled corridor. He would then dash upstairs, change into his best suit and tie, and reappear as the Headmaster; and although an occasional visitor would give him an odd look, as if they thought they surely must know him from *somewhere*, he was virtually unrecognizable as the tramp-like figure who had greeted them only a few minutes earlier.

It was on the roundabout that I finally learned to ride the small blue bicycle from which I had fallen so many times during our last weeks at White Hazel. This was achieved by Mummy promising to retain her hold on the back of the bicycle seat while I rode along, and then suddenly, without any warning, letting go. I had travelled several more yards before realizing to my huge delight that I had found my balance and was at last bicycling unaided.

We often cycled here, me on my blue two-wheeler and Simon on his tricycle; and occasionally we laid our cycles to one side and walked down the path beside the Nissen Hut which led into an area of woodland. This was chiefly notable in our eyes because, within five yards of the Nissen Hut, at the very edge of the other trees, it contained a horse chestnut tree which always bore a huge crop of excellent conkers. A particular advantage, in our view, was that its branches came down so low that it was easy enough to throw sticks to knock down the green, spiky fruits; and often, as they hit the bare earth of the ground below, one segment of the green outer shell would fall away revealing a conker that was already browning nicely inside.

In several other directions we had explored much further away from the main school buildings. To the north-east, for example, we had gone beyond Mr. Hills's shed and the compost-heap and the Tool shed, and walked along beside thick clumps of bamboo on our left and a tall hedge on our right. Here, the previous autumn, we had discovered another one of the best of the seven Holme Grange conker trees, almost unbelievably superior to the one in the compost heap, though not quite so prolific as the one near the roundabout. This one by the bamboos not only had a good crop each year of ordinary-sized conkers which came inside tender green shells that peeled off easily, but also produced a number of giant-sized conkers for which in my eyes and Simon's eyes it had soon become famous.

Beyond this conker tree, at the very end of the tall hedge, there was an opening which led into an apple orchard. This had been planted back in the 1890s with three varieties of cooking apples and six varieties of the most delicious eating apples that I have ever tasted. My father loved apples and was delighted by finding himself the owner of these traditional varieties; and during the apple season, almost whenever Simon and I came across him somewhere in the grounds, he would magically produce a small knife and a couple of eating apples from his pockets, and sit us down either on the grass if it was dry enough or on a handy bench or tree-trunk.

Then with his large strong hands he would very neatly slice the apples one by one into four quarters, cut out with a quick twist of his knife the sections of the core that remained, and hand the quarters to us one at a time as a special treat to be eaten there and then, while all the time giving us a running commentary on the variety. "You should like this one", he'd say as he sliced and handed out. "Do you see the bright red skin? It's a Worcester Pearmain. Tastes a little of strawberry, don't you think? Now this is quite different but it's one of my favourites. It not only tastes good, but it smells good. And just look at this skin: it's an orangey-red with some green. That's a Cox's Orange Pippin, and one of the most famous apples in England!"

Over to the west of Holme Grange, the large roughly-grassed area with its two oak trees which lay on the way to the rented football fields had become another favourite area, because Mr. Hills had been asked to attach a swing with stout ropes and a wooden seat to one of the branches of the right-hand oak. Once Daddy had taught us how to gain momentum and height by tucking in our legs as we swung back, and then shooting them straight out as we swung forward, Simon and I spent many happy hours taking turns to swing up and down in this isolated spot.

There was another good reason for coming here: we found that each spring this whole area was thickly carpeted with masses of flowering daffodils. They were invisible from the western terrace, but as soon as we had walked across the sunken garden, and negotiated the staggered exit through the centre of the tall yew hedge at its back, there they were, 'all at once' just as our family friend William Wordsworth writes of a similar occasion in his own life:

> I wandered lonely as a cloud
> That floats on high o'er vales and hills,
> When all at once I saw a cloud,
> A host of golden daffodils...
>
> Ten thousand saw I at a glance,
> Tossing their heads in sprightly dance

This golden acre was a beautiful sight never to be forgotten and it had been planted by the Weston family with numerous different varieties of daffodil.

By the way, those of you who are keen gardeners will know that technically all daffodils are narcissi, but my father taught us to use the word daffodil only for those flowers like the golden-yellow King Alfreds whose cups or trumpets are as long as, or even longer than, their petals. These were in the majority, and included varieties which either had white petals or were all-white; but sadly, they had no discernible scent. I much preferred the narcissi, a word we were taught to reserve for those flowers which had white petals, very much smaller cups of yellow edged with orange or red, and a delicious sweet scent.

South of the daffodils, the grassy area led back towards the azaleas at the edge of the southern lawn; but first there was a patch of bulbs at that time so rare in the wild that they were often described as an endangered species: I refer to specimens of the beautiful snake's head fritillary, with bell-like flowers in purple and white, which we were enjoined never under any circumstances to pick, but simply to admire. These were invested by my father with almost sacred significance, and it was of the fritillary rather than the lily that I thought when I later heard the words: 'Solomon in all his glory was not arrayed like one of these'.

North of the daffodils, there was another large clump of rhododendrons, coming up very close to the sunken garden, and standing among yet more rough woodland. Although Simon and I delighted in all the great rhododendron shrubberies, it was this one by the corner of the sunken garden that we found by far the most satisfying, for it contained both a look-out point and a secret room.

The rhododendrons here rose up to fifteen feet above the ground, a solid mass of thick green leaves overlaid, each spring, by a glorious profusion of different coloured blooms. From a starting-point close to the sunken garden we found that it was possible, after pushing a little way into the shrubbery, to climb up from branch to branch until, some eight or nine feet above the ground, we had reached a very good solid thick branch on which we could stand and peer out through the leaves. Secretly spying on people had become one of our favourite games, and from here we could easily spy on anyone who happened to be passing by in the nearby grounds.

After a while, we would turn towards the middle of the shrubbery, first walking along the branch we were on, and then moving across to another branch, before beginning a gradual downward climb. Once we had by-passed a particularly difficult upright branch that threatened to block our way, we were able to move on, lower and lower, until we were within a few inches of the ground, where we found ourselves in a hollowed-out cavern within the very heart of the shrubbery where we could meet in secret to discuss our plans.

Elizabeth's nannies continued to exercise a restraining function from time to time. One of them was relatively easy to avoid. Despite not being with us for very long, she achieved long-lasting notoriety through her insane determination that Lilibet should be potty-trained at an unreasonably early age. My sister, who was beginning to show that she had considerable spirit, rebelled against this, and the result was that she was often made to sit on her large pink potty in the middle of the Nursery floor for what seemed like hours, looking on sadly while we older children either played games nearby, or managed to escape completely into the outside world.

Another Nanny, also not with us for long, seems to have regarded herself as a kind of Pioneer. She was certainly tougher and more successful than most in corralling us, and she began taking us on walks with a pushchair for Elizabeth, a fearsome-looking scythe for herself, and a small whetstone with which to keep that scythe razor-sharp. Her favourite route lay past the woodshed and down the back drive.

To our right, more than one track led off into desolate woodland, and we had soon passed the second most disappointing conker tree at Holme Grange. Its shells refused to be peeled. They were huge and thick. Treading hard on them simply pushed them into the ground. If one stamped on them on a hard surface, they still would not break until one stamped so hard that they were totally squashed. And on the rare occasions that the shells could be forced off, they revealed only two or three very small conkers inside, not fit to be used for anything, so after a year or two we gave up on them completely.

To our left, we passed by the entrance-gate into that long field containing about a dozen apple trees which I regularly passed through on my way to the football field at its top. These ancient trees, dotted about in a seemingly random manner, had not done as well as the apple trees in the orchard. They produced very little fruit, and they were surrounded by equally ancient iron grilles, many of which now leant over at the crazy angles to which the growing trees had bent them.

There was no scope here for a pioneer, so we carried on, following a track which led south alongside the field, but was separated from it at first by a row of laurel bushes. As the slope grew steeper, the laurel bushes to our left came to an end, and then on our right we passed by a row of three more Nissen huts. The first two of these huts had narrow doors set at the centre of their semi-circular façade and were completely empty; the third had large wide doors, and was used as a staff garage.

Beyond these huts, the track narrowed and narrowed until there was only just room to walk in single file, and it was at this point that Pioneer Nanny delegated me to take over her push-chair duties, and began to wield her scythe with almost frightening enthusiasm. Sometimes she swung out at the undergrowth on each side of the narrow path, and sometimes she massacred any plants that had grown up in the middle of the path ahead and were blocking our way.

I suspect that she must have seen one of those films in which intrepid explorers hack their way through African or Far-Eastern jungles while exotic birds fly overhead and dangerous animals roar horribly from close by, and that she would much rather have been somewhere out there than looking after the three of us.

Eventually, at the very bottom of the slope, we came to a place where two or three planks offered a precarious route over a narrow shallow stream; on the other side of which the path completely petered out. At length, after more ferocious scything in this general area, and more equally ferocious sharpening of her scythe – personally I began to suspect her of having homicidal tendencies and felt much more secure after she had moved on – Pioneer Nanny would lead us back up the slope to the safety of Elizabeth's bedtime and Simon's and my High Tea.

CHAPTER SEVEN
Summertime

During the summer, Cricket replaced Football as our principal sport, and this was played on a large Cricket Field in the most northerly part of the Holme Grange grounds, the part furthest away from the school, closest to the lake, closest to Wokingham and containing the most visible Holme Grange landmark, a massive Giant Sequoia that could be seen from miles away.

To reach this field, we trudged down the drive wearing games shorts, a white games shirt, cricket shoes and a grey felt broad-brimmed sun-hat, considered essential for protecting us from sun-stroke whenever we were outside during the summer term. More senior boys than me also had to carry their own bats and pads and white cricket gloves reinforced on the backs of the fingers with rubber spikes; but those of us in the lowest game did without the gloves and shared communal bats and pads which were loaded into one of the trolleys and pushed down the drive.

Having reached the oak-tree junction, instead of turning left towards the Lodge or right into the driveway of what had once been the Stables, then the Dower House, and was now the Garden House, we carried straight on into an area that Simon and I had as yet hardly begun to explore. To our right, beyond the strip of grass two or three feet wide which was owned by us, there was a low wooden fence just this side of a thick belt of trees and scrub which formed part of the grounds of the Garden House; while to our left was a triangle of rough ground which lay between us, the driveway leading to the Lodge, and the line of trees and shrubs bordering the Lake. It was a somewhat desolate and I thought wasted space and I often wondered how it could be improved.

Soon the drive began curving round to the left and, as we passed very close to the north-eastern end of the Lake, we could look down almost its entire length. Our end was shallow and full of leaves, many of them shed each autumn by another Horse-Chestnut. This one had perfectly good conkers, but most of them fell into the water and rotted while a few, germinating in a nutritious mush of old leaves, took root and had to be pulled up each year while it was still easy to do so, when they were still only a few inches tall, and showing their first distinctive set of green leaves, five or seven leaflets to each stalk.

The rest of the lake was attractively edged with willows and silver birch and an occasional clump of bamboo. In the spring there were also a few sprinklings of golden daffodils on the banks of the lake; and on the surface of the grey-blue water itself swam families of moor-hens: the young ones who had been hatched in the spring with their brown beaks and their brown and grey feathers, and their much more colourful parents with their red and yellow beaks, and their brown and purplish-black feathers, some of them edged with white markings. Usually there was nothing to hear apart from the soft lapping of the water when the wind was upon it, but sometimes these lovely birds disturbed the tranquillity of this secret and magical lake with their nervous gargling calls.

Immediately beyond the lake's end, we came to the corner of the Cricket Field and here, just ahead of us and a little to our left, stood the vast red trunk of our Giant Sequoia, by far the most amazing of all the specimen trees in the Holme Grange grounds. The largest tree in the world, with a trunk whose diameter at its base can eventually be over 25 feet, and which can reach a height of more than 300 feet, the Giant Sequoia is a survivor from prehistoric times, and now grows naturally only on the western slopes of the Sierra Nevada mountains in California.

Although well-known to the local tribes of what we called in those days 'Red Indians', it had remained unseen and undiscovered by any western eye until the 1830s, when explorers from the outside world brought back tales to an incredulous Europe of its huge girth and height. Then in

1852 large quantities of its seed were imported by an enterprising plant collector into England, where for the next ten years or so growing a Giant Sequoia became the height of fashion for those with large enough Estates. Our own specimen, planted by the Westons in the 1890s, was a relative late-comer, but it was also extremely healthy. This was because it had been planted in exactly the right location. Even in the driest of summers its roots could soak up all the water it needed from the nearby Lake, with the result that after only sixty years or so its trunk was already five or six feet in diameter.

The Cricket field itself was perfectly flat and relatively easy to manage. It was bounded on the south by the Lake, on the north and west by the Heathlands Road, and on the east by the drive which ran on to an exit on the Easthampstead Road, from which it was separated by a locked wooden gate. The First Game Pitch was situated half-way down the field relatively close to the drive, and several more pitches had been measured out all around. Incidentally, no tape measures were needed for this. Daddy knew from long experience that a well-judged adult stride is exactly equal to a yard, and so he had paced out each 22-yard cricket-pitch himself. The only thing seriously lacking for any self-respecting Preparatory School hoping to play matches against other Preparatory Schools was a Cricket Pavilion.

Fortunately, between the right-hand-side of the drive and the Easthampstead Road there was a wide area of trees and scrub. The part closest to the lake was already occupied by a fairly primitive flat-roofed outside latrine, invisible from the drive, reached by a path that led between two eating chestnut trees (of which more later), and made just like the Nissen Huts and the woodshed of corrugated iron.

A little further on, however, there was plenty of room, and my father had a concrete base laid down beside the drive. Not long afterwards, sections of a prefabricated Pavilion arrived on a lorry and were dumped onto this base. There they stayed for a while, until the day came when Mr. Hills and Simmy, (with a good deal of help from Daddy, and closely watched by Simon and me), unwrapped the various sections, fitted them together with huge nuts and bolts, and fixed them into place. The result was a surprisingly superior-looking building, its central door flanked by two windows that could be shuttered during the winter months; and, after being kitted out with such necessities as a table, a number of chairs and a portable scoring board, it was soon in regular use.

The most junior cricket pitch, the one on which I played, was in the top right-hand corner of the field not far from the wooden gate leading out onto the Easthampstead Road. Unfortunately, although I had come to enjoy football, with its opportunity for displaying a certain amount of tactical cunning, cricket simply bored me. Or was it simply that it was another skill, like singing or playing the piano, for which I had absolutely no talent?

Success in cricket requires being able either to bowl or to bat successfully, preferably both; and it is also useful if one can throw a ball accurately and catch it easily. However, even as a despised under-arm bowler my accuracy left a great deal to be desired; I was so bad at judging the speed and direction of an incoming ball that my bat hardly ever made contact with it; I could not throw a ball accurately to save my life; and there was never more than the briefest of intervals between my having a very good chance of catching someone out, and disgusted cries from my team-mates of "Butter-fingers!"

So it was a considerable relief to me when from about the beginning of June onwards one of our cricketing sessions each week was replaced with swimming. Not that we had a pool of our own. Behind the first Nissen Hut on the back drive, beside a track leading in the direction of the azaleas at the south-western corner of the great southern lawn, Simon and I had discovered a huge swimming-pool shaped hole in the ground which was all that was left of Gordon Walker's efforts in this direction. As usual where he was concerned, this had been another colossal failure, notable only for a small colony of the most beautiful black bulrushes which had somehow seeded themselves in its watery base.

No, our swimming cannot begin until those in charge of Martin's swimming-pool, situated behind elaborate wrought-iron gates down Milton Lane at the far end of Wokingham, have decided that the weather is warm enough for them to open for business. And when they do, my father reserves their pool each week for a private Holme Grange School session.

Older boys with bicycles cycle all the way from Holme Grange in convoy, the rest of us are ferried here by car and minibus and taxi; and for an hour-and-a-half the whole establishment is ours and ours alone. We can't see much of it at first, for having entered the gates and been decanted from our transport, we are diverted down a path with shrubberies to each side into a large artificial and somewhat gloomy underground cavern. This is lined with pegs from which hang steel frames in which to store our clothes and, having changed into our bathing-trunks, we walk out of the other end of the cavern up a slope and into the light.

What we see in front of us is now the property of the local Council, who have been in charge of it for five or six years; but so far, apart from removing an Art Deco diving stage considered to be hazardous, and replacing it with something more modern, they have done very little damage to what is something of a local treasure. Built back in the 1920s by wealthy philanthropist Mr. Martin, it seems less like a civic establishment and more like a private swimming pool that has been very kindly opened to the public.

The main pool is huge, fifty yards long, and set in beautiful lawns and flower-gardens surrounded by poplars. Its best feature, from my point of view, is a splendid slide, set in the centre of the shallow end just in front of a cascade. This cascade pours water in all directions, some of it over the blocks one must climb up to reach the top of the slide, some of it down the broad flight of steps leading into the pool, and a good deal of it down the slide itself. What I like doing is to climb onto the top of the slide, whoosh down it and land in the water with a terrific splash, hoping that enough water is thrown up to splatter anyone who happens to be swimming nearby. There is also a large round paddling pool, fed by another cascade, where the water is only eighteen inches deep, and often very warm after a morning in the sun.

A more complete escape from cricket came during the last few weeks of the summer term when the cricket field was entirely given over to preparations for Sports Day. First the square of the First XI pitch was taped off so that it could be preserved as a sacrosanct patch of turf, and then the line-marking applicator was brought out of Mr. Hill's shed. This was a kind of small box on two wheels from which white marker paint could be transferred to the ground by a set of rollers as it was pushed along. Both Daddy and Mr. Hills were expert users, and before long the cricket field had been marked out with numerous sets of running lanes, some of which ran in straight lines parallel to the Heathlands Road, others of which circled the First XI square. Hurdles were also found at the back of Mr. Hills's shed, and small areas were dug out and filled with sand in the corner of the field between the Lake and Heathlands Road to make them ready for the Long Jump and the High Jump.

Soon we were busily practising both for these jumps and for a wide variety of races: not only 100 yards, 220 yards and 440 yards races, but also hurdle races, three-legged races, sack races, and even egg-and-spoon races. Unfortunately for me, the china egg wouldn't stay in my spoon, I could only manage a very Low Jump, I crashed into the Hurdles instead of jumping over them – and in general as the days went on and I tried and failed at almost everything, I could only compare myself to Tigger finding yet another food that Tiggers don't like.

By the time Sports Day arrived, I had been eliminated from every single event; and the following summer it would be almost as bad. My sole achievement, watched by my cousins Rowan and Judith who had come over for the day, would be to take part in the semi-final of the Junior Sack Race. This was only because, in the previous heat, two of my strongest and most determined opponents had crashed into each other and fallen over half-way down the track; and, naturally enough, I never reached the final.

CHAPTER EIGHT
Wokingham

Wokingham was so close to us that we made frequent visits, driving north-westward along the Easthampstead Road until we had passed the White Horse, the turning to Ludgrove, the level crossing, Murdoch Road, and the Ritz Cinema and reached the T-junction on the very edge of the shopping area where the Easthampstead Road meets Peach Street. After this, our first stop was very often the Garage just around the corner to the left.

Turning into the forecourt, we parked beside an open-air row of three freestanding individual petrol pumps, each standing on a plinth about three feet square, and each advertising its own brand of petrol in a more or less distinctive manner: at the top of the Shell pump, for example, I could see a huge yellow plastic scallop shell on which the word SHELL stood out in dark red. There would also be notices telling us the price per gallon, which in 1953 was around 3/6d (three shillings and sixpence).

Garages were dirty places, where it would have been unthinkable for any of us to get out of the car, let alone serve ourselves. Instead, we waited for one of the garage attendants to emerge in his filthy overalls from the big shed at the back of the forecourt and walk up to the driver's window to ask what was wanted. "Three gallons of the Shell, please, and could you check the oil?" Mummy or Daddy might say. The attendant would nod, unclip the petrol dispenser from the side of the pump, and insert its nozzle into EPB 223's petrol tank. As he did so, I would look up eagerly at the large round dial on the front of the pump, on which I could see a notice near its top telling the attendant: 'SEE THAT BOTH HANDS ARE AT ZERO BEFORE DELIVERY COMMENCES'; and then the delivery began, and the hands began whizzing round, the longer hand going once round for each gallon, while the shorter hand pointed to the number of gallons.

At any other Garage, after delivering the petrol and checking the oil, the attendant would have taken the money and brought back any change; but we were regulars here, so when it was time to pay, Mummy or Daddy would simply say "Put it down to my account, please – Holme Grange School." And then we would drive south-west down Peach Street into the market-place at the centre of Wokingham where, in our early Holme Grange days, there were no yellow lines and so few cars that my parents expected to be able to park immediately outside any shop they wished to visit.

Peach Street, by the way, was one of the three main shopping-streets in Wokingham. It led off to the north-east of the market-place and the Town Hall, as Denmark Street did to the south-west, and Broad Street to the north-west, and each of them had its special attraction for me personally.

Besides the garage that we used, Peach Street had not only the finest fruit and vegetable shop imaginable, but also a branch of F.W. Woolworth Co Ltd, a general store in which a great deal was for sale at pocket-money prices; Denmark Street had its bookshop, a branch of W.H. Smith situated in a beautiful old eighteenth-century building with bow windows on each side of its entrance; while Broad Street had a toy-shop, just over the other side of the road from the Post Office, and conveniently close to the Off-licence, where I would call in with Daddy when he went there to buy an occasional bottle of sherry or gin.

I thoroughly enjoyed these visits to Wokingham, especially when I had any book tokens to exchange or pocket-money to spend. Even my weekly 6d was enough for a bag of marbles or a packet of gummed strips for making paper-chains at Woolworths, or a painted plastic Red Indian in the toyshop, and I liked buying things. In this I was turning out to be very different from my brother Simon, who was a thrifty child. Extremely generous when it came to buying presents for others, he normally chose to spend very little money on himself. He preferred saving it up, and in due course he would begin investing it (as we were both encouraged to do) in Government-issued interest-bearing National Savings Certificates.

Had I been given a substantial present of £1 or more, I myself would have felt somewhat reluctantly constrained to accompany Mummy into the Post Office in Broad Street, and watch as the counter clerk took my money and converted it into a 15/- [fifteen shillings] National Savings Certificate. He would then stick it into the booklet which Mummy had brought with her, and which immediately disappeared back into her handbag for safe keeping. But while my first such booklet remained half-empty, Simon's was soon full, and before long he had moved onto a second or even a third. At times I was a little jealous as I saw his wealth accumulating so much faster than mine; but not very jealous: I much preferred spending my money on things I wanted now, rather than saving it up for some unknowable future.

CHAPTER NINE

The Worst News Possible

Broad Street also contained two major family landmarks both of which have an important part to play in our story. The first landmark, on the eastern side of Broad Street not far from the town centre was a branch of the Westminster Bank, for which as children we learned the most profound respect. For one thing, it was the only place from which our father could collect the banknotes and coins that he needed, for there were no cash machines or debit cards in those days. For another, it was clear that he felt almost as loyal to this particular bank as he did to the various educational establishments by which he had been nurtured. Others of his generation felt exactly the same. Within these hallowed walls a solemn near-silence was observed by the bank's customers; even the bank clerks talked in hushed tones and, apart from the Rector of All Saints (of whom more later) there was no-one we knew in Wokingham who seemed closer to God than our Bank Manager.

We depended upon him personally for all our financial dealings and especially for our mortgage; and in this respect my father had good news. After an appallingly difficult first two years, during which there has been so little income to pay for the running expenses of the school that both my parents had been doing the work of several normal people, Holme Grange School was at long last beginning to prosper, mainly because we had begun taking in more of the sons of serving officers in the army, navy or air force.

These children had routinely suffered from a very unsettled education as they followed their parents from posting to posting, which often meant not only moving from place to place in the United Kingdom, but also spells in Germany or even further afield. However, they enjoyed being dayboys at Holme Grange so much that when they faced the prospect of yet another move, it was comparatively easy for my father to persuade their parents to let them stay on at Holme Grange as Boarders. And since being a Boarder at Holme Grange was in those days a little like being a member of a large and happy family, this proved to be a great success, word of it spread, and even service children who had never been dayboys at Holme Grange began joining us as Boarders.

This was just as well, since during the summer term of 1953, less than two years after we had moved in, it was learned that whoever had surveyed Holme Grange on our behalf had failed to notice traces of incipient dry rot. Dry rot! A name calculated to strike almost as much terror into any owner of an old building as that of the death-watch beetle. And at least one can hear the death-watch beetle tapping away in the rafters on summer nights. But dry rot in houses is more sinister, being so utterly secret and utterly silent that it has often been compared with cancer in human beings: there may be few signs of it at first, but the longer it is left unchecked the more likely it is to lead to disaster. Dry rot, for those of you lucky enough never to have come across it, is basically a fungus that eats wood. Dry rot spores are widespread, and they can germinate and grow on any timber that has become damp, especially if ventilation is poor.

The discovery was first made when faulty plumbing in the Boarder's cloakroom had needed attention. This was the room which lay behind that door in the Front Hall just next to the Front Door. To the right of the entrance were washbasins, with two lavatories in separate cubicles just beyond them; and when part of the cloakroom floor had been taken up, the characteristic fine orange dust of the dry-rot spores had been detected on some underlying timbers. When this was professionally investigated, it was found that the worst part of the infestation lay in the supporting beams beneath the floor of the main Hall; but since there was no immediate danger of the floor collapsing, work could be delayed until the start of the summer holidays.

Apart from Daddy, we were all away at Rottingdean when the remedial work began, but you can see the horror on all our faces on the day when we returned home to find that large parts both of the Hall floor and of the floors of all the immediately surrounding rooms had been stripped out, and that panelling and plaster had also been removed from the walls here and there in order to discover how far the dry rot had spread. There were small outlying colonies in Daddy's study, (where part of one wall had had to be removed), and beneath the floor of the red-tiled corridor.

Fortunately, the Bank Manager by this time knew my father well enough to trust him with an additional mortgage, because the expense of dealing with this dry rot was huge. At the same time, the visible desolation must have been heart-breaking for both my parents, yet I never heard a word of complaint from either of them. Their Christian faith and their loyalty to each other had made them amazingly resilient. They described it only as 'bad luck', and told us not to worry (though of course we did) and that it would soon be put right. Which it was. Although there would be several further visitations of this dreadful disease before it was entirely conquered, they were comparatively minor. It was this first visitation that was incomparably the most severe.

Yet even this was far from being the worst news possible, as we will discover when we move on to our second landmark.

This is Tudor House, the timber-framed 16th-century building which faces directly back into the centre of the town from the very top of Broad Street, in the space between the main road leading on towards Reading, and the much narrower Milton Road which led down to Martin's Swimming Pool. It was in Tudor House that the excellent Dr. Hargrove, who was both our family doctor and the official Holme Grange School doctor, shared his medical practice with two other GPs; and although at various times it had been two private houses, a school and the premises of an antique dealer, the interior had been altered very little over the centuries.

It was within these ancient rooms with their odd shapes and low ceilings that we were taken for our consultations, and it was here that in the early autumn of 1953 Mummy first learned some very serious news about Lilibet. She was now two-and-a-half years old, but although her personality was bright and cheerful, her energy levels had begun to seem quite abnormally low. Dr. Hargrove, having heard a heart murmur while listening to her chest with a stethoscope, had thought it prudent to send her for tests to the Hospital for Sick Children in London's Great Ormond Street, where there was a specialist heart and lung unit.

Alarmingly, for she already knew very well how to read his mood, when Mummy was called into the surgery to hear the Great Ormond Street report, and was directed into Dr. Hargrove's long, narrow consulting room, she found that he had altogether shed his normal brusque manner, and was at his most kind and considerate. "Mrs. Graves,' he said, "I'm afraid the news isn't good, and you're going to have to be brave. I am very sorry to have to tell you that your daughter appears to have been born with what we call a hole in the heart."

He explained what this meant. A hole in the heart, technically known as a ventricular septal defect, occurs when there is a hole in the wall or septum that separates the two lower chambers or ventricles of the heart. "In the current state of medical knowledge," Hargrove went on, "Elizabeth has a very limited life expectancy. However, a great deal of work is being done on this, and although no operation is available now, it's more than likely that one will become available within the next few years. We must hope and pray that it doesn't come too late for Elizabeth. And in the meantime, you must treat her as normally as possible while making every allowance for her weakness."

So my poor parents, having lost Rosemary, now faced the prospect of also losing her twin. I suspect that in private they wept when they first shared this news. My father, for all his apparently tough exterior, had a very tender heart; and my mother's love for each of her children was deep and passionate. Once again, it was their Christian faith that sustained them. Their ability to manage Holme Grange appeared to be quite unaffected; and Simon and I, who were very wisely told nothing, had no idea that anything was wrong.

Here, as an aside, is a word-picture of our happy little family, painted by my Aunt Clarissa some five months before anyone knew about what might lie ahead. It is Clarissa's conscientious and somewhat formal report of a day spent looking after us all, some five months earlier during the

Easter Holidays of 1953. Beginning with 'Richard Perceval Graves', she describes me as:

> co-operative. He helped me to make the beds & to look after Elizabeth, whom he loves tenderly. He understands money, & giving change, as was proved when we played "shops". His drawing was poor when we played Heads, Bodies & Tails. But he is well-disposed & helpful.

Moving on to 'Simon William Graves', she finds him:

> Not so co-operative as Richard, but will go off & work hard on his own initiative. Tidied the toy-cupboard without being asked, but refused to clear up the mess on the floor! A true Puck, but knows the difference between right & wrong. A fearful tease to Elizabeth, who seldom cried when slapped or upset. Possibly a budding poet, poor lad.

When it comes to 'Elizabeth Graves', she has little more to add, just that she 'Called her Mummy once or twice, then settled down & was quite surprisingly good.'

Lilibet was indeed very lovable and good-natured, and although we knew nothing about Dr. Hargrove's terrible revelation, as the months went by it came as little surprise to us that she had begun to acquire a kind of 'most highly favoured nation' status within the family. Her wishes, for example, were far more likely to be acceded to than ours. Simon and I put this down to her being the youngest, and decided not to mind. After all, we would always have each other.

BOOK FIVE

HOLME GRANGE: 'THEN FACE TO FACE' 1953–1954

When I was a child, I spake as a child, I understood as a child, I thought as a child: but when I became a man, I put away childish things.

For now we see through a glass, darkly; but then face to face: now I know in part; but then shall I know even as also I am known.

1 Corinthians 13, King James Version

CHAPTER ONE

Joining Mr. Hinton

When the summer of 1953 had come and gone, and term was about to begin again, my friend David Over and I felt very much like old hands after a whole year at Holme Grange School. We were part of the throng of Boarders in the Hall waiting for new arrivals, and asking their names as they came in. How unkindly we howled with laughter (though not to his face) when we discovered that one of the new boys was called 'Rose'! What an unlucky name, we thought, for a boy!

By now I had progressed beyond the two upstairs classrooms and come to rest downstairs in Form 4a, which was based in the half of the old drawing-room closest to the Hall and was run by the kindly though occasionally irascible Mr. Hinton. My new form-teacher was a married man but his wife was far away, and during term-time he chose to live like a bachelor, staying in rooms at Ye Old Rose Inn.

This was situated at the top of Denmark Street in the very centre of Wokingham. Having started life as two separate fifteenth century houses, by the mid-nineteenth century these had been enlarged and joined together and it had become a coaching Inn known as the Rose Hotel and offering 'accommodation and comfort for the nobility, gentry and public'. More recently, where the coaches had once passed beneath the upper floor of the Hotel to the yard and stables at the back, a new front entrance had been created leading into a broad internal paved walkway at the side of which an eighteenth-century sedan chair was proudly displayed as a reminder of Ye Olde Rose Inn's antiquity.

It was from this elegant establishment that Mr. Hinton motored up to Holme Grange each morning. He himself always looked very presentable, with his beard neatly trimmed and a red check handkerchief carefully folded in the breast-pocket of his jacket; but although I had once enjoyed watching him prepare footballs for use, I was never quite on his wavelength, or perhaps on that of any of my teachers that autumn.

This was a shame: I was by far the youngest in the class, and should have had a wonderful opportunity to power ahead. I certainly made a good start in Latin under the watchful eye of my father who first introduced me to those Roman worthies Cotta and Labienus; but in other subjects my progress was uneven and disappointing, and was fairly summed up at the end of the term when Mr. Hinton reported that although I had made some progress in French, 'his attention is apt to wander rather frequently and the standard of his neatness is very low'.

As to my attention wandering: I well remember sitting in the classroom on the other side of the dividing wall, the one that looked out over the sunken garden, being taught by a young master called Craig, who was always so exceptionally dull that a single thirty-minute lesson seemed to last a lifetime. In an attempt to fill at least a part of that lifetime, in an attempt not to die almost at once of sheer boredom, I would construct elaborate mental fantasies, or dream waking dreams.

In one of these, no doubt inspired by the adventures of Dan Dare, (since we had now begun taking *The Eagle* each week), I day-dreamed that the wall immediately outside the window had acquired supports, along which metal rails ran. On these rails a spaceship was waiting for me, and I imagined myself slipping out of the window and into the spaceship and then either whizzing around the outside of the school or actually taking off and heading for outer space.

In another fantasy, I imagined that there were secret levers hidden in the room, possibly controlled by Mr. Craig as he sat there droning on at his desk, with the glass-fronted bookcase behind him and a blackboard between him and the doorway. And when these levers were pulled, a whole section of the classroom floor would suddenly open up, so that a boy and his desk and chair (mine of course!) could disappear from view, and slide down into some underground chamber beneath the school, a chamber which led into the hidden passage that ran, or so some of the Boarders believed, from just underneath the school all the way to Wokingham.

I already knew in my conscious mind that the real way to get to the secret passage, if there was one, was not by sliding through the floor, but by walking to the Boarders' cloakroom where, just before the macs and caps on the left, there was a low entrance into the wall. This led into a mysterious area immediately beneath the main school stairs at the back of the Hall, where all the trunks were stored once they had been unpacked before the start of each term; and it was from here that the secret passage was said to run.

As for my 'standard of neatness', I was indeed dreadfully untidy. The fact that I been promoted to occasionally using an old-fashioned pen which I could dip into the inkwell on my new desk, had not helped matters – in fact it had made them considerably worse, since many of the pages of my exercise books were now covered with large ink-blots. 'Rewrite & show to me again if you want any marks. Too untidy to read' Mr. Craig wrote angrily in red ink in my English exercise book, having already put a thick red line all the way through one of my essays; but I was still the Headmaster's son, and when I had penned what I hoped was a 'Fair Copy', but which was almost as bad as the original, he only added rather hopelessly: 'Not very fair!'

I had sporadic enthusiasms, for example for the French Revolution of 1789, as taught to me by Miss Robinson. This inspired me with a brief but ferocious bout of revolutionary fervour, during which I wrote:

> Rousseau's famous book was something which everybody liked. "Who cares for Kings?" they grumbled. Indeed all the churchmen were terribly selfish and forgot their work. Well at a time when Louis wanted money the people just said "We will not pay anything to the King until we have a right to vote for parliament." When Louis broke down, they broke down a great prison and set all the prisoners free. The King and Queen tried to escape but were captured and beheaded so were all the nobles.

But most of what happened in the classroom I regarded as a tedious distraction from my real life which lay in my books and in Children's Hour and in my ongoing exploration of the school grounds. It didn't help that despite the improvement in the school finances, both my parents were still far too busy to exercise much supervision. Daddy in particular seemed to be everywhere at once, keeping the whole day-to-day running of the school absolutely under his control. Although he was overworked, this meant that there was not a happier or more well-run school anywhere in the south of England. Mummy was also working at full stretch, and was not above washing dishes in the Pantry, preparing vegetables in the Scullery, or even acting as a temporary Chef during those not infrequent periods when sickness, sacking or resignation led to there being no-one else available for one of these tasks.

The result of this lack of supervision was that I spent as little time on my homework as possible. This became very clear when one morning, in Mr. Craig's absence, Mr. Hinton took us for English, and asked us one by one to stand beside his desk and read out to the whole class the essays that we were meant to have written the previous evening.

When my turn came, I faced a serious problem, because when I opened my exercise book to start reading, I found that I had only written a single paragraph of four or five lines. I stretched those lines out as much as possible by reading them very slowly and very carefully. It was then far too embarrassing to come to a dead stop, so I continued with what turned into a ghost story, making it up as I went along while pretending to be continuing to read it out. This was quite successful for a few minutes and, as my story became more and more sinister, I soon had the whole class under my spell. But instead of bringing it to a dramatic end and possibly getting away with it, I made the mistake of playing to my audience and going on for too long.

"Just a moment, Graves!" said Mr. Hinton at last, stretching out a hand for my exercise book. "Let me see that!" I handed it to him, and he showed that he too knew how to play to an audience. First, he examined my single paragraph very closely and then, after making a humorous pretence of looking everywhere for the missing part of the story, he said: "What a shame. But never mind. You may have actually *written* only five lines."

Mild laughter from some of the class. "But we were all enjoying your story, weren't we?" Much more laughter. "Would you like to continue?" Raucous and prolonged laughter. Overcome with embarrassment, I was unable to say another word, and slunk back to my desk in silence.

The spring term of 1954, was even worse, because I had a succession of childhood illnesses which kept me out of the classroom for much of the time. There was still one teacher for whom I worked hard whenever I saw him. This was Mr. MacGowran, a small tough Scotsman already in his fifties and with a lined, careworn face who took Physical Education for the whole school and Boxing for those like me who had been signed up to it.

We boys knew almost nothing about MacGowran, except that he was probably an ex-serviceman. He was also rumoured to be living in a caravan, and in my mind's eye I conjured up an elegant caravan like the one I had once glimpsed through trees at the edge of the bluebell wood near White Hazel. In any case, children are often better judges of character than adults – which reminds me of that line 'For now we see through a glass, darkly; but then face to face'; so we did not mind very much where he lived, or what his past had been like, for we found him an immensely kindly and thoroughly good man, full of wisdom and humanity.

Since there was no Gymnasium, Boxing lessons took place in the Hall; and I thoroughly admired the way in which MacGowran made Boxing so gentlemanly an art. He ensured that learning new skills was the most important part of his training, that there was always good feeling on both sides and that thickly-gloved hands were warmly shaken before and after each fight. His greatest virtue in our eyes, since children very much want everything to be fair, was that he brought a huge sense of fair play to everything he did – and that included his role both in the run-up to Sports Day and on Sports Day itself, when he carried a clip-board with him and personally oversaw and recorded the results of most of the races.

PE lessons were also given in the Hall, though on a fine summer's day they might be adjourned to the great south lawn. Many bending, stretching and turning from side-to-side exercises were done while standing in disciplined rows holding in our hands each end of a four-feet-long wooden pole. There was also a traditional wooden horse stored at the side of the Hall and, whenever this was brought out, much to our excitement, we were encouraged to undertake all sorts of running and jumping and balancing manoeuvres, safe in the knowledge that MacGowran was always ready to catch us without recrimination should we fall.

During the autumn and spring terms, lectures and films were also regular features of our school life.

One of the lecturers in particular made a great impression upon me. He was a deep-sea diver, and deep-sea divers in those days were almost as much respected as astronauts would become in the 1960s when they were the first to travel into space, and then the first to land upon the moon. Both types of men risked their lives travelling into alien environments within which they had to take with them the very air they needed to stay alive; and at that time the deep-sea diver was distinguished by having to wear the most monstrous-looking helmet made of copper and brass and with only a small round visor in front for looking out.

While he alarmed us with stories about his terrifying experiences beneath the waves, our visitor, with the help of two powerfully-built assistants, gradually donned his standard diving dress. First came his baggy water-proofed canvas diving suit, with air pipes attached, a line on which he could pull to summon help, outsize gloves, a chest weight and heavily weighted boots for moving around on the ocean floor. This was strange enough but, with his head still protruding above his diving gear, our lecturer still looked vaguely human. And then his helmet was attached, and he became an altogether inhuman and thoroughly frightening spectacle.

In addition, as soon as the autumn evenings were dark enough, my father had begun arranging for a projectionist to come up from the town once a fortnight, bringing with him a portable screen, a pile of square boxes each containing a reel of film, and a large reel-to-reel film projector. Mr. Hinton's classroom would be turned into a cinema for the evening, with the screen taking the place of the blackboard, the desks pushed close together and supplemented by seats from the Hall, and the projector set up at the Boarders' tuck-boxes end of the room.

While the lights are still up, I like to sit as near to the back of the room as possible, so that I can watch the projectionist at work. He seems like a magician practicing the darkest of arts as he lovingly checks that everything is in place, loads a reel of film onto the front of the projector, threads the film all the way through the projector and attaches it to the centre of the empty reel at the back. Then the lights are switched off, the projector begins making a whirring noise as the film runs from reel to reel, a widening beam of light fills the darkness between the projector and the screen, and a few numbers start appearing on the screen like the count-down for one of the space-launches we read about in Dan Dare.

A few seconds later we hear a powerful theme tune from the speaker close to the screen, and watch as a cockerel crows vigorously from inside a large inverted triangle over which the words PATHE NEWS have appeared. After which a plummy voice narrates the events of the past week, while politicians, actors, actresses, world leaders, and celebrities of all kinds flit across the screen.

I am briefly introduced to figures such as our Prime Minister Sir Winston Churchill, the American President Dwight D. Eisenhower, and the Shah of Iran; I can see actors and actresses like Humphrey Bogart or James Stewart or Marilyn Monroe or our own Diana Dors arriving at first nights with flashbulbs popping all around them and then on occasion being presented to the Queen; I can watch the racing-driver Stirling Moss speed round a track, or the footballer Stanley Matthews completely outwitting opponent after opponent as he races down the wing.

Then there would be a series of educational features, taking us perhaps to coffee-planting in Kenya or to pearl-diving off the coast of Western Australia; and finally, if we were very lucky, one of the films from the Children's Film Foundation such as Lewis Gilbert's *Johnny on the Run* which gave us glimpses of Edinburgh and the area of Perthshire around Loch Earn.

By this time, I have already begun reading *The Daily Mail* on a regular basis, but nothing can compare with Pathé News and the educational films that followed it for opening a vivid series of windows onto the wider world.

CHAPTER TWO

Going to Church

There was a weekly route-march to Church each Sunday. On the morning of that day, after breakfast, all the Boarders who were fit and well had to go to the Boarders' cloakroom to change into their outdoor shoes and collect their macs and caps before the master-on-duty walked them the two miles or so down to All Saints' Church, Wokingham.

I was spared this trek, since although I lived at Holme Grange I somehow counted not as a Boarder but as a Day-boy; so there I am being driven down with Simon in EPB 223. I am sorry to say that I could never avoid a shameful sense of elation when somewhere along the way, usually not far beyond the level-crossing, we passed a line of Boarders walking dismally along the pavement two-by two with a couple of trusties in front and Mr. Rushton or one of the other masters bringing up the rear.

Driving straight past them without waving (I was often tempted, but wisely felt that it would have seemed too triumphalist) we carried on to the T-junction at the very end of Easthampstead Road. Here, instead of turning left towards the town centre, we turned right into the narrowest stretch of Peach Street, with old houses on each side of the road; and very soon we had our first sight of All Saints' Church, which dominates the junction of Peach Street, Wiltshire Road and the London Road.

The first thing you notice about this handsome building is the crenellated fifteenth-century stone tower, surmounted by a stair turret which rises above the south-east corner to a stone pinnacle and an iron weather-vane; and it stands in more than five acres of churchyard, set within a low semicircular wall of brick-and-flint that reminded me very much of the walls at Rottingdean.

Having parked in the London Road, we entered the churchyard through a lych-gate set in the wall on its southern side, and walked round to the main entrance beneath the tower at its western end. "Caps off, boys", Daddy would remind us, before we walked into this very traditional place of worship.

Although the body of the church had been largely restored in the mid-nineteenth century, the roof was supported by massive stone pillars, the bases of which were said to date back to the twelfth century; light shone in through high windows mostly filled with lovely stained glass; and at ground level there were four substantial blocks of wooden pews, divided both by a central aisle (the nave), and by a further aisle to each side.

Having been issued with prayer-books and hymn books, if we needed them, our route lay down the left-hand or northern aisle to where, at the very front, a block of pews had been cordoned off just beneath the northern wall for the sole use of our Holme Grange contingent. As soon as Daddy had been spotted, an usher would hurry on ahead of us and remove the rope so that we could take our seats in the pew right at the front and wait for the walkers to catch up with us.

This corner of the church was an appropriate place for us Holme Grangers, because it was also the children's corner. From the paneled wall beside our pews hung a well-known painting for children by the illustrator Margaret Tarrant, who had become famous for her depiction of religious subjects. It shows three angels standing at the front of a wood, the one on the left holding flowers, the one on the right holding a plate piled high with fruit, and the one in the middle encouraging her audience to listen by holding out both arms towards them. This audience consists partly of various woodland creatures such as rabbits and deer, and partly of three small children, one standing and two others sitting on the grass just in front of her.

I had become particularly glad to see this picture ever since my eighth birthday, on 21 December 1953, when my godmother Nancy Biddle had sent me a small blue prayer-book that was full of beautiful pictures by

Margaret Tarrant, including the one on the wall beside us. The caption, running partly above and partly below the painting, reads:

> All things bright and beautiful, All creatures great and small,
> All things wise and wonderful, The Lord God made them all.

This is the first verse of one of Cecil Frances Alexander's 1887 *Hymns for Little Children*. It had been incorporated into *Hymns Ancient and Modern*, and had become one of my favourite hymns, accepting and celebrating the whole of God's creation in the most simple and delightful manner.

The second verse continues with this theme:

> Each little flower that opens,
> Each little bird that sings,
> He made their glowing colours,
> He made their tiny wings.

After it, we repeated the first verse as a refrain, and then sang a third verse in which, having celebrated the flora and fauna of the natural world, we moved on to celebrate mankind, considered by Christians to be the summit of God's creation:

> The rich man in his castle,
> The poor man at his gate,
> God made them, high or lowly,
> And ordered their estate.

We were perfectly happy whenever we sang this third verse, although its apparent endorsement of the existing social order or class structure had already made it anathema to every socialist or communist ear; and it would later be rejected as disgraceful by all those of first 'progressive' and then 'politically correct' views, for whom, fatuously, every rich man is almost by definition a bad man, and every poor man is a victim of capitalist oppression.

Immediately in front of us was the door to the vestry, with organ pipes on the wall above it; and the first sign that the service was about to start was a musical flourish. Then the number of the first Hymn would be announced, we would rise to our feet, the vestry door would be flung open by an unseen hand, and through it would come, (dipped right down at first), a long black pole with a large silver Cross at its head, borne aloft by the tallest and strongest member of the choir, wearing his white choral surplice edged with purple. Then came eight or ten much smaller choir-boys also in their surplices, holding their hymn books in front of them as they began singing; and they were followed first by the adult members of the choir, both male and female; then by the curate and any visiting clergymen; and finally by the Rector of All Saints' Church the Rev. F.A. Steer.

This Rector was a man who was below average height, but who carried himself with great natural dignity and therefore never failed to impress. He had a sharp nose and bright eyes and a surprisingly deep mellifluous voice; and he was an earnest, well-educated man some three years younger than my father who radiated an unusual combination of great kindliness and extreme moral rectitude. Wearing a white surplice over his ankle-length cassock, holding his hymn-book in front of him and singing as he walked, he followed the others as they processed down the aisle next to us to the very back of the church, and returned up the nave to the front. Here the Cross was set up by its carrier in a fixed position to one side, while the rest of the procession moved beneath the rood-screen into the stalls on each side of the Chancel. This much-admired wooden rood-screen, with its delicate open tracery, was one of the most beautiful features of the church, an ornate partition between the nave and the chancel.

I forgot to mention that my new blue prayer-book, of which I was intensely proud, featured a crown on its front, beneath which was the name 'Elizabeth R' and the date '1953'; while inside the front cover there was a photograph of our young Queen. This connection between the royal family, our national religion and the social order was further underlined by the prayer for the royal family that was intoned by the Rector each Sunday morning, from his position at this end of the back row of the Choir on the right-hand side of the Chancel.

> Almighty God, the Fountain of all Goodness, we humbly beseech thee to bless Elizabeth the Queen Mother, Queen Mary, Philip

> Duke of Edinburgh, Charles Duke of Cornwall and all the Royal Family: Endue them with thy Holy Spirit; enrich them with thy Heavenly Grace; prosper them with all happiness; and bring them to thine everlasting kingdom, through Jesus Christ our Lord. *Amen.*

The sermon, to which I always looked forward, was also delivered by the Rector, who emerged from his place in the Chancel, bowed towards the altar, strode in our direction and climbed up into a handsome stone pulpit very close to where we were sitting. This good man then turned towards a small wooden cross on the wall behind him and made the sign of the cross while intoning: 'In the name of the Father, the Son and the Holy Ghost'. When he turned back to face his audience, whatever he said to us was carefully thought-out and clearly rooted in the most profound scholarship. This was not surprising, since after ordination training at St. Boniface Missionary College in Warminster he had gone on to study Theology at Hatfield College, Durham.

His sermons were beautifully delivered in simple, straightforward English that was easy even for an eight-year-old to understand; while his moral and spiritual instruction was never dull, but was always illustrated with flashes of good humour and with vivid examples taken sometimes from the Bible, and sometimes from everyday life.

Other parts of the service also had their interesting moments. When it was time, for example, for the General Confession, I found it not just strange but frankly astonishing to kneel beside Daddy, he on his hassock and me on mine, and to hear him declare:

> Almighty and most merciful Father, we have erred and strayed from thy ways like lost sheep. We have followed too much the devices and desires of our own hearts. We have offended against thy holy laws. We have left undone those things which we ought to have done; And we have done those things which we ought not to have done; And there is no health in us. But thou, O Lord, have mercy upon us, miserable offenders.... And grant, O most merciful Father, for his sake, that we may hereafter live a godly, righteous, and sober life...

I was unable to think of anything that Daddy could possibly have done to offend against God's holy laws. As for his being a 'miserable offender', the very idea was ridiculous. And if there was anyone in the world (apart perhaps from the Rector) who already led the 'godly, righteous and sober life' that we all promised to lead 'hereafter', then surely it was him!

After the Confession came the Lord's Prayer, which was well-known territory since we recited it every night. What followed included the Venite – rather dull, I thought – and the Te Deum, which I found more interesting, with its drama of the 'noble army of martyrs', and its triumphant cry: 'Thou art the King of Glory: O Christ. Thou art the everlasting Son of the Father'.

The Te Deum also included the words: 'When thou tookest upon thee to deliver man: thou didst not abhor the Virgin's womb'. Like most eight-year-olds of my background, I had only a very vague idea of what it meant to be a Virgin, which seemed to be the name given to any woman who had had little or nothing to do with men; and no idea at all about what a womb was, except that it was some mysterious part of a woman within which a baby lived before it was born.

Later on, when we came to the Creed, we all said that we believed in 'God the Father Almighty, Maker of heaven and earth: And in Jesus Christ his only Son our Lord: who was conceived by the Holy Ghost, Born of the Virgin Mary', and so on. Yet I knew nothing about conception and very little about birth, except that these would be forbidden subjects until I was very much older; and one of the great attractions of the church liturgy was that it touched upon so many of these hidden mysteries.

Over the years I would become extremely fond of the Collects for Peace and Grace, written in such beautiful and timeless English:

A Collect for Peace.

> O God, who art the author of peace and lover of concord, in knowledge of whom standeth our eternal life, whose service is perfect freedom; Defend us thy humble servants in all assaults of our enemies; that we, surely trusting in thy defence, may not fear the power of any adversaries, through the might of Jesus Christ our Lord. Amen.

A Collect for Grace.

O Lord, our heavenly Father, Almighty and everlasting God, who hast safely brought us to the beginning of this day; Defend us in the same with thy mighty power; and grant that this day we fall into no sin, neither run into any kind of danger; but that all our doings, being ordered by thy governance, may be righteous in thy sight; through Jesus Christ our Lord. Amen.

No special allowance was made for us children during Morning Prayer, nor did we expect that one should be made. But on Christmas Day there would always be a point in the service at which the Rector would ask all the children in the congregation under the age of ten to stand up and sing:

Away in a manger, no crib for a bed,
The little Lord Jesus laid down his sweet head.
The stars in the bright sky looked down where he lay,
The little Lord Jesus asleep on the hay.

The cattle are lowing, the baby awakes,
But little Lord Jesus, no crying he makes.
I love thee, Lord Jesus! look down from the sky,
And stay by my cradle till morning is nigh.

Be near me, Lord Jesus; I ask thee to stay
Close by me forever, and love me I pray.
Bless all the dear children in thy tender care,
And take us to heaven to live with thee there.

I found it embarrassing to be singled out like this, but Simon and I stood up and did our not very tuneful best; and, more important, I began using part of this carol as a special charm to ward off evil. Should I be troubled by a bad dream at night, for example, I would shut my eyes very tightly and sing to myself:

Be near me, Lord Jesus; I ask thee to stay
Close by me forever, and love me I pray.

As for the Notices: many of them were extremely tedious messages about such things as meetings of the Mothers' Union, which were of no interest to me whatever; but I always pricked up my ears when the Rector read out the Banns of Marriage. This involved him telling us the full names of a couple who hoped to be married in All Saints in a few weeks' time, and then instructing us in no uncertain terms that if we knew what sounded to me like 'any cause or justin pediment' (whatever that was) why these two persons should not be gathered together in Holy Matrimony, 'Ye are to declare it'. During the long dramatic silence that followed these words I always hoped against hope that some member of the congregation would get to his feet and declare an objection, but they never did; and indeed, I have never in my life seen it happen except in films, where it always causes a sensation.

Mummy almost never joined us, since her duties on a Sunday morning lay elsewhere; but she and Daddy would sometimes go together to an early morning Holy Communion Service; and before long Daddy had bound himself still more closely to All Saints' Church by volunteering to read an occasional lesson. The Rector tried him out, was delighted to find how good he was, and soon had him reading both lessons at Morning Prayer each Sunday.

So twice during the service we saw Daddy leave our pew, walk across to the other side of the Church, and take his stand behind a sturdy brass lectern on which an extremely large Bible was supported by a great Golden Eagle with outstretched wings. Fortunately, Daddy had not only produced numerous plays as a schoolmaster (he was always understandably proud of having been the man who had first put Dennis Price on the stage); but he had also trodden the boards himself, notably alongside many members of his family in the Harlech Castle Masques back in the 1920s. Like every competent actor in the days before microphones, he had learned how to project his voice, and he could be heard clearly and distinctly in every corner of the church.

The readings were always taken from the Authorized Version of the Bible, published back in 1611 during the reign of King James VI of Scotland, and I of England and often called the King James Bible. Should you be reading these memoirs of mine in some future century then the language in which the Authorized Version is written may seem as remote to you, my dear reader, as Chaucer now does to me. However, it is an undisputable masterpiece. Often claimed as an example of how well committees can write, it is in fact very largely drawn from the work of one man, William Tyndale, a brilliant Oxford scholar who had produced an incomplete translation of the Bible before being strangled and then burnt at the stake for heresy back in October 1536.

Sir Thomas More, a good Roman Catholic who would later be executed himself for his religious beliefs, commented unkindly while Tyndale was still alive that searching for errors in the Tyndale Bible was like searching for water in the sea; and numerous scholars in more recent times have equally correctly and equally stupidly explained that the Authorised Version is not a very accurate translation. To which one can only reply: 'So what?' It remains one of the very finest works of Literature in the English Language and I implore you to give it a try.

Perhaps after my death God may allow me to venture back in Time and once again watch my beloved father standing up to announce (for example) that: 'The First Lesson is taken from the First Chapter of the Book of Genesis, beginning at the First Verse' and then to declaim in his beautifully modulated voice, which gave every line its full weight and meaning, one of the greatest passages of the King James Bible:

> 'In the beginning, God created the heaven and the earth. And the earth was without form, and void; and darkness was upon the face of the deep. And the Spirit of God moved upon the face of the waters. And God said, Let there be light: and there was light.'

Or again:

> 'For unto us a child is born, unto us a son is given: and the government shall be upon his shoulder: and his name shall be called Wonderful, Counsellor, The mighty God, The everlasting Father, The Prince of Peace.'

Or again:

> 'Tell it not in Gath, publish it not in the streets of Askelon; lest the daughters of the Philistines rejoice, lest the daughters of the uncircumcised triumph.'

Or again:

> 'Suffer little children, and forbid them not, to come unto me: for of such is the kingdom of heaven.'

Or again,

> 'In the beginning was the Word, and the Word was with God, and the Word was God.'

Or again:

> 'And I saw a new heaven and a new earth: for the first heaven and the first earth were passed away; and there was no more sea. And I John saw the holy city, new Jerusalem, coming down from God out of heaven, prepared as a bride adorned for her husband. And I heard a great voice out of heaven saying, Behold, the tabernacle of God is with men, and he will dwell with them, and they shall be his people, and God himself shall be with them, and be their God. And God shall wipe away all tears from their eyes; and there shall be no more death, neither sorrow, nor crying, neither shall there be any more pain: for the former things are passed away.'

And then, after a suitable pause, my father would say 'Here endeth the First [or Second] Lesson' before returning to join us where we sat proudly waiting for him in our pew.

It was not long before the Rector had also learned about the profusion of flowering bulbs and shrubs at Holme Grange with the result that, in the run-up to Easter Day each year, the whole family would spend part of an afternoon filling half-a-dozen buckets with daffodils, while Daddy would also cut some blooms of whatever happened to be in flower. It would be too early for the rhododendrons, but there would always be plenty of azaleas with their delicate pink, red and purple flowers, and perhaps some sprigs of golden-yellow forsythia; and these would all be ferried down to All Saints to form the heart of a glorious Easter display.

We were considered far too young to be taken to any part of the three-hour service on Good Friday, when the whole of creation groans as it shares in the suffering of Christ upon the Cross; but Easter Day, the day of His resurrection, was wonderfully cheerful. "Happy Easter!" we all wished each other as soon as we were properly awake. For breakfast there were hard-boiled eggs whose shells we had carefully painted with elaborate patterns the evening before. After breakfast there were delicious chocolate Easter eggs. And when we had been driven to Church, we could enjoy singing another of Mrs. Alexander's hymns:

> There is a green hill far away,
>   Without a city wall,
> Where the dear Lord was crucified,
>   Who died to save us all
>
> We may not know, we cannot tell,
>   What pains he had to bear;
> But we believe it was for us
>   He hung and suffered there.
>
> There was no other good enough
>   To pay the price of sin.
> He only could unlock the gate
>   Of heav'n and let us in.
>
> Oh, dearly, dearly has he loved!
>   And we must love him too,
> And trust in his redeeming blood,
>   And try his works to do.

This was another of my favourites, though it was some years before I understood that 'Without' here meant 'Outside' rather than 'Lacking', and that the green hill was perfectly happy not to be walled-in.

When the end of the service approached, and we were singing the final hymn, a collection was taken and Daddy, who never put in less than a 10/- (ten shilling) note himself, gave us a sixpence each to put into the collection bag that was passed into our pew by one of the churchwardens. Then the Rector dismissed us with his blessing:

> The grace of our Lord Jesus Christ, and the love of God, and the fellowship of the Holy Ghost, be with us all evermore. Amen.

The procession once more wound its way through the church until it left as it had arrived through the vestry door just opposite; and we ourselves walked out of the church into the light where, with a strong sense of friendship and peace and happiness, we drove home to rejoin Mummy and Elizabeth and to enjoy our Sunday lunch.

CHAPTER THREE

Winter Excitements

On Christmas Eve 1953, just a few days after I had been given my blue Coronation prayer-book, we had the excitement of a visit from Jennifer and Barbara Ranger, two girls several years older than me who were distant relatives on my mother's side. They joined us in putting out stockings at the end of their beds for Father Christmas to fill with presents during the night, and I woke up at about half-past-seven to find that my own stocking was full of good things, including several small toys, some chocolate, and an orange.

Our main family presents were not given out until after breakfast, when there was a grand and greedy opening session in the Nursery, during which, since my parents knew how devoted I had become to the *Eagle* comic, I found that I was now the proud owner of an Eagle hairbrush, a Dan Dare card game, and an Eagle Diary for 1954. Then came the Christmas Day service at All Saints, at which Simon and I dutifully stood up to sing 'There is a green hill far away'; and then we all returned to Holme Grange for lunch.

Because there were so many of us, our Christmas turkey was eaten not upstairs in the Nursery, but downstairs in the school dining-room at the large table in the window looking out over our private garden. This was the high table at the eastern end of the room where Daddy usually ate all his meals in term-time, together with his most senior pupils.

I have already mentioned that the dining-room was a large handsome room, and that it was full of Graves and von Ranke family portraits; but its great feature was a magnificent fireplace which had been tiled on each side of the hearth with a double-row of the most wonderful Victorian tiles that I have ever seen. They had on them what appeared at first sight to be monochrome reddish-pink pictures of Galleons and strange sea creatures on a white background; but, as I showed Jennifer and Barbara, when these pictures caught the light at a certain angle, they suddenly became quite miraculously rainbow-coloured.

Their creator was that great ceramicist William de Morgan who, before he wisely enriched himself by writing popular novels, was not only the friend of William Morris but the most innovative designer of the Arts and Crafts movement. He designed his own kilns and used his own chemical research to produce glazes of a kind that no-one else had even dreamed could exist, with the result that those tiles in the dining room at Holme Grange were one of the most glorious wonders of my childhood.

A few weeks later I wrote in my Eagle Diary how much I had enjoyed the turkey, and described this as 'The best day of my holyday'. To be sure, I had found the afternoon less interesting than the morning because, after bothering Mummy for my sweets, of which she always gave us a small ration after lunch, I had found myself: 'in one of my don't-know-what-to-do moods. I wasted all the time till tea. I did not like the Christmas cake [this was because I hated Marzipan] but would have given anything for the icing. I only had two bread-and-butters myself. I envied the others who were eating the icing. After that I wasted some more time and soon it was seven time to go to bed.'

However, the New Year of 1954 brought with it three novelties: a period of exceptionally cold weather, a new serial on Children's Hour, and the consequences of a notice to quit our main football field.

The freezing conditions in January and February led to ice forming on the Lake. After a while it became so thick that Simon and I and the Boarders were allowed to slide about on its surface, and my father put on his skating boots and took a few turns on the ice. I had never seen him skating before, but it turned out that as a young man he had been so keen on Winter Sports, that in 1936 he had travelled by boat and train all the way to Bavaria to be a spectator at the Winter Olympics held in

Garmisch-Partenkirchen. Nor, although he chivalrously claimed never to have been interested in anyone but my mother, had he been immune to feminine beauty. Spectators and participants mingled far more freely in those days, and he had taken numerous photographs of the beautiful 24-year-old Norwegian figure-skating star Sonja Henie before watching her win her third consecutive gold medal in women's figure skating.

The frozen Holme Grange lake must have reminded Daddy vividly of how much he had enjoyed ice-skating and, when the freezing weather continued, he arranged one weekend for a large party of us to be ferried several miles away to the edge of Heath Lake. This was a shallow 7-acre mere not far from Crowthorne, with forest all around and a mysterious island at its centre. Here he donned his skates (perhaps for the last time – I never saw him skate again) and, while the rest of us had great fun sliding about on the ice in our outdoor shoes, he glided elegantly around the lake performing a series of the turns and spins and jumps that had given him so much pleasure in his youth.

Watching Daddy perform his complicated skating manoeuvres so expertly and apparently so effortlessly made me admire him all the more, especially as I had become utterly entranced by a new play in six fifty-minute instalments that had arrived on Children's Hour on Wednesday evenings, and had figure-skating at its heart. This was *White Boots*, and it was based on Noel Streatfield's children's novel of the same name, which had been published as recently as 1951 and which begins:

> Even when the last of the medicine bottles were cleared away and she was supposed to have "had" convalescence, Harriet did not get well. She was a thin child with brown eyes and a lot of reddish hair that did not exactly curl, but had a wiriness that made it stand back from her face rather like Alice's hair in "Alice in Wonderland".

White Boots is the story of Harriet Johnson, who comes from a good family that has fallen on hard times, so that she and her three brothers and their parents are reduced to living over the greengrocer's shop that her father runs. Despite being poor, they lead an enviably happy family life; and eventually, through putting on the white boots of an ice-skater,

Harriet finds not only good health but also her purpose in life. More important, it is the story of Harriet's friendship, turbulent at times, with another girl, the vivacious Lalla Ward, whose family life is far from happy since although the aunt who cares for her is wealthy, she is also determined that Lalla should follow in her late father's footsteps by becoming a skating champion.

Although this was a story aimed largely at girls, it is not difficult to see why it appealed to me so much, with its vivid descriptions of a family living in somewhat straitened circumstances, and of what it was like trying to live up to family expectations. In any case I had always taken an interest in the feminine point of view, finding conversations with Jancis at the White House or with my cousin Judith at Kerry House far more absorbing than most of those with my masculine contemporaries.

Since we had moved to Holme Grange, we had been close enough to Farnborough for my mother to drive over occasionally to see my Aunt Betty and, knowing how fond I was of Judith, she began including me on these early evening expeditions. A pattern was soon established: after one of Betty's warm, throaty greetings I would rush down the corridor to the living-room next to the kitchen, hoping that for once I would find the parrot ready to be inspected, but at this time of the evening it was almost always hidden away under its night-time awning. Uncle Geoffrey would put in a brief appearance and then retreat to the front room, where he was relaxing after a long day at the Bank and perhaps listening to some classical music on the wireless. Rowan was normally away at Boarding School, and Mummy and Aunt Betty would soon be drinking coffee in the living-room and filling the air around with them cigarette smoke, while talking nineteen to the dozen about matters in which I had absolutely no interest.

After a short while it was usually Aunt Betty who would break off from her conversation with Mummy and say to me: "Ricky, this must be terribly dull for you. Why not run along upstairs and have a chat with Judith? You'll find her reading in her room. You know where it is." This was the part of the visit to which I always looked forward, since as I have already mentioned, Judith's bedroom was always filled with exciting reading matter. This now included numerous stories either about girls or set in girls' schools and, if I was lucky, the latest two or three editions of a comic called simply *Girl*. This had been launched by Marcus Morris in November 1951 as the feminine counterpart of *Eagle*, shared many of the same contributors, and was full of exciting stories in which girls or women were the chief protagonists. To begin with this approach had been too radical for popular taste, so that its first front page serial, *Kitty Hawke and her all-girl crew*, had had to be replaced by a schoolgirl cartoon strip called *Wendy and Jinx*. But as well as being entertaining – one of its regular features was a set of comical stories about *Lettice Leefe, The Greenest Girl in School* – it was keen to show that the world was full of exciting possibilities for women outside the traditional home.

As for the notice to quit our main football field, it was given to us by Jack Robbins, who had received a much better offer for the land. This came from another member of the Robbins clan, who wished to use it for the game bird production in which his wife was already an expert. He also took over the Lodge as the headquarters of his new business, which in due course became known as Holme Park Game Hatcheries and has continued in business to this day.

In many ways, the ending of the lease suited my father very well. He had always suspected that it would not last forever, and he had already ear-marked an alternative site for several new football pitches on our own land. This was the part of the large south-eastern field that was dotted with indifferent apple-trees. The two most productive of them, the ones closest to the back drive, were retained; but a tractor was brought in to pull up all the rest.

I was there to watch; and for trees that had been so long established, and had always seemed to me to occupy such a secure position within the landscape, they came out of the ground with alarming ease. Their iron grilles, intended to protect them from any molestation, were taken away on the back of a lorry to be sold as scrap metal. And then the trees themselves were dragged over to the side of the field furthest away from the school, where for many months Simon and I enjoyed climbing about over them.

As time went by, they were removed one by one to the area near Mr. Hills's shed and cut up to make logs for the woodshed and kindling for the bunker in the kitchen yard; but some of them presided over our new football field for a year or more. Even in sunlight it seemed strange to see this row of leafless skeletons of trees; and under the moon, or in winter mists, they seemed eerily like the ghosts of their former selves.

One more excitement at this time was that during the Christmas holidays, Daddy decided to teach Simon and me both Chess and Draughts. I took to both games avidly, and learning from my father was a particular pleasure given how busy he usually was with school affairs. He also had a keen ear for any mispronunciation on our part. If for example he heard one of us overstretching a word, he would shake his head very sadly and say what he later explained had been said to him when he was a child by his own father: 'The Berlue Perlum came tumberling down the chimerney'. Daddy would also come into the Nursery and read to us, a chapter at a time, from the books he himself had once enjoyed.

Charles Kingsley, the Church of England clergyman author, was a frequent choice. 'Do as you would be done by' had always been one of Daddy's favourite admonitions to us children, and we first heard of Mrs. Doasyouwouldbedoneby' when he read us Kingsley's *The Water Babies* (1863), in part a tract against child labour, but also the tale of Tom, a young chimney-sweep transformed into a water-baby, whose amazing adventures underwater teach him all kinds of moral lessons. Daddy had already read us *Madam How and Lady Why* (1869), Kingsley's introduction for young children to scientific thought in general and geology in particular; and in due course he would enthrall us with Kingsley's *Westward Ho!* (1855), an exciting historical novel set in Elizabethan times which, almost a hundred years after publication, remained one of the best-loved children's stories of all time.

Daddy's next choice was Harriet Beecher Stowe's novel *Uncle Tom's Cabin* (1852), which opened my eyes to the evils of black slavery. It was already more than five years since the good ship HMT [His Majesty's Transport] Empire Windrush had docked at Tilbury on 22 June 1948, bringing with it some 800 passengers from Jamaica, Trinidad and Tobago and other Caribbean islands, but the vast bulk of the British population was still white, and so, like most children of my age, I had reached the age of eight without having ever come across anyone in real life whose skin was coloured differently from my own. My only experience of such people had come from seeing photographs of them in *The Times* or *The Daily Mail*, seeing film of them in Pathé newsreels, or reading about them in books.

Of these books, the best-known was Helen Bannerman's *Little Black Sambo*, published back in October 1899 by A.E. Housman's friend Grant Richards. This is the exotic tale of how an English lady in India, 'where black children abound and tigers are everyday affairs' amuses her two little girls on a long railway journey in India by telling them Sambo's story. His mother makes him a beautiful red coat and blue trousers, while his father buys him a green umbrella and a pair of purple shoes with crimson soles and linings. But when he goes for a walk wearing or holding all these wonderful gifts, he is pursued by four ferocious tigers each of whom says to him:

> Little Black Sambo I am going to eat you up

Placating them one by one with the presents he has been given, he is saved from death only when the victorious tigers fall out with each other, and chase each other so fast around a tree that they turn into a pool of melted butter or "ghee", and are used to cook pancakes.

Personally, I thought this was a very silly story, since it was obvious to me that the tigers would have torn little black Sambo from limb to limb. Far more enjoyable were the *Epaminondas* stories. Originated by Sara Cone Bryant back in 1911, the stories on our Nursery shelves had been written much more recently by Constance Egan. They concern the humorous misadventures of Epaminondas, a coal-black child with fuzzy hair who wears shorts and a T-shirt and usually has bare feet. He and his fat black Mammy, always pictured with a long dress down to her shoes, a huge apron and her hair tied up in a scarf, lead a simple life, sharing a somewhat broken-down cottage with broken-down wooden fencing around it. Here they keep chickens and grow vegetables, and their most valuable possessions are the donkey and the donkey-cart in which Epaminondas's Mammy drives to market to sell her produce.

The attraction of Epaminondas is that he is always trying to do the right thing but usually failing, with comical consequences, as a result of misunderstanding the instructions that have been given to him, just as I had done when I stuffed the hollow tree at White Hazel with cabbages. For example, in *Epaminondas Helps in the House*, having complained earlier in the day about having been kept awake by a banging door, his Mammy has to declare to her son:

> "Oh! My sakes alive! You ain't got the sense you was born with. You won't never have the sense you was born with! To go an' screw up the sittin'room door so we can't get into the room, to prevent the door from bangin'! Laws a massey me, you foolish chile."

But she is not unkind, and when her outburst reduces Epaminondas to tears, she declares:

> "There, there, honey! Don' you cry any. I'd sooner have a piccaninny make the biggest mistakes ever over trying' to help his Mammy, than one that didn't never think of helping his Mammy at all."

The simplicity of the life led by Epaminondas and his Mammy was curiously appealing; and Mummy, who read these books to us, had soon adopted as her own one of Mammy's favourite sayings, so that when one of us did something particularly foolish she would turn to us and say, only half in jest: 'Oh! My sakes alive! Epaminondas, you ain't got the sense you was born with.'

Sadly, however amusing these stories may be, they reflect the mistaken assumption of their day that black people, with some exceptions, are generally less intelligent than their white counterparts, and even in some cases are so fundamentally child-like that they need looking after: a point of view not confined to children's books but very evident in, for example, Joyce Carey's *Mister Johnson* (1939). This meant that on the rare occasions when Mummy had good cause to be moderately angry with one of us, she would say very loudly and firmly: 'Don't be a fat-head!' or, when very angry indeed: 'Don't be a fat-headed cooner!' 'Fat-head' was such a common term of abuse in the 1940s and 1950s that it was normally uttered without any thought of prejudice against black people; while I am sorry to say that 'coon' is a dreadfully derogatory name for a black person, with its origins in Portuguese colonialism: a 'baracoon' being the word for a slave barracks.

It was within this context that I was first introduced to the horrors of slavery by my father's reading of *Uncle Tom's Cabin*. Whether or not it portrays the slave-owners of the southern states fairly was hotly contested almost from the day of publication, especially by those who believed in Aristotelian vein that African Americans were a child-like people who needed to be overseen by others for their own good; and later on I would gain what may have been a more balanced view of these matters by contrasting the evils of the ante-bellum south portrayed by Harriet Beecher Stowe with the same world as it appears in another best-selling novel, Margaret Mitchell's *Gone with the Wind*, first published in 1936.

At the time, I was simply swept up in the compelling melodrama of Stowe's story, which begins with the good Christian slave Uncle Tom being separated from his wife and children through no fault of his own, when he is literally 'sold down the river' to settle his employer's debts; and ends with him being whipped to death on the orders of the evil slave-owner Simon Legree. Throughout these and other misadventures he retains his Christian faith with which, even as he lies dying, he inspires the overseers who have whipped him, by forgiving them wholeheartedly for what they have just done.

As well as listening to what Daddy read to us, I was still devouring books at a great rate on my own account, as is evident from my first English essay of the spring term of 1954, on the subject of *Exploring an unexplored island*, which runs:

> We were on a house boat and I was wondering what to do. I was having a holiday with a friend "Joe" and his cronys Bill and Roger. It was night time the stars were shining, and I could not get to sleep when I felt the boat sudden jerk, and we began moving down the river past rowing boats steamers and other house-boats.
>
> I woke the others but we kept on and on. I had a chart so followed our cours up about lunchtime we landed on somewhere that was not marked on the map. We looked around but instead of Fir Beech Oak and Ash trees we found we were stareing at a funny

sort of Garland trees with a fruit which we tried because we were so hungry that we could not resist it. The ideia suddenly dawned upon me we-had-discovered-a-new-island.

We searched the island and meashed it. It was a mile wide and two miles long and covered with such fruits as had never before been known to the world and we discovered some prehistoric monsters.

After ransacking the place we made for home. When we reached it we phoned the Government and soon we had reporters coming in streams. We had found an island!!!

The children in a drifting boat are clearly an echo of Arthur Ransome's *We Didn't Mean to Go to Sea,* while the prehistoric monsters come straight from the pages of Sir Arthur Conan Doyle's *The Lost World.* Yet underneath, Mr. Craig has written only:

I CAN'T READ THIS
You are using a hard pencil again
Your work is still disgustingly untidy

He was quite right about the untidiness, but after all my hard work his angry comments rankled, and once this particular exercise book was safely back in my possession I added very rudely after 'I CAN'T READ THIS', 'I'm glad you can't'; and after 'disgustingly untidy', 'yes Ha Ha'.

I was away for much of this term with various childhood illnesses, as I have already mentioned, and many of my teachers pointed out at the end of the term that I had done too little work for them to be able to write me a report. However, my constant daydreaming had added to my problems, and even my father was a little dispirited, writing in his report of my Latin that: 'He has lost a good deal of ground through absence, though poor attention contributed. Harder work will be required if he is not to be left behind when the others move up.'

I was now very far from being the star pupil of my father's expectations. For some time, he had been hoping that despite the substantial fees of over £70 per term he could afford to give me a better education than was available at Holme Grange by sending me off to be a Boarder at Copthorne School, which had done so well for him when he was a child, and he opened a correspondence with the Copthorne authorities on this subject. Whatever my mother felt about sending one of her children away from home, in matters of this importance, my father's word was law; and in any case how could the wife of a prep-school Headmaster possibly object to one of her own children being sent away to school?

In addition, with my dislike of some teachers and my increasingly dreamy disregard for the school rules, I was becoming an embarrassment. Years later, she would tell me how badly it had affected her when she was sitting in the drawing-room one day and suddenly heard Mr. Hinton, who had caught me out in some petty misdemeanour or other, angrily shouting out "GRAVES!!" in his most stentorian tones down the red-tiled corridor just outside her door.

Eventually, in the first week of April 1954, my father wrote to Copthorne saying that he would be able after all to send me there in September, and that he hoped to make an introductory visit with me towards the end of the month. He must have been relieved that a combination of his ferociously hard work, his modest tastes and his entrepreneurial skill had finally made this possible.

CHAPTER FOUR

Estate Work

There was one area in particular in which my father had been able to combine considerable savings with perhaps the most valuable of his educational projects. The twenty-one acres of the Holme Grange grounds had been in a state of terrible neglect when we arrived, and looking after them properly was a task which he soon realized was well beyond the capability of Mr. Hills and Simmy, even with a good deal of help from himself. Yet he could not afford to employ more gardeners.

The solution was to be found in modifying for Preparatory School use the long-standing tradition within Public Schools that the senior boys should be more or less in charge of the day-to-day running of their Houses, while under their command the junior boys carried out a wide variety of practical tasks such as sweeping the floors, cleaning the silver cups and even handing out the milk.

And so 'Estate Work' was born.

This meant that the entire school, whether Boarders or Day-boys, spent one afternoon a week not playing organised games but, dressed in dungarees and either gumboots or stout outdoor shoes, working in the school grounds. On the whole, we thoroughly enjoyed ourselves doing Estate Work, while also gaining a great deal of practical experience in managing the large garden or even the small estate to which most of us could look forward in later life. The reaction from Parents was also positive, with many of them reporting that they were astonished and delighted by the fact that their sons were suddenly showing a keen interest at home in outdoor work of a kind which they had previously done their best to avoid.

It was not for nothing that my father had been in the Officers' Training Corps at Charterhouse, and Estate Work was as well-organised as any military operation. He was in overall charge, a kind of Regimental Colonel; selected members of the Staff Room such as Mr. Rushton were his Majors; and the senior boys, his Captains and Lieutenants. Every boy wore a badge to denote his particular Estate-work rank, from Team Leader down to ordinary Helper, and once it had been decided what tasks needed doing that afternoon, the Team Leaders were told what was expected of them, allocated a squad of appropriate helpers and sent along to the Tool Shed or to the Garage to collect whatever was needed for the work in hand.

One of the jobs I enjoyed most, because I knew exactly where to look for it, was collecting kindling for the Common Room fires which burned from dawn to dusk throughout the year except during the heat of summer. My team leader would sub-divide us into several two-boy teams, and each team would be given one of the wooden boxes that had been used to deliver vegetables. In my team, I usually led the way past the far side of Mr. Hills's shed, where we immediately came to a broad path. To the left, this led within a few paces to the roundabout, just past the tall syringa which flowered so beautifully each spring. To the right, it led almost immediately to an ancient, mysterious and very overgrown bamboo walk, with four or five large clumps of bamboo on each side of the track, which sadly led to the dead-end of an iron fence when it reached the edge of the Garden House property.

We however went neither to left nor right, but straight across, plunging into an intriguing strip of woodland with a narrow path at its centre that wound along beside the main drive, but was completely hidden from it. Here we could walk in secret if we wished all the way down to the meeting of the four drives, where it suddenly opened out beneath one of the better Holme Grange conker trees. As we walked along, talking of this and that, we occasionally put down the box and rummaged around on the ground for twigs and sticks which we then broke if necessary into suitable lengths and put into the box. When the box was full, we carried it to the kitchen yard, walking back along the drive this time. On the right-hand-side of the yard, just beyond the first doorway leading into the kitchens, there was an outside bunker. I swung open the two halves of the black door which covered the upper half of this bunker, and together we tipped in the kindling under the approving eye of our team leader, and set off again to look for more.

Another favourite task was sawing up wood, of which for many years, as the grounds of Holme Grange were gradually restored to a former beauty of which Colonel Watson would have been proud, there was a constant supply. Three or four sturdy wooden sawhorses had already been constructed by Mr. Hills, and placed by him in the area between his shed and the garage, where there would almost always be heaps of large branches or even small tree-trunks that needed sawing up into logs.

Teams of three would be chosen by my father, who took personal charge because of the risks involved, and were given strict instructions about how to hold a saw safely and how to manage a sawhorse. One boy would hold the branch firmly in place where it rested between the splayed uprights of the sawhorse, and move it along another foot each time a log was sawn off at the protruding end; while the other two did the actual sawing, each holding one end of a large bow-saw.

How satisfying it was to saw through the wood and hear the rasping noise of the sawing and watch the sawdust fly out, and finally see the log crash to the ground. We soon learned the texture and other properties of the different kinds of wood, apple-tree wood being the easiest to cut and having the sweetest smell. Finally, when we had enough logs, there was the job of loading them into a wheelbarrow, pushing them across to the woodshed, and hurling them one by one to the back of the piles of wood inside.

Raking up leaves each autumn was another task that I enjoyed. First a team of four of us would go to the Toolshed where we would collect one of the wooden trolleys, two large wooden rakes, and two sets of wooden boards or 'hands'. All four of us would then push and pull the trolley to one of the numerous places where the ground was thick with leaves, for example by the side of the drive, or beneath the trees near the roundabout. Then two of us would rake the leaves into piles, and two of us would use the 'hands' to transfer the piles of leaves into the trolley until it was full. Then came the most enjoyable part, which was pushing the trolley back to the compost heap and emptying it out which, unless we were closely watched and forced to be more sensible, we did by throwing great piles of leaves into the air and watching them as they drifted lazily down again onto the heap.

Another task was dealing with undergrowth that needed clearing back, but much to my disappointment it was only very senior boys who could do this, since only they were allowed to use the long scythes, known by us as 'slashers'. These, kept well-sharpened by Mr. Hills, sliced easily through nettles and brambles and even small self-seeded saplings.

The only part of Estate Work that I really disliked was weeding either on the drive immediately in front of the school or on the golden gravel of the terrace. Weedkiller was never used and, armed with a hoe like my two companions, it seemed a thankless task trying to decapitate and clear the endless profusion of tiny weeds which regularly appeared after even the slightest shower.

Far more enjoyable were the autumnal afternoons when we were given bowls and sent out blackberrying. At first, the best blackberries were to be found along the edges of the field that we rented for football. It was exciting finding the dark purple fruit, trying to fill one's bowl faster than anyone else, and trying (although this was strictly forbidden) to eat at least a few of them without leaving too many tell-tale blackberry-juice stains on one's lips.

Later on, when the track past the Nissen Huts at the back of the school had become more negotiable, blackberrying more often than not involved walking down it, crossing the stream over which a more substantial bridge of thick planking had now been laid, and carrying on between thick woodland to the southern edge of the grounds. This was bordered by a narrow public highway, known locally in those days as Splash Lane because cyclists or drivers had to splash their way through the Ford that it contained. To the left, it only ran for thirty yards or so straight onto the main Easthampstead Road which bordered so much of the eastern edge of Holme Grange. To the right, this country lane, on which one hardly ever saw a car, and on which the only turnings-off were into farmer's fields, was perfect blackberrying territory. The sides of the lane were mainly bordered not with formal hedges but with a rough and unruly mixture of trees and shrubs. These were only rarely cut back and were full of brambles which produced excellent large blackberries each autumn.

Blackberries on their own were delicious, but what we all preferred was a blackberry-and-apple pie, and another seasonal Estate work task was apple-picking. As with the sawing, in view of the potential risk to life and limb, this was always organized personally by my father, and involved perhaps a dozen or fifteen of us. Several long ladders were stored just beyond the paraffin tank on the right-hand-side of the Garage. These were collected, two senior boys to a ladder, and carried up to the orchard, while the rest of us followed with one of the trolleys, several wheelbarrows, and numerous wooden vegetable boxes.

Daddy would have already decided on which trees the apples were ready to be picked; but first there was some education to be done, and he would remind us how to pick an apple very carefully by holding it in the palm of one's hand and moving it gently around to ease its stalk away from the branch. This was a skill that needed to be learned, since any apple that was too firmly attached was not yet ripe and should be left for another time; and, much worse, any apple that was disturbed in such a way that it simply hit the ground immediately joined the windfalls. Our aim, Daddy explained, was storage. The top Nissen Hut beside the drive at the back of Holme Grange had already been converted into a giant apple store, and windfalls couldn't be stored.

Some of them could still be used, he conceded, and several of us were chosen to clear the ground beneath the apple trees of any windfalls that had already fallen and had not yet either rotted too extensively or been too badly eaten by wasps or slugs; and then our job was to watch out for additions to their ranks, and to keep the ground as clear as possible. So we gathered them into boxes, loaded the boxes into wheelbarrows, and took them immediately to the kitchens, where they were cored and peeled and trimmed and put into home-made apple or apple-and-blackberry pies for the staff supper that very evening and for the school luncheon the next day.

Now for the actual picking. To anyone who was used to climbing trees (and that included most boys in those days unless they were city-bred) several of the apple trees had branches growing out from the main trunk in such a way that they were not at all difficult to negotiate. How we longed to be chosen to climb up into one of those apple trees without a ladder or harness of any kind, to pick all the apples we could reach, and to throw them down one by one to be caught very carefully by one of our acolytes below, who would then place each apple very gently (to avoid bruising) in one of the wooden boxes that were waiting to be filled and placed in the trolley.

It was almost as exciting to do the same from one of the long ladders that were set up so that we could reach the apples that couldn't easily be reached from the centre of the tree. First the ladder would be raised from the ground by Daddy, who would ask two boys to stand on its lowest rung while he walked it up from the other end; then he would manhandle the ladder into place, leaning it against a convenient tall branch before sending one of the lighter boys climbing up it. This boy would be instructed never to lean out too far and always to keep one arm safely round the back of the ladder, while some heavier comrade remained below with one or both feet on the lowest rung of the ladder to steady it and make it safe. In this manner, we learned the principles of safe ladder work as well as of successful apple-picking, and during the twenty years of my father's Headmastership I never once heard of an accident.

Once the trolley was full of boxes of apples, four of us would wheel it all the way to the new Apple Store. Here Daddy had arranged for an enormous wooden rack to be constructed, six feet tall and almost as long as the Nissen Hut itself, and under his watchful eye we would lay each apple gently in one of the long grooves between the wooden slats. Different varieties of apple had to be stored in different areas, for some were best eaten within a month or two, while others would develop more delicious flavours as they aged. Most important of all, we had to make sure that no apple touched another so that if, despite all our care, one apple had been bruised and began to go rotten, it could not infect the ones next to it.

Soon the whole shed smelled deliciously of apples and, after a good autumn, there would be enough of them to provide fruit right through the winter. Some of them did go bad of course, and had to be picked out and thrown away, and occasionally Simon and I would join Daddy on one of his weekly apple-shed patrols to see that this was done.

I mentioned that Mr. Rushton (who had been so helpful at the time of the leaking electricity incident, and who was now both my maths teacher and my football coach) took a leading part in Estate Work. His enthusiasm for this was partly derived from his love of carpentry. Looking at that triangle of waste ground on this side of the Lake, and the dozens of young trees it contained, he immediately saw an opportunity to practice his woodworking skills and to pass them on to his pupils. Under his direction, the trees were pollarded, cut back almost to the ground; and once the fallen timber had been trimmed, it was taken up in a trolley to the area near Mr. Hills's shed where it was sawed into suitable lengths.

From these, Mr. Rushton had soon constructed four or five lovely garden seats which were placed at various vantage points around the school grounds. The best of them was set on some grass at the south-western corner of the roundabout, just next to another of his creations. The lowest six feet or so of the trunk of the felled Scots Pine had already been placed here as a rustic seat; next to it my father had planted a rambling rose, and at the back of the seat Mr. Rushton now added a wooden framework up which the rose climbed happily for many years. All these constructions were very much admired and, together with his youth and his skill on the games field, they helped to make Mr. Rushton one of our most popular masters.

CHAPTER FIVE

Alice Through the Looking-Glass

Listening to episodes of *White Boots* was one of my greatest pleasures during that largely unsuccessful spring term of 1954; and quoting as I did from its opening passage in which the heroine of *White Boots* is described as having hair that stands back from her face 'rather like Alice's hair in "Alice in Wonderland" ', has reminded me that by now I had been exposed by my father not only to Lewis Carroll's 1865 *Alice's Adventures in Wonderland* but also to its 1871 sequel *Through the Looking-Glass, and What Alice Found There* (commonly *Alice Through the Looking-Glass*).

I should mention at this point that the word 'looking-glass', which dictionaries now define as 'archaic or poetic' remained in common usage in all upper-class and in many professional families throughout my childhood. In the 1950s, calling a looking-glass: 'a mirror' was considered just as irredeemably common as calling a table-napkin: 'a serviette'; or calling luncheon 'dinner'.

Alice Through the Looking-glass begins with a brilliantly surreal coup de théâtre which I imagine influenced both Jean Cocteau's cinematic masterpiece *Orphée* and Robert Hamer's 'Haunted Mirror' section of *Dead of Night*. Alice discovers that the looking-glass above the fireplace in her room does not merely reflect her own world, but can be used as a portal to a different one. It begins with make-believe: "Let's pretend", she says to her black kitten, "there's a way of getting through into" what she calls 'Looking-glass house'. She goes on: "Let's pretend the glass has got all soft like gauze, so that we can get through." And then, miraculously,

> "Why, it's turning into a sort of mist now, I declare! It'll be easy enough to get through—" She was up on the chimney-piece while she said this, though she hardly knew how she had got there. And certainly the glass *was* beginning to melt away, just like a bright silvery mist.
>
> In another moment Alice was through the glass, and had jumped lightly down into the Looking-glass room... Then she began looking about, and noticed that what could be seen from the old room was quite common and uninteresting, but that all the rest was as different as possible.

In this alternative reality (or dream as it later turns out) an elaborate game of chess is taking place, in which Alice begins as a humble pawn and, after many bizarre encounters, ends up as a Queen. To this day I still think of any curiously mismatched pair of friends as Tweedledum and Tweedledee, while any eccentric artist or absent-minded Professor (or even me if I catch an unexpected glimpse of myself in a shop-window as I grow older) immediately brings to mind the White Knight; and I still recite many of the nonsense verses that appear throughout the book. My favourite is the first verse of Jabberwocky, which runs:

> 'Twas brillig and the slithy toves
> Did gyre and gimble in the wabe;
> All mimsy were the borogoves,
> And the mome raths outgrabe.

Lines from *The Walrus and the Carpenter* come a close second, because any particularly futile philosophical discussion, of which there is always plenty about, immediately brings to mind:

> "The time has come", the Walrus said,
> "To talk of many things:

Of shoes — and ships — and sealing wax —
Of cabbages — and Kings —
And why the Sea is boiling hot —
And whether pigs have wings."

And I also recall its final verses, partly because the world is full of hypocrites, and partly because I have such happy memories of my father's wonderfully lugubrious rendition:

"I weep for you," the Walrus said.
  "I deeply sympathize."
With sobs and tears he sorted out
  Those of the largest size.
Holding his pocket handkerchief
  Before his streaming eyes.

"O Oysters," said the Carpenter.
  "You've had a pleasant run!
Shall we be trotting home again?"
  But answer came there none—
And that was scarcely odd, because
  They'd eaten every one.

It was listening carefully to the nuances of Daddy's reading, whether he was sitting in an easy chair in the Nursery at home, or standing behind the Lectern at All Saints, that helped me to win the only prize of any kind that I won during my two years as a pupil at Holme Grange School. This was the Junior School Reading Prize, for which we competed towards the end of the Spring term and, since I was so much better at reading out loud than any of my fellow-contestants, it was clear that I was the winner well before the result was declared. This was extremely fortunate because, had there been any other serious contender, choosing me, the Headmaster's son, as the winner, would have appeared like the most blatant kind of nepotism.

A day or two after the competition had been held, Daddy asked me privately what book I would like to be awarded as my prize; and although it was clearly a girls' book, so he asked me once or twice: "Are you sure?" I had so much enjoyed the wireless adaptation of Noel Streatfield's *White Boots* earlier in the year that I had no hesitation in asking for it.

When Prize-Giving came a few weeks later, there were so many visitors that my class was sitting half-way-up the stairs at the back of the Hall, and I had a long way to go when my name was called out. 'Well done, Graves!' Daddy said to me when at last I reached his desk; and it was a wonderful moment for me when he shook my hand and presented me with my prize and regarded me very proudly and lovingly. I had opened *White Boots* and begun reading it almost before the applause had died down and I had returned to my place on the stairs.

Winning was a new experience for me, and I must admit that I liked being a winner, and I liked the applause that went with it. The result was, that although I only had one more term to look forward to at Holme Grange, I began working very much harder, which in many ways was just as well.

CHAPTER SIX

My first visit to Copthorne School

Once it had been decided that he could afford to send me away to boarding school, it had been inevitable that my father's preference would be for Copthorne School, on the borders of Surrey and Sussex, the prep-school that he himself had attended long ago and to which he felt the tremendous loyalty that well-run institutions can inspire. His elder brothers Robert and Charles had preceded him, and all three were fortunate to have had as their Headmaster the wise and kindly Bernard Rendall. John had risen to be Head Boy by the time he left in the summer of 1916; but, as I have already intimated, that was not the end of his connection with Copthorne.

When Bernard Rendall retired in 1928, he was succeeded by his 50-year-old colleague Skeete Workman, the son of a clergyman and an equally devoted schoolmaster who had been teaching at Copthorne for many years, had only recently married, rather late in life, and had a son, always known as Tim, who was less than a year old. Skeete had great ambitions for Copthorne, and almost his first action as Headmaster was to ask my father, who had once been his pupil, to move on from his teaching job at Sandroyd and to accept a more senior position as an assistant master in charge of both Classics and Soccer.

John had been more than happy to accept this invitation, though the following year it led to a very wounding passage in his brother Robert's *Good-bye to All That* in which John's conventional outlook was brutally mocked. By the constant repetition of the words 'typical', 'good' and 'normal', Robert successfully conveyed the unkind and very misleading impression that his youngest brother lacked all interest as a human being. Writing about Copthorne School, Robert declares:

> How good and typical the school was can best be seen in the case of my youngest brother, who is a typical good, normal person, and, as I say, went straight from home to the school without other school influences. He spent five or six years there – and played in the elevens – and got the top scholarship at a public school – and became head boy with athletic distinctions – and won a scholarship at Oxford and further athletic distinctions – and a degree – and then what did he do? Because he was such a good normal person he naturally went back as a master to his old typically good preparatory school, and now that he has been there some years and wants a change he is applying for a mastership at his old public school and, if he gets it and becomes a housemaster after a few years, he will at last, I suppose, become a headmaster and eventually take the next step and become the head of his old college at Oxford. That is the sort of typically good preparatory school it was.

At the time, this thoroughly unpleasant attack led to a two-year estrangement between the brothers; though eventually, after a further argument over John having dedicated a book to Robert without his permission, there was a kind of reconciliation. In any case, John's career had followed a different path from the one predicted by his brother. After an intriguing period as a private tutor, during the course of which he had travelled on the Continent with a wealthy family, attended the 1936 Winter Olympics, and fallen madly in love with a woman whom he pursued unsuccessfully across several European countries, John did indeed move on to a Public School, but not to Charterhouse. He went instead, as you know, to Malvern College and thence to the Ministry of Education, to Sandroyd (a second time and in a new location) and finally to Holme Grange.

In the meantime, Skeete Workman had continued as Headmaster of Copthorne School until his death in March 1952 at the age of 73, leaving his widow and their son in charge of the school. And now, in the Easter holidays of 1954, Daddy had arranged to drive me down to Copthorne, ostensibly to judge for himself whether or not the school was still in safe hands and could therefore be trusted with me as one of its pupils; though in practice I believe that his decision had already been taken.

It was a two-hour journey which we began by turning left out of the back drive, and immediately right again onto the Easthampstead Road. At first, we travelled through open farmland before turning right onto the Old Wokingham Road and then plunging southwards into an area which, apart from an occasional small cluster of dwellings, largely consisted of thick forest.

When we turned eastward onto the Nine Mile Ride, Daddy began his usual running commentary about everything of interest in the landscape through which we passed. First, he told me about the excitingly named Road Research Laboratory, of whose substantial tract of land in this remote place we had some intriguing glimpses. Not much further on, we passed a sign on the right with the words 'Caesar's Camp' on it, and Daddy explained that the track to which it pointed led up to an ancient Iron Age fort. "It has absolutely nothing to do with Julius Caesar", he told me. "It was built hundreds of years before his arrival, and it probably went on being used until the Roman invasion of AD43."

We turned south-eastward along the A322 on our way to Guildford, and the next landmark, which I came to know well, was the Cricketer's at Bagshot, in whose grounds Daddy told me that he himself had played cricket more than once. From outside this grand roadside Inn the great A30, one of the most important main roads in England, ran all the way up to London in the north-east or all the way down to Salisbury, Exeter and eventually Lands' End in the extreme south-west. We crossed over it on this occasion, following first the A322 all the way to Guildford, and then the A25 through Dorking and Reigate.

Dorking intrigued me simply because in the Nursery at home there was a children's book called *The Donkey from Dorking* which I had thoroughly enjoyed. It told the story of how it was a donkey from Dorking who, having somehow travelled all the way to Palestine, had been the donkey upon whose back Jesus had ridden on the day of his triumphal entry into Jerusalem.

As we travelled on to Reigate and then turned sharply south along the A217, Daddy began telling me about his own time at Copthorne. "It was a good school", he told me,

> "and helped all three of us, Robert and Charles and me, to get scholarships to Charterhouse. Just as well, because we couldn't have gone there otherwise. I was there during the First World War. Of course, it wasn't the First World War in those days, because the Second World War hadn't happened. We called it the Great War. It was a terrible war – huge casualties. Your Uncle Robert was reported dead. I still remember my mother's shriek of joy when she found out that he was still alive!
>
> "And poor Bernard Rendall. A great Headmaster. He always sat at the Head of the senior dining-room table, just in front of the fireplace, and when I was Head Boy I sat next to him on his left. He liked to bring *The Times* into breakfast, so that he could discuss any interesting items of news with his senior boys. But now from time to time there was news of the death of an old Copthornian, and he would stand up and read out his name to the whole school and then there would be a minute's silence while we bowed our heads before he sat down again and talked to us about the dead man, often with tears running down his cheeks."

At length, past Horley, we began driving down quieter and quieter roads, until we turned off the B3208 into what was no more than a lane. To the left were seven or eight large detached houses; to the right were open fields; and the lane was lined with huge elm trees, their branches filled with large untidy crows' nests.

"Look, there it is!" said Daddy, "That's it! That's Copthorne!", as he gestured excitedly to a somewhat unprepossessing range of brick buildings in the distance. And then, as we drew closer, and there was about to be a very sharp turn to the right, just under the walls of Copthorne School, we left the road and swept straight ahead into a short driveway, before scrunching to a halt on the untidy gravel of an irregular oval parking area. Daddy switched off the engine, and for a moment or two there was silence and we both looked around.

There was nothing at all to our left except the intriguing wilderness of Copthorne Common stretching out into the distance. Ahead of us, a rough track made its way beyond what looked like a church tower and along the northern edge of the Common. To our right, we had just driven past the south-east wing of the school, which jutted out almost as far as the hedge beside the driveway, and now the main building was some twenty yards away to our right, a tall undistinguished three-story pile, brick-built with a slate roof. From where the original front door must have been, at the centre of this building, protruded an aesthetically displeasing narrow single-storey construction with a pitched roof, which ran out all the way to the parking area. At its front was the new entrance, and when Daddy had rung the bell and a servant had opened it for us, I found myself walking along a broad entrance corridor, with two or three doors leading off to the left.

I would soon discover that this corridor was almost never used by the boys except at the very beginning and end of term, or on leave-outs, or on a frightening visit to the Headmaster's Study: frightening because any summons to this room with its neat desk standing diagonally across the room facing the door and its low bookshelves all around the walls meant that one might be in danger of a caning, or 'six-of-the-best'.

At the very end of this corridor, there was an ante-room with a fireplace which must have been the former entrance Hall. To the right of it were the private apartments; while to our left a door led directly into the central school corridor. On this occasion there was no fire in the grate; but Daddy was delighted to be back and he received a very warm welcome from Skeete Workman's widow Margaret, an elderly but still formidable creature, rather stocky with a plump pink face, grey curly hair, intense blue eyes and a powerful handshake.

Ten or eleven years older than my father (so to me she seemed ancient), 60-year-old Mrs. Workman had known him for over a quarter of a century, and regarded him with a mildly proprietorial air as she advanced towards him. It was then that I heard for the first time the distinctive strangulated tones of her high rasping voice, with her s's slightly slurred into a 'sh' sound, as she called out: 'Johnnie! How good to shee you again after all thish time!' As they clasped arms in a kind of embrace, she went on: "And of courshe, you haven't sheen Tim shince he wash a boy!"

It was now that I noticed for the first time the other figure who had just come into the room and who stepped out of the shadows into the light: this was Mrs. Workman's son who, when he had become Headmaster of Copthorne just two years previously at the age of 25, had been the youngest Headmaster in the whole of the Independent Association of Preparatory Schools (IAPS). Now, I know that in 1783 William Pitt the Younger became Prime Minister of Great Britain at the age of only 24, but then he was a man of outstanding administrative and political genius. Unfortunately, P.H.P. Workman had turned out to be deeply second-rate in almost every way.

Sure, he was a large man with a fresh, well-scrubbed appearance as though he had only just shaved and showered; but his straight dark hair that was so carefully parted sat above surprisingly weak blue eyes in a face that was plump and flabby-looking; and his smart, double-breasted blue blazer, with its large silvery buttons, could not hide the fact that although not actually fat he was certainly overweight and he looked physically out-of-condition. To put it another way: it was impossible to imagine him refereeing a football match; and I felt immediately, with the clear insight of a child ('now through a glass darkly' etcetera), that he was far too young and inexperienced to make a good Headmaster.

He was now shaking Daddy's hand, but it seemed to me that although he was very much in awe of my father, he had no particular liking for him. I guess he had heard far more than he wanted to from his mother about the days when his father had worked with mine for the good of Copthorne school. He was certainly very deferential to Daddy, and occasionally flashed a jolly smile while speaking to him in a deep bass voice quite unlike his mother's, but it seemed to me that just below the surface he was seething with annoyance.

At this moment Mrs. Workman turned away to walk into her long drawing-room, leaving her son to take us on a brief tour of the school; and no doubt hoping to give my father the impression that Tim Workman was very much in charge: which was far from true.

Many years later I would learn that Tim Workman had originally wanted to be not a schoolmaster but a pig-farmer. As a schoolmaster, how could be possibly live up either to his father's excellence or to his mother's expectations? However, after studying at Cambridge he had joined the teaching staff in order to help out the family at a time when his father was becoming old and ill; and on Skeete's death, when his mother had absolutely insisted that he should become the new Headmaster, he had capitulated.

I almost wrote 'feebly capitulated', but it would have taken extraordinary strength to resist this ferocious woman. During Skeete's declining years, she had gradually taken over the reins of power, and she had no intention of relinquishing them. She saw only one minor difficulty. If she was to remain very largely in charge as Mrs. Workman, how could her son be allowed to become Mr. Workman in his own right? No, Tim had been her nickname for him when he was a child and completely under her control; Mr. Tim he had become when he had joined the school under his father's Headmastership, for how could there be two Mr. Workmans? And on Skeete's death she had insisted that her son should continue to be addressed by teaching staff and pupils alike not as Mr. Workman, but as 'Mr. Tim'.

It may be that Tim Workman had once been in reality the cheerful person of the large jolly smile; but if so, that core of his personality was already in the process of being hollowed out and replaced with anger and bitterness. He had inherited his mother's lust for power, so some aspects of his new role were not altogether disagreeable. But he did not really like boys, and he did not really like being Headmaster.

As Mr. Tim led us around the school grounds, which is where we began our tour, he said almost nothing to me, but made occasional deferential remarks to my father, who was mainly talking about his own happy memories of Copthorne School as it had been many years ago. The grounds were certainly much less interesting than those of Holme Grange: not a rhododendron or a horse-chestnut tree in sight, let alone a mysterious lake with its own moorhens. However, Copthorne had a number of facilities we lacked, including tennis-courts, an open-air swimming pool and even a small rifle-range. We came back into the school buildings through a side-door close to what had looked to me like a church, but was in fact the school Chapel, and then walked up beneath a roofed-over passageway. This led first into a very new Library, packed with books that I longed to read; and then into an immensely long room, with a stage at its far end.

I looked at the rows and rows of empty desks and smelled the particular brand of pungent floor-polish then in use at Copthorne and noticed that there were no pictures to be seen on the walls apart from two rather beautiful framed posters calling themselves Shell Guides to June and November. And then: "This is Big School", Daddy began explaining to me:

> "Do you see over there on each side of the room those tall oak panels going all the way up to the ceiling? And some more at this end of the stage? Those are parts of two huge partitions, and when you pull them out, they slide across Big School and convert it into three separate classrooms."

To me, this was the most interesting thing I had learned all day, apart from Daddy's description of his wartime breakfasts with Bernard Rendall.

Indeed, by the time we left Copthorne and set out on our long return journey, I had formed very little impression of what life would be like for me at Copthorne. Emptied of boys and masters, all I could see in the main school buildings was another collection of classrooms and dormitories. I did wonder a little nervously what it would be like to be in a school where there were as many as ninety boarders, and secretly I wished that it might have been possible to remain at Holme Grange amongst my family and friends.

But I loved Daddy, and as we drove home it was clear that he was convinced that all was well at his old school. He assured me that being a Boarder at Copthorne School would be an immense benefit to me. He added that he was delighted to be in a position to pay the fees so that I could follow in his footsteps and in due course, all going well, win a scholarship to Charterhouse as he had done.

Before long I had been properly enrolled, an entrance fee had been paid and that summer intensive preparations were put in hand for my departure from everything that I most loved. Barring accidents, I was now fated to spend the better part of the next five years immured for months at a time in an institution of which I still knew almost nothing, except that I had taken an instant dislike to the man who would be my new Headmaster.

CHAPTER SEVEN

Last Term at Holme Grange

My six-and-a-half-year-old brother Simon remained my best friend and my constant companion. He was so clever that he always had something interesting to say, we almost never quarreled or even disagreed, and there was nothing we enjoyed more than being out in the grounds. As season followed season there was always something new to see and to enjoy, and after less than three full years at Holme Grange there were still unexplored corners, especially in the land on each side of the stream at the bottom of the back drive. Usually we were out alone together, but sometimes Daddy came with us and showed us something new, like a small clump of double-white daffodils that he had found near one of the Nissen Huts on the back drive, or a second group of fritillaries which flowered each spring between the Nissen Hut by the roundabout and the rhododendron bushes near the top of the front drive.

Once, back in November, he had even walked with us all the way down the drive to gather eating chestnuts from the two trees that stood close to the urinals by the cricket-field. The chestnuts were so ripe that they had begun falling to the ground, and while Simon and I picked up all the ones that we could find at our feet, Daddy reached up to pick any of the spiky burrs that had turned from green to yellow-brown, and had begun to split open to reveal the hard brown tear-shaped nuts inside. Extracting the chestnuts from their burrs proved to be much more difficult than removing conkers from their shells, but Daddy was an expert and showed us how to do it.

Later that day, when the chestnuts had been carried home and soaked for half-an-hour in a large bowl of cold water that he had placed on the kitchen table, Daddy showed us how to use a small sharp serrated knife to make a shallow cut along the side of each chestnut. The chestnuts were then placed on a baking tray, and baked in one of the ovens for a further half-an-hour. Finally, when they had cooled a little, we were able to carry a bowl of chestnuts up to the Nursery, where we peeled off the thin outer skin, dipped the yellowish nuts in a little salt, and ate them as they should be eaten: warm, fresh and utterly delicious.

More recently, during the Easter holidays, Daddy had decided that Simon and I were old enough to take on more responsibility within the grounds that we loved so much. As you know, we already had our own gardens, and now he gave us each a 'wood'. Mine was the rough area between the southern side of the sunken garden and the western azaleas: not very prepossessing, though it had just enough trees to be called a wood; and at some stage in the spring it would be carpeted in bright red Valerian, of which, although it is usually considered to be a weed, I became inordinately fond.

Simon's wood was at to the east of the great southern lawn, and was in many ways far more interesting. At one end of this thick oblong clump of woodland, not far from the flight of steps leading down from the eastern end of the terrace, was a very curious tree, a weeping silver-leaved ornamental pear, with creamy-white flowers that appeared in April at the same time as its willow-like leaves, grey-white and velvety. At the other end was a small plantation of damson trees which most years produced a large crop of delicious damsons that were sweet enough to eat when fully ripe; and somewhere in the middle was a massive Ash tree. It was in every way a wonderful wood, and Simon was quite rightly very pleased with it.

Three-year-old Elizabeth, or 'Lizzie' as we had begun to call her instead of 'Lilibet' had been considered too young to own a wood, but as some small compensation Daddy gave her a new flowerbed in the garden that lay just below the Library windows, and just above the Sunken Garden. At the centre of this small garden was a round bed that became hers and that was named 'the cartwheel flowerbed' because a cartwheel had been inserted into it, creating twelve little flowerbeds between its spokes.

Because she was so young, Lizzie rarely accompanied Simon and me on our expeditions into the Grounds. And very sadly, Simon had continued to tease her quite dreadfully at times. One evening, after a particularly savage bout of teasing in the Nursery, Lizzie had burst into such floods of tears and such loud wails that Daddy came rushing into the room, found out what had happened, bent Simon over his lap, punished him with three or four smacks on his bottom and, when Simon's own wails had died down, told him that he must never again be so cruel to his sister. This was the only time that Daddy ever smacked one of us, and although it was unpleasant, it appears to have worked, because Simon's attitude to our sister underwent a complete transformation for the better.

Of course, Simon and I still had no idea how ill Lizzie really was, though we had grown used to the fact that after even a very short walk she would 'run out of puff', and her physical deterioration continued gradually but remorselessly from month to month. After a while, I trained her to climb on a chair and then onto my back, so that if we wanted her to come outside with us, perhaps to sit on the grass not far from her garden and enjoy some fresh air, I could carry her down the back stairs and through the side door and out into the light. This was heavy work, since from lack of exercise she was gradually becoming plump.

She too had no idea how ill she was. There she is one sunny afternoon soon after the start of the summer term, a small stout figure being held by her Nanny and watched by me while she kneels on the Nursery windowsill and looks out over the lawn. She can see that Mr. MacGowran is taking a PE class, with rows of boys bending and stretching and flinging their arms out in unison. And because she can no longer do things like this herself, she can't imagine anyone else being so foolish as to take so much exercise. "Silly boys", she says a little breathily, "very silly boys!"

This would be my last term as a pupil at Holme Grange, and it was chiefly memorable for the arrival of a new senior Matron, for my short-lived friendship with Hubert Preston and for a gradual improvement in the quality of my schoolwork. This was still variable, but by the end of the term, although I had made almost no progress in French (due, considered

Mr. Hinton, to 'insufficient interest') Mr. Rushton observed that my work in Mathematics was much better, I had managed to come top in the English exams, and my father was able to conclude in his Headmaster's Report that I had made good progress in most of the school subjects, but that Richard 'must now learn to put his back into subjects that do not, at first sight, attract him.'

As for our new matron, she was an unusual, one might almost say exotic, member of her clan, not only hard-working, but deeply feminine, and with a great love of literature that she was determined to impart to the boys in her charge. To this end, she somehow or other persuaded my father who, though always utterly correct in these matters, may not have been altogether insensible to her charms, to allow her to conduct reading and cocoa sessions with select groups of boys in her private bed-sitting-room. These sessions took place late in the evening just before bedtime when we were all dressed in pyjamas and dressing-gowns and slippers, which made it all the more intimate, and I well remember the excitement of entering her room, which was normally out-of-bounds, through the door on the landing half-way up the main stairs.

It felt like a tremendous privilege to have been invited into the inner sanctum of this remarkably warm-hearted and yet at the same time erudite woman. With its functional wardrobe, chest of drawers, one or two armchairs, a small table and chair under the window looking out over the roundabout, a gas-fire where a fireplace had once been opposite the door, a single bed along one wall, and a second door leading conveniently into the sickroom, this was normally the most anonymous of rooms. Yet with a few deft touches here and there, including a colourful bed-spread and rug, pictures of the countryside on her walls, and piles of books wherever one looked, she had magically transformed it into a home from home.

Here it was that she sat us down either on the edge of her bed or in one of her arm chairs or (in my case) on the rug. When we were all comfortably settled, she produced mugs of cocoa: she had a gas-ring and kettle in her room, and there was water in a hand-basin in the sick-room next-door; and then she began reading to us from an extraordinary 1937 novel with the haunting title of *The Far-Distant Oxus*.

Written by two schoolgirls, Katharine Hull and Pamela Whitlock, each girl had taken it in turns to draft a chapter, which the other then revised; and its very considerable emotional power comes from the fact that 16-year-old Katharine's mother had died the year before they began writing. The story, about a group of pony-loving children and their adventures without adults, is set in the West Country; and a surreal quality is given to it by Katharine and Pamela projecting onto the real Exmoor, the Persian place-names of a long narrative poem by which they had both been entranced. This was *Sohrab and Rustum: An Episode*, a long narrative poem by Matthew Arnold. First published in 1853, it tells the tragic story of how the famous Persian warrior Rustum fights a man in single combat, not realising until he has fatally wounded him that this man is his long-lost son Sohrab: of whom Matthew Arnold writes the line:

By the far-distant Oxus, he is slain.

While Matron read to us most beautifully, I did not really understand how Persia and England had somehow become inter-mingled, but the glamour of it caught my imagination and the words *The Far-Distant Oxus* somehow lingered on in my mind where they have remained as a kind of talisman, a magical and evocative gateway into some mysterious world that is more real than normal reality.

Finally, let me describe my brief and unsatisfactory friendship with Hubert Preston, a Holme Grange day-boy, which I can only explain by telling you about my recent enthusiasm (which I shared with Simon and which had been encouraged by our parents) for what were known as *I-Spy* books.

In my childhood, and for many years afterwards, playing I-Spy was a favourite family game with which to while away a dull afternoon or a long car journey. By the way, do please skip the rest of this paragraph if the game is well known-to you; but in case in your day it has passed out of living memory, just as has happened in my day to many of the games routinely played by Victorian children, let me explain how it works. The person volunteering to start the game begins by looking around, choosing an object and then using its first letter in the prescribed manner. For example, had you been looking through our Nursery window, seen a cloud in the sky and chosen that as your object, you would have begun by saying:

> I spy with my little eye, something beginning with.... [these dots represent a pause for dramatic effect]... c!!!

The other players would then take turns to look around and suggest what you might have seen that began with the letter c: 'carpet' perhaps? Or (if Budge happened to be present) 'cat'? The first one to guess 'cloud' would be the winner and would have the excitement of starting a new round.

This game had been cleverly adapted for commercial purposes by Charles Warrell, a Headmaster nearing retirement who had reinvented himself as Big Chief I-SPY. The basis of his business was a series of small I-SPY booklets which could be bought in most newsagents or bookshops for the pocket-money price of 6d. Each booklet, which began with a welcoming message from Big Chief I-SPY himself, covered a different subject: for example, *At the Seaside, On the Farm, On a Train Journey* and *In the Street*; and each booklet had over forty pages of drawings of people or objects that could be I-SPY-ed.

Each drawing was accompanied by a text description, by the number of points you could acquire for having I-SPY-ed it, and an area into which you could enter the details of when and where you had done so. The subjects were varied: *I-SPY in the Street* includes a mounted policeman (25 points); a Steeplejack (25 points); a Barrel Organ (20 points); the Bank signs of Westminster Bank, Barclays Bank and Martin's Bank (20 points each); a plain telephone box (10 points); and a Police Telephone Box, (just like the one which would later feature in *Dr. Who*) (15 points).

Mummy and Daddy liked these booklets not only because they were a useful distraction on a long car journey but also because they had educational value: they trained us to be observant, and they passed on information. For example, the text accompanying the picture of the Police Telephone Box (one of which I knew well from the southern end of the High Street in Rottingdean) explains that:

> The little door opens to disclose a telephone. The policeman

– or you in case of emergency – can use it to ring up the local police station. A winking light at the top, and a loud bell, tell the policeman that Headquarters want to talk to him. In the telephone box there is often some First-aid equipment.

Simon and I liked them too. To I-SPY something that was in the booklet for the first time, to record it in the proper manner and to add the points you had earned to your current total was great fun; and it became more and more of a challenge as each book was gradually filled up, and the remaining objects became harder and harder to find.

By 1954, when we bought our first I-SPY books, the business was a huge success and, with Worrall still nominally in charge as Big Chief I-SPY, it had become the property of a popular daily newspaper called *The News Chronicle*. Our next step could have been to join the I-SPY Tribe, already more than half a million strong, and become one of Big Chief I-SPY's 'REDSKINS'. I was considering doing this when I learned that my class-mate Hubert Preston had already signed up.

Mainly because they shared the same Christian name, Hubert always made me think of the fictional Hubert Lane whose gang rivalled William Brown's Outlaws. However, this Hubert could never have been the leader of a gang. He was the plump, self-absorbed, mildly unpopular and extremely lonely son of a wealthy Wokingham family; and on learning that I had been seen with an I-SPY book in my hand, he became tremendously excited and made a bee-line for me one day immediately after lunch. I noticed for the first time that he was wearing an I-SPY badge in his jacket lapel, and I was soon being invited to have tea with him at his home in Murdoch Road to discuss I-SPY matters. To begin with I was quite interested, so I agreed to this, and Mummy kindly drove me there on the appointed afternoon, and left me at the door.

A few moments later, I was standing in the vast hallway of one of the most prestigious-looking private houses into which I had ever been invited, and deferentially shaking hands with Mrs. Preston. Even more overweight than her son, she was a massive presence both in the hallway and at the tea-table, where she consumed a large number of the chocolate buns that her cook had prepared for the occasion, and looked on approvingly while

Hubert (who was also demolishing buns at a great rate) began telling me about the progress he had been making since he had first enlisted as a REDSKIN.

"You should do the same", he told me enthusiastically, in between mouthfuls of chocolate bun. "All you have to do is to go to Smith's and buy an I-SPY membership packet. It only costs a shilling and then you get a membership number and a badge and a book of secret codes and all sorts of useful things. It's mostly secret until you're a member, but there's one book that I can show you straight away!" And he passed me a red booklet headed:

NEWS CHRONICLE

I-SPY

THE

GREAT

TRIBE

A Book

For REDSKINS AND PALEFACES

I began looking through it rather anxiously, thinking that perhaps I might after all prefer to remain a PALEFACE if becoming a REDSKIN involved forking-out a whole two weeks' pocket-money; and at this point his mother intervened.

"Hubert", she said, "Go and show him the totem-pole!" She turned to me. "It's all very exciting, isn't it? I know Hubert's hoping that you're going to help him set up a Wokingham branch. And he's already got two feathers from the large Chief!"

"It's *Big* Chief I-SPY, Mother," said Hubert reprovingly, "not *large* Chief!" And then he led me up to his bedroom, which was about four times the size of mine. "There's the totem-pole", he said carelessly, "What do you think?" And then without waiting for my reply he donned a headband into which he had already stuck two feathers and began explaining that once you were a member you could send off completed I-SPY booklets to Big Chief I_SPY and receive in return... But I didn't take in much more of what he was saying, because I was staring in amazement at the corner of his bedroom in which I could see the totem-pole to which Mrs. Preston had referred.

It was at least five feet tall, with elaborate wooden carvings on it and a colourful winged creature of some sort near the top. I began to feel uneasily not only that his parents had more money than sense but also that there was something both about Hubert's involvement with the I-SPY movement and about his sudden attachment to me that was far too intense for my liking. The attention that he paid me was flattering, but there was no doubt that he was extremely odd, and I felt that if I spent much time in his company, I would soon be tarred with the same brush of eccentricity.

After a while I refocused on what Hubert was telling me, which was that he hoped to become a Tribe Recruiting Officer (TRO), which would mean winning an Order of Merit and a special green feather. "All we have to do", he said, looking at me adoringly, "is to recruit five new members. I'll have the first TRO feather, and then you can have one when we recruit the next five. And then of course we must all buy *The News Chronicle* every day, so that we can use our code books to read the secret messages and start winning some of the prizes for good I-SPYing."

His mention of *The News Chronicle* was the last straw. We already took *The Times* and *The Daily Mail*, and I felt certain that there would be no chance of persuading Daddy to add *The News Chronicle* to this list. After politely showing moderate enthusiasm for Hubert's ideas for another ten or fifteen minutes, I asked him what the time was, and when he had looked at his wrist-watch and told me, I suddenly discovered that it was exactly the right time for me to go home. Mrs. Preston offered to drive me, but by this time I was so keen to escape completely from the entire mildly deranged Preston family that I said I would walk.

Back home I explained the situation to Mummy, telling her that I wanted to avoid having to take part in Hubert's plans without hurting his feelings too much. She thought for a moment or two before giving me some sound advice. "It's all quite simple, really", she said. "You just have to explain that you're off to Copthorne next term, so it would be much more sensible for him to find someone who's still at Holme Grange to help him."

A day or two later, at the end of a sunny but boring afternoon on the cricket-field, Hubert caught up with me near the Giant Sequoia, and immediately launched into a new set of ideas for recruiting members to 'our' I-SPY club. I explained about my becoming a Boarder at Copthorne and, as we walked along in the shade of the trees that overhung the driveway beside the lake, I added that I would have to leave everything in his hands. It was disagreeable to have to tell him this and, even as I spoke, I felt guiltily that I was letting him down badly. Poor Hubert said that he would see what he could do, but he looked dreadfully disappointed. I had the strong impression that without my help he would in fact do nothing at all, and that was how it turned out. In the meantime, he was like a distressingly unbounced Tigger, and we walked the rest of the way back to the school in almost complete silence.

CHAPTER EIGHT
Visiting Pearce-Powell

When we had left White Hazel behind, we had also, much to my relief, left behind our Shaftesbury Dentist; and since we were now so close to London, Daddy had decided that rather than find someone in Wokingham, it was time for us all to benefit from the services of a truly first-class London Dentist. It was my Uncle Charles who had pointed him in the direction of Mr. Pearce-Powell, who plied his somewhat disagreeable trade from the ground floor of a splendid six-storey town house at 98 Gloucester Road, a little to the north of the Cromwell Road, and so prestigious an address that many years later it would become for a time the Embassy of the Kingdom of Bahrain.

At the front of No 98, which is one of a terrace of six similar properties, two large columns support a splendid portico, above which is a balcony and beneath which six stone steps lead up to the front-door. Almost as soon as we had rung the bell, this door would be opened by a pretty young dental nurse wearing a formidably well-starched white uniform with a nurse's cap in her hair, and she admitted us into a world so elegant and luxurious that it was difficult not to feel that it was a great privilege to have been invited in. She led us a short distance along the narrow but beautifully-tiled hallway and ushered us into a thickly-carpeted reception room immediately to our left.

In between the large window at one end looking out over the street, and the massive sideboard with an equally massive mirror above it at the other end, there was a great profusion of expensive-looking sofas and armchairs, and a side-table covered with high-quality magazines such as *Country Life* or *The Illustrated London News*. Pearce-Powell spaced out his patients so very carefully, that usually we were the only people in the room; but despite this it was all so impressive that we found ourselves talking in hushed voices as though we had just entered a church or a bank.

Pearce-Powell himself was a large, clean-shaven, softly-spoken man, bald on top and with very short black hair above his ears on each side. He also had the kindliest of eyes, set in a slightly pudgy face; and over his trousers he wore a large white garment that reached from his neck to his knees and instead of being buttoned down the front was somehow fastened at the side.

I had been only six years old on my first visit to No. 98, and slightly to my annoyance Pearce-Powell had treated me as even younger than I was. As soon as I had been called next door into the dental surgery to be introduced to him by my father, I had held out my right hand and said 'How d'ye do?' in the prescribed manner when meeting anyone for the first time, but instead of saying 'How d'ye do?' back, he had responded by lifting me bodily into his dentist's chair and working its mechanical handle so that I shot up and up until I felt that I had almost reached the ceiling.

Any new dentist normally takes very little time to discover that the work done by his or her predecessor has left much to be desired; and Pearce-Powell, though in most other respects a very genial human being, was no exception to this rule. It was not long before he was explaining to my father, in a version of his softly-spoken voice that cleverly succeeded in being both delightfully deferential and amazingly authoritative, that the extraction of four of my teeth by our Shaftesbury Dentist a few years earlier had been most abominably mismanaged.

Not only was there still evident overcrowding but also, as he pointed out sadly but sympathetically, some of my remaining teeth were beginning to point in odd directions. He would of course have to make a start by dealing with a number of cavities which urgently needed filling; and to be certain about exactly what was needed he would need to see for himself how the situation developed over the next eighteen months; but it was already very clear to him that in due course a dental plate would become necessary.

From now on, we had regular six-monthly appointments with Pearce Powell and, despite brushing my teeth with great regularity morning and evening, I had to put up with numerous fillings. This was to some extent an inherited problem. Children are said to inherit their mother's teeth, and my mother's had never been good. But it was mainly because I was eating far more sugar than was good for me.

At breakfast I sprinkled white sugar liberally on my porridge or Kellogg's Corn Flakes; at elevenses I did my best to eat at least two delicious biscuits, chocolate if possible; one of my favourite treats was to be given a whole orange with a hole cut in the top, so that I could push two white sugar-lumps into it and then suck out the juice; after lunch each day Mummy gave me a liberal ration of sweets, to which I looked forward with such enthusiasm that if denied them for any reason I became as bad-tempered as a drug addict deprived of his daily fix; and there was nothing I liked more at tea-time than bread-and-butter covered with a thick layer of Lyle's Golden Syrup. How eagerly I spooned this out from one of those iconic green and gold tins featuring a dead lion, a swarm of bees and those mysterious words, taken from the Biblical story of Samson: 'Out of the strong came forth sweetness'.

This problem of eating too much sugar was not ours alone: there had been an epidemic of tooth-decay in Great Britain for many years, with the result that dentists were kept hard at work. Most of their patients came either to have teeth extracted or to have false teeth fitted, rather than to have cavities filled, and by the age of thirty almost one in five adults had lost all their teeth. Things had become even worse when sugar and sweets rationing were ended in September 1953, but despite this, on the very rare occasions when we came across families in which no sweets were allowed, we regarded the children with pity and their parents as monsters.

I can of course understand from personal experience why people preferred extractions to fillings, because fillings involved a kind of torture. It is true that by this time many dentists were offering injections into the gums to numb the nerves before they began drilling; but Pearce-Powell was not one of them. He knew that anaesthetic injections could have unpleasant and even dangerous side-effects; and he firmly believed that he could drill more safely and more effectively if he allowed himself to be guided by his patients' unfiltered suffering.

I would therefore begin each session feeling extremely apprehensive as I sat in the dentist's chair and, sitting on his stool just behind me, Pearce Powell first examined my teeth and then, having decided which of them were in need of attention, placed a suction tube in my mouth, switched on his noisy ancient whirring drill, and began pulling it closer and closer to my mouth. Then the noise from the drill altered, and it became a sudden high-pitched scream as it began grinding its way into a decaying tooth.

Provided that I was not in too much pain, the grinding continued; but if it became so acute that I called out in agony, then it almost certainly meant that Pearce Powell was getting too near some vital nerve. It would be safer for him not to go any further in that direction, and he would pause for a short while to let me recover; and before he went on again, he would suggest that I had a 'rinse-out' from the glass of pink water that stood on its little holder conveniently close to my left hand.

And then, early in 1954, Pearce-Powell finally decided that it was time for me to be fitted for that long-threatened corrective dental plate. For normal family dentist appointments Daddy would drive all five of us up to London in EPB 223, and park immediately outside No. 98. But since the plate involved only me, Mummy and I travelled up to London together by train.

We begin by driving through Wokingham to the end of Broad Street, carrying on past the surgery in the Reading direction, and then turning sharp left down the long slope of Station Road. A quarter of a mile later, and Wokingham railway station is just over to our right: a lovely brick-built Victorian building with a sloping slate roof.

We park on the station forecourt between the station itself and a local Inn. As always, I do my best not to stare for too long at the almost unbelievably busty portrait of Molly Millar wearing a very low-cut top, an Inn sign which swings from a tall wooden stand just in front of the establishment for which it is such a striking advertisement.

Turning in the other direction towards the station, we walk through its large front door into a small square room with three further doors. One of these, immediately to our left, leads into a waiting room with padded benches around the edge of the walls, and a fireplace, in which, because it is now the dead of winter, a coal fire blazes. Over to our right, a second door, always closed, leads into the ticket office, from which uniformed staff sell tickets and answer enquiries while standing at counters behind two glass windows set into the wall, each window with an oval hole cut in the centre for ease of communication, and a gap along the bottom through which tickets can be exchanged for notes and coins or a very occasional signed cheque.

The third door, ahead and to the right, is usually kept open and leads directly onto the south-facing London platform. This is protected from the elements, like the Reading platform opposite, by a tiled wooden roof, edged by a decorative fascia daggerboard painted in cream with a band of dark green above it, and supported by occasional iron pillars also painted green.

Once we have bought out tickets and walked out onto the platform, if we look over to our left we can see the station's most dramatic feature, its massive iron footbridge. This spans the tracks beside the level crossing over which the main road continues southward; and I have already learned that when the level crossing gates have been closed (they are controlled from a large signal-box just beside the track on the other side of the gates) it is exciting to stand on the bridge and lean over the railings as a steam-engine passes below, making its fierce chuffing noise and briefly enveloping the whole bridge in thick clouds of steam and smoke.

However, the main line up to London had been electrified back in 1933 by Southern Railway (replaced since nationalization in 1948 by British Railways) using a third live rail, and this means that when our train arrives from Reading it is an electric train with three or four carriages painted light green, a driver's cab at the front of the first carriage, and a Guard's Van for luggage at the back. We step into one of the carriage compartments, the Guard blows his whistle and waves his green flag, and we are off. And before very long, we are passing over the Easthampstead Road level crossing, where it is tempting to open the carriage door into the corridor and look out through the windows to see our Giant Sequoia towering above the line of trees in the far distance.

After the Giant Sequoia has disappeared from view, there is nothing very exciting to see until almost exactly an hour later, by which time the countryside has been entirely replaced with buildings, and we begin pulling into Waterloo, in those days my favourite London Railway Station. I remember it for the excitement of its hustle and bustle; for its vast crowds of people; for its twenty-one long platforms, divided between platforms 11 and 12 by a road for taxicabs, which comes right into the middle of the station; for the cries of 'Porter! Porter!' and its swarms of uniformed porters with their hand-trucks, all standing ready and willing for a suitable tip to transport luggage to and from the trains; for the occasional loud whooshes of steam from the steam-engines; and for the tall iron grille separating the platforms from the concourse, with the entrance and exit to each platform either impenetrably shut, or closely guarded by one of the ticket inspectors who carefully examine every single ticket used by every single arriving or departing passenger.

Soon we are out onto the concourse which is lined with kiosks, and full of comfortable wooden benches. Above us we can see a huge four-sided clock, with black Roman numerals on a white background. This is a well-known place of rendezvous; and above the clock is the roof from which it hangs, a massive construction of iron girders and sloping glass which covers both platforms and concourse at a height of some fifty feet.

The item which fascinates me the most, however, is an imposing advertisement for Johnnie Walker Red Label Whisky which dominates a large part of concourse. It comes in the form of the larger-than-life figure of Johnnie Walker himself, with his cane under his arm, striding forward in his distinctive costume of Top Hat, red tailcoat, white trousers and long black boots. He stands high up on a plinth above a kiosk selling theatre tickets, while a large caption just below him reads: 'Born 1820 – still going strong'.

Mummy always seemed happy to be back in the London that she had known so well during her days at the Royal College of Music, and from within Waterloo she led us confidently onto the escalator which took us down into the depths of the London Underground. Here, she showed me on the London Transport map the route we would be taking: first the Northern line (black on the map)) or the Bakerloo line (brown) only one stop north to Charing Cross, and then the District line (green) or the Circle line (yellow) four stops west to Gloucester Road, from where it would be only a short walk across the Cromwell Road to Number 98.

The process of being fitted for a corrective plate was awkward and uncomfortable, but not at all painful. First Pearce-Powell took two or three X-ray pictures of my upper jaw. For each one of these, I had to hold in my mouth a disc of some white material behind the teeth that were about to be photographed, while he pulled down from its green stand, to which it was attached by jointed steel rods, the heavy X-ray machine, about two feet wide and two feet deep and several inches thick, with a protuberance like an ancient arrow-head that had to be manoeuvred into the correct place against my cheek before the photographs could be taken.

Once this had been done, the dental nurse added water to some special powder. This created a white clay-like substance with which she filled a dental tray before handing it to Pearce-Powell, who told me to "Open wide!" before pushing it so far into my mouth so that I felt I was on the verge of choking. "Now bite down on it", he said; and I had to sink my teeth into this repulsive mixture, and hold the position for a minute or more until it was judged to have 'set', when with a quick practised movement Pearce-Powell would suddenly remove the whole tray from my mouth. In due course a dental laboratory was able to use the photographs and the dental impression to create the dental plate that was needed, and which I saw for the first time on my next visit.

It was a strange pink object, manufactured to the shape of the roof of my mouth, and with various metal wires protruding from it, the longest one of which, when I inserted the plate into my mouth for the first time, fitted neatly around the front of my upper teeth. "That's good", said Pearce-Powell encouragingly. "Now, take it out again and I'll show you how it works. There", he said, taking it from me and turning it upside down. "Do you see that little piece of metal near the back with a hole in it? I'm going to give you a special key which fits into that, and you've got to promise me to insert it and turn it once every evening *without fail* just before you go to sleep. Do you think you can manage that?"

"I'm sure he can do that, can't you Ricky?" Mummy, who had been allowed to be present, intervened protectively.

"I'd like to hear it from him", said Pearce-Powell looking a little doubtfully at me.

So naturally I promised, and I was stuck with and to some extent defined by this wretched piece of pink plastic and steel wires for at least the next two years of my life. I tried not to mind it too much, despite its drawbacks: chief of which was that food was far too easily trapped in it; and that wearing it, altered the interior shape of my mouth, so that for several months it was extremely difficult for me to speak clearly enough to be understood.

On our way home that day, Mummy led me into a shop somewhere near Waterloo that sold a bewildering variety of wrist-watches and pocket-watches. "You'll need a watch at Copthorne", she said. "What kind would you like?" I already knew that most children who wore a watch had a wrist-watch, just like Hubert Preston, who had the most expensive-looking wrist-watch I had ever seen; but I had often thought to myself that wrist-watches were a bad idea, because in the normal rough-and-tumble of school life it would be too easy for them to be broken. A pocket-watch which would be kept safe in the top pocket of my jacket seemed more sensible, and that was what I asked for. Mummy said that would be fine, and began pointing out the ones whose faces were heavily decorated. "Look at this one, Ricky – it's got a steam engine on the front! Or this one, with a picture of Donald Duck!"

"No thanks", I replied, "I don't really like those." What I was thinking to myself was that they looked terribly childish, and would very likely lead to my being teased by my new schoolfellows, which would be a bad start to my time at Copthorne. Finally, the choice was between a completely plain pocket-watch, or one which had luminous green paint on the hands and numbers. I would have quite liked to be able to tell the time in the dark, but I had already noticed that the luminous watches were far more expensive than the non-luminous ones, and I was genuinely worried that Mummy might be spending more on me than she could really afford.

So although she kept asking me whether I was quite sure, I settled on a plain Ingersoll pocket watch. It had a winder at the top with a metal loop just above it, silvery back and sides, a white dial with black hands for the minutes and hours, and a small inset dial with a second-hand. Not only was this considerably less expensive but, although I didn't know this at the time, it was also much safer, since the luminous green paint in common use in those days contained enough radio-active radon to set a Geiger counter buzzing.

When we returned home, I was keen to show Daddy my new watch, of which I already felt very proud, and he sat down with me at the Nursery table after high tea that evening and looked at it carefully. 'A good second hand', he commented.

> "I probably haven't told you that the second-hand was an invention of one of our ancestors, Robert James Graves, a first cousin of my great-grandfather John Crosbie Graves. Robert James was known in his day, back in the 1840s, for having made the Dublin School of Medicine world-famous. He also had the idea that a second-hand would be useful in his medical work, when he was timing a pulse for example, and he had a watch with a second hand specially made for him by a Dublin watchmaking company. Unfortunately, like many of our family, he didn't have much of a head for business, so he never patented the device himself, and after his death in 1853 it was the watchmaking company which began selling watches with second-hands and made a fortune."

Daddy looked at my new watch again. Normally one would have expected a boy's watch like this to come with a simple leather strap, which would have at one end an Albert swivel clasp by which it could be attached to the metal loop above the winder, and at the other end a T-bar clasp, a short metal bar that could be pushed through the button-hole of the lapel to keep the strap in place. For some unaccountable reason, Mummy and I had forgotten all about this, but Daddy came to the rescue. "What you need now", he said, "is something to hang it on!" And he left my new watch on the table and hurried mysteriously from the room.

When he returned a few minutes later he was carrying something in his closed fist. He sat down beside me again. "Look what I've got here!" he said, and opened up his fist to reveal an Edwardian silver double-Albert chain. "I bought this for myself as a boy", he told me. "I had to cycle a long way for it! You can have it now." I picked it out of his palm with a sense of awe. Three lengths of beautiful silver chain hung from a silver T-bar: two of them were long, and I immediately used their swivel clasps to attach them to my new watch; and a third was pure ornament, a small decorative chain of no more than a dozen links to hang from my lapel buttonhole.

Before he left the Nursery to return to his Headmasterly duties, Daddy showed me that every single small link of my new silver chain, just like every piece of our Graves family cutlery, was stamped with a lion to prove that it was made of silver. The combination of watch and chain was now my most precious possession, a sign of my parents' love for me despite the fact that they were planning to send me away from home; and, when I was far away, it would become a talisman to defend me from all perils and dangers of either the day or the night.

CHAPTER NINE

Childhood's End

We had heard back in March that my 30-year-old architect cousin Sam, Robert's youngest child by his first wife Nancy Nicholson, had become engaged to Anneliese Hildebrandt, a warm-hearted children's nurse whom he had known for just over twelve months, and who came from the German-speaking part of Switzerland. They were married at Caxton Hall Registry Office on 9 July 1954, and later that day, together with a host of others, Daddy and Simon and I attended their wedding reception. Thanks to the kindness of Lord Wilmot, a Labour Party politician who had been elevated to the peerage earlier that year, this reception took place on the terrace floor of the House of Lords. It was a very grand affair, with white table-cloths and uniformed waiters and champagne; though as I look down upon it, and see us spilling out from Room number 6 onto the peers' terrace, I wish very much that I had been ten years older. Why? Because it was also the occasion of my only meeting with Sam's elder sister, my cousin Jenny. She was a formidable journalist and, years later, when writing about her in my biography of her father, I would grow to love her very much for her wisdom and humanity.

But do spare a thought at this point for poor Anneliese. She must have thought when she married into the family of Robert Graves, at that time one of the most famous poets in the world, that her life would never be less than interesting; but she did not receive the warm welcome she had expected when, at Robert's invitation, she and Sam travelled out to Deya for their honeymoon. Unfortunately, on first meeting Anneliese, Robert and Beryl simply took against her. After all, she was neither an artist nor a writer and her opinions seemed uninteresting, so they ignored her as much as they could and, when they did meet, were only minimally polite. To be treated like this by her parents-in-law was both cruel and humiliating and so, after that one visit, Anneliese never returned. If Sam wanted to visit his father after that, he had to do so without her.

At any rate, term came to an end and for the next seven or eight weeks, having finished at Holme Grange but not yet begun at Copthorne. I felt wonderfully free, and enjoyed the remainder of that summer with unusual intensity.

First, Daddy drove us down to Rottingdean where, instead of sharing a bedroom with Simon at the very top of Braemar, I was given a small bedroom of my own, up one flight of stairs and at the end of the corridor past the cuckoo clock and the bathroom on the first floor. Another difference, far more dramatic, was that part of the ground floor of The Grange had been turned into a Public Library.

This large, white, two-storeyed Georgian House, with its porticoed front door and its long tall windows with external shutters, stood ten yards or so behind a flint wall in the corner of land between Whiteway and the road past the Pond. It had some family interest, having been owned in the years leading up to the Great War by my Uncle Robert's father-in-law, the artist Sir William Nicholson; but for me its principal virtue was that it contained the largest and most wonderful collection of children's books that I had ever seen.

Elizabeth, who was feeling particularly 'short of puff' on the morning of our first visit to the library, had been left behind at Braemar with Grandad and the Aunts, so it was Mummy and Simon and I who walked through the entrance gate, with its square stone columns topped by stone balls on each side, down a narrow path over the lawn, and went on through the front door into a large entrance hall with stairs at the back of it and doors to left and right.

The left-hand door took us into the Library, where the Children's Section was immediately on our left and, as soon as I was able, I fell upon it with all the enthusiasm of a pirate who has unexpectedly stumbled upon a hoard of Treasure, or a wine-lover who has been given the freedom of a cellar full of vintage wines. The only difficulty would be deciding where to begin, especially as I had already learned while filling out a form at the central desk nearby that I could take out no more than two books at a time.

But then I spotted almost a complete set of the twelve children's novels of Arthur Ransome. I had already found several of these in the Holme Grange School Library, and on reading *Swallows and Amazons* for the first time I had been transported in my imagination far away to The Lake District where the four Walker children, John, Susan, Titty and Roger have received a telegram from their absent naval officer father giving them permission to go sailing alone on one of the lakes, without any adult help, telling them in effect that if they are idiots they would be better off dead, but if they are not idiots they won't come to any serious harm.

This gives the children an extraordinary amount of freedom to fend for themselves on their sailing holiday. Before long they are camping on Wild Cat Island at night, sailing by day in their dinghy *Swallow*, and sharing adventures with their piratical rivals Nancy and Peggy Blackett of *Amazon*. 12-year-old John, so much more practical and capable than me, was my hero; but I also much admired the resourceful Nancy, a tomboy whose real name is Ruth, but who has adopted the name of Nancy after being told that pirates are 'ruthless'.

I now began systematically reading my way through the remainder of Ransome's stories, returning to The Grange if humanly possible every day that it was open, taking out two more books and immediately devouring them from cover to cover.

By the time we returned from Rottingdean, it was not long before I would be leaving for Copthorne, and Simon and I made the most of our remaining time together, visiting many of our favourite places in the grounds, especially the rhododendrons near the sunken garden where we climbed once again to the very top; and we even explored one or two completely new places.

In the far south, for example, on the other side of the stream, we found in the wilderness on the right-hand side of the back drive an amazing tree. Some kind of fir, it had been so battered by a storm that its trunk, instead of being vertical, projected from the ground at an angle of fifty-five or sixty degrees. This made it easier to climb, and on my very first attempt I climbed almost twenty feet into the air, watched from below by my adored and adoring brother.

In the meantime, preparations for my move to Copthorne had been stepped up when the envelope containing the bill for my first term at Copthorne (£73 10/- payable in advance), brought with it a long, narrow sheet of paper on which was a detailed and formidable list of everything that I needed to bring with me in September. It was a list that demanded the most scrupulous adherence to its requirements. In particular, all items of clothing must have name-tapes sewn into them, and everything else from hairbrush to football boots must be clearly marked not only with my name but also with the school number that had been allocated to me: 82.

A very few items such as the school cap (orangey-red) and the school tie (orangey-red with diagonal black stripes), could only be bought from the official school supplier. This meant a special journey to London, this time to visit Frederick Gorringe's Ltd., or 'Gorringes', a long-established and extremely fashionable Department Store based in Buckingham Palace Road.

Fortunately, however, most of what was needed could be supplied by a local company that was now part of the John Lewis Partnership (and hence 'never knowingly undersold') but had been allowed to retain the name of Heelas under which its Department Stores in Wokingham and Reading had been extremely well-known for many years. Mummy had been delighted when we first came to live at Holme Grange to discover that Wokingham had its own Department Store; but it was very much smaller than its Reading counterpart and so when it came to dealing with Copthorne's stringent requirements, she drove me the seven miles westward on a special expedition to Heelas of Reading.

Back in 1954 Reading was probably one of the dullest towns in England, widely known only for its biscuits (Huntley and Palmer: good); its University (red brick: indifferent); and its connection with a writer of genius, Oscar Wilde, who had written a very fine poem about his imprisonment in Reading Gaol (morally equivocal). Even John Betjeman, the poet and architectural critic, could only write despairingly that 'No town in the south of England hides its attractions more successfully from the visitor'. However, to enter the swing-doors of Heelas of Reading was to enter a small corner of the fashionable world, somehow transported here all the way from the heart of London.

We make our way full of eager anticipation into the Men's Department, conveniently situated on the ground floor, and presided over by the dapper Mr. Castle, a small thin man with a thin face and a deep booming voice who invariably wears a well-made dark suit and well-polished black shoes. He also wears heavy black-rimmed glasses beneath dark black hair which is brushed well back from his forehead and liberally coated with hair-oil: probably Brylcreem.

Mr. Castle always remembers my mother, who is younger, prettier and far more amusing than most of his regular clientèle, and he treats her like royalty, whisking out a chair for her to sit on in front of his counter as soon as he sees her coming. Yet however deferential Mr. Castle's tone of voice, and here you should observe him in characteristic pose, leaning slightly forward with his hands clasped together just beneath his chin and saying: "Oh, *Mrs. Graves!*" in response to some pleasantry or other; he has a host of lesser mortals at his command, and he leaves us in no doubt at all as to the importance of relying absolutely upon his judgment.

Mummy and her devoted admirer and mentor spend much of the next hour gradually working their way through the lengthy Copthorne list, with Mr. Castle busily sending off his assistants in all directions to gather samples of everything that is required, samples which are then laid out on the counter for Mummy's inspection. When her choices have all been made and it has been agreed that everything will be boxed up and safely transported by Heelas to Holme Grange School, Mummy suddenly remembers the name-tapes.

Mr. Castle immediately produces with something like a magician's flourish a book with examples of all the different styles of Cash's name-tapes. I am called in to examine them closely, a welcome relief after so much boredom, and before long we settle on blue capital letters in Times New Roman on a white background thus:

RICHARD GRAVES

Finally, it is time to settle up; and as soon as Mr. Castle has produced a hand-written bill, and Mummy has written out a cheque, he rolls up both bill and cheque and places them into a round metal container. He then screws this container into its holder, or car, which is part of a 'rapid wire cash railway' system located high up on the wall at the back of his counter. After which (as I look on enviously, because I would like to be doing this myself), he gives a sharp tug to the handle of a cord which is attached to the system. The car, propelled by compressed air, immediately whooshes away at top speed along a wire until it goes through a hole in the wall and disappears from sight.

Several minutes later, having reached the cashier's office and been dealt with, the car whooshes back again along its wire, making a 'ding' on its return; and when it is unscrewed it can be seen that both cheque and bill have been taken out and replaced with a formal receipt. This receipt is carefully examined by Mr. Castle, and then handed to Mrs. Graves with a slight bow, together with many devout and flattering protestations about how wonderful it has been to see her, and what a great pleasure her visits always are, and how he hopes very much to see her again soon.

Mummy accepts these compliments gracefully, and then she and I move on to the Men's Shoe Department, where we go through the usual tedious preliminaries. These consist of waiting for a shop assistant to be free, which can take some time, then having him approach me with a shoe-fitting stool. He sits just opposite me on one end of this while I remove the shoe from my right foot and place it on the sloping end of the stool. Then he measures my foot with a calibrated steel measuring-tool and, having enquired what exactly we are looking for, he goes off to fetch a first box of new shoes in what he hopes will be the right shape and size.

Unfortunately for him, my feet are very broad in comparison with their length: so anything that is the right length tends to be too narrow, and anything that is broad enough tends to be too short, and nothing seems to be a particularly good fit. All the while, as the shop assistant gradually becomes more and more hot-and-bothered, and the floor around us becomes a sea of shoes and of half-empty shoe-boxes, Mummy regales us both with a constant series of anxious questions: "How does that feel?" "What do you mean, 'I'm not sure'?" "Is there room for his feet to grow?" "Could we try half-a-size larger?"

Eventually, when we have found a pair of shoes that might be all right (though it is difficult to tell, even after walking up and down in them a few times, because all new shoes feel a little stiff at first), it is time to make a final check by visiting the shoe-fitting fluoroscope. This is an X-ray machine housed in a vertical wooden cabinet, with a step on one side and an opening just above that step into which I can insert both my feet. The box tapers towards the top, on which there are three raised viewing ports, one for the salesman, one for Mummy and one for me.

With my feet in place, I am now standing on top of an X-ray tube, from which I am shielded only by a thin layer of aluminium; and as soon as the machine is switched on, we can all see through our respective viewing ports a green-ish fluorescent image of the bones of my feet and the outline of my shoes. For me, knowing nothing of the radiation hazard, this is the highlight of our shopping expedition. Not only can I see for myself that my new shoes really are a good fit, but also I have the slightly eerie and unforgettable experience of wiggling my toes and watching my bones move, of viewing part of my own skeleton while I am still alive.

It was at about this time that my parents decided to promote me to the privileges of a grown-up supper. So, one evening, instead of having high-tea with Simon and Elizabeth in the Nursery at around five o'clock, I was allowed to join Mummy and Daddy for their supper in the drawing-room at 6:45 sharp. When I knocked on the door and went in a few minutes early, I found that the gate-leg table had already been pulled out a little, one end of it had been covered with a white linen table-cloth and it had been laid up by one of the servants with the family silver for a three-course supper for three. The wireless was on, and Mummy was already sitting on her chair. "Well, this is something new!" she said to me with a welcoming smile, "How lovely to have you with us!" A moment later there was another knock on the door and the soup was brought in; and then, at the very last minute, Daddy hurried in, removed his academic gown, muttered "Sorry darling!" and sat down in his chair. At that very moment, some music familiar from our White Hazel days began playing on the wireless and I heard an announcer say: "We present *The Archers*, an everyday story of country-folk."

Although I remembered the music, this was the first time that I had taken any interest in the story, and I was soon being introduced to the village of Ambridge and its principal characters. These included the stalwart Dan and Doris Archer of Brookfield Farm, and their friend and delightfully feckless small-holder, the elderly Walter Gabriel, whose catch-phrase 'Me old pal, me old beauty', uttered in the broadest of west-country accents, had soon been copied by me and become a family favourite.

When only fifteen minutes later *The Archers* had ended on a cliff-hanging dramatic moment, we listened to the start of the 6 o'clock news. Daddy commented knowledgeably on what was happening in the world, and I was thoroughly enjoying being a part of all this, when suddenly we heard running footsteps outside and Simon burst into the room.

"It's not fair! I want to be here too!" he shouted at the three of us, "It's not fair! It's not fair!" A moment later, he was weeping and sobbing and howling with rage. Daddy, looking extremely displeased, said nothing at all but caught hold of him and carried him kicking and screaming out of the room; and then Mummy, who looked devastated, followed Daddy upstairs, telling me that she was going 'to calm Simon down'. Indeed, the fuss that my brother had made was so upsetting to my parents, and especially to my mother, that on the very next evening the privilege that I had only just been awarded was extended to him too.

This seemed to me to be so desperately unfair that more than twenty years later, I wrote very bitterly about this incident: 'So much for the joys of being the first-born!' Now that you have watched this scene for yourself, what do you think? Should my parents have given in to this emotional blackmail or not? I am no longer certain. Simon was certainly very jealous of me on this occasion, and unreasonable jealousy should never be rewarded; but he had shown occasional signs of being very highly-strung ever since we had first moved to Holme Grange, so perhaps my parents were wiser than I knew.

Moving on a few days, it is now only a week before the start of the Copthorne School term, only a week, though I do not yet know it, before childhood's end. That is of course if we think of childhood in its romantic nineteenth and early twentieth century incarnation, at least within most upper and middle-class families within the Christian West, as a time of trust and security and innocent happiness. Only a week.

The RICHARD GRAVES name-tapes have all been sewn on, and

the long list of requirements has been carefully checked by Mummy one last time while every item upon it is carefully ticked and then packed into an old leather trunk of Daddy's. The list itself is the final item to be included before the trunk is closed up, and my father himself comes into the Nursery to fasten a leather strap all the way round it for extra security. It must be the same well-travelled trunk with which he had visited Europe back in the 1920s and 1930s, because it is covered with exotic labels: Paris, Rome, Vienna, Kitzbühel. It now sits at one side of the front hall, with a new label, not at all exotic, declaring simply: 'IN ADVANCE Wokingham to Horley R.P. GRAVES, Copthorne School, Sussex'.

Next to it, with a similar label attached, is a small wooden tuck-box with black metal corners and with R.P.GRAVES 82 painted clearly on the top in large black letters on a white background. Apart from a quantity of tuck that Mummy has transferred into it from the school supply, it contains my new tartan rug and a brand-new dark-red leather writing case of which I am already very proud. Mummy had bought it for me, and when she handed it to me for the first time I had unzipped it in great excitement. I found that on the right side she had placed a thick pad of light-blue Basildon Bond note-paper which fitted neatly over the leather straps provided; in the middle was a brand-new fountain pen in its holder; and on the left, in various compartments, were some Basildon Bond envelopes, and a small address book into which she had already written the addresses of several family members, and a booklet of 2d stamps. She had added at the top a label written in her own hand: 'R.P. GRAVES' and carefully pasted and sellotaped into place. "You will write every week, won't you darling?" For once she had sounded a little forlorn, so I had hugged her and promised that I would.

Within 24 hours, both trunk and tuck-box have been collected by two men in a lorry who drive up from Wokingham Station. Sending luggage by train 'In Advance' is at this time a widely-used and inexpensive way of transporting more than can easily be carried, and Copthorne insists upon it because it means that their school matrons have time to unpack everything before we pupils have arrived.

At last comes the day for my own departure. After an early lunch I rinse out my new plate, which as usual has become clogged-up with food, and replace it in my mouth. Then I go along to my bedroom and dress carefully in my new school uniform, which Mummy has laid out on my bed. Using the looking-glass on top of my chest-of-drawers I tie my new school tie very carefully. Then I put on my new school jacket and place in its breast pocket my new pocket-watch, which is already fully wound up and attached to its beautiful silver chain, the T-bar of which I insert carefully into the button-hole in my lapel.

Daddy has already summoned me into the drawing-room for a final pep-talk. "Remember", he says,

> "there are only two things that boys really hate: a cry-baby and a sneak. You'll probably be homesick for a while, but that's natural. Try not to be too knocked over by it, and remember that it will pass. Mrs. Workman should be a good friend if you ever need someone to talk to. She's a remarkable woman, you know. Did I tell you that she's famous for being able to tell whether or not a child is ill simply by shaking his hand? She's done it every night to the whole school ever since she and Skeete first arrived at Copthorne. She'll probably do it to you this evening on your way to bed. And that reminds me, whatever you do, remember that you know right from wrong and remember that God loves you and loves your family and don't forget to kneel down and say your prayers every night before you get into bed."

I say goodbye to Simon and Elizabeth in the Nursery. Lizzie is cheerful enough, but Simon looks very miserable, and despite his recent bad behaviour over supper, I tell him truthfully how much I will miss him and assure him that it won't be long before my return. And then Mummy drives me to the station and travels with me first up to Waterloo and then across London to Victoria Station, from which we have been told that the school train will be departing at 3:45pm.

The right platform is easy to find, and there beside the school train, clip-board in hand, is a member of the Copthorne School staff. He is a good-natured-looking character in his forties, slightly plump, with a check jacket rather like Mr. Hinton's but less colourful, and a large school-boyish face the shape of an inverted turnip surmounted by thinning black hair.

"Ah, Mrs. Graves!" he says, smiling amiably as Mummy introduces herself. "Yes, I'm Mr. Bineham, and your son is quite safe with me now!" He ticks off my name on the list on his clipboard. Mummy, with tears in her eyes, tells me once again "Don't forget to write!" before hurrying off; and I am directed into one of our reserved carriages.

Knowing no-one, I sit quietly in a corner. As the train leaves the station, the other boys talk animatedly to each other about all the exciting things they did in the holidays. I notice that several of them are busily scoffing sweets which they do their best to hide whenever Mr. Bineham hoves into view. He spends most of the journey pacing anxiously up and down the corridor, looking in on us compartment by compartment and doing his best to keep us all in order.

The only real excitement comes on our third or fourth stop when our train pulls into Earlswood Station, and there are general cries from one person to another of: "This is your stop! This is where you get off!" Mr. Bineham does his best to quell this outbreak, but it proves impossible. In due course I will learn that these cries have probably been made ever since the time of Copthorne's founding, when Earlswood had been home to The Asylum for Idiots; and although it has come to be known as The Royal Earlswood Hospital, and actually caters for those whom it describes as mental defectives (who would now be called more kindly 'the learning disabled'), to all Copthorne schoolboys it is simply a lunatic asylum or looney-bin.

A few minutes later, as our train began to move out of the station, there are more cries of: "Oh no! You missed your stop! You'd better pull the communication cord. Quick someone, stop the train!" And from Mr. Bineham, with a rueful grin on his face: "Silly boys! Do be quiet! You'll give the school a bad name!"

Two stops further on, we leave the train at Horley, the nearest railway station to Copthorne, and swarm over the covered bridge to the exit, where a single-decker bus is waiting for us. The final stage of our journey lies on narrow country roads through green fields until at last we turn right into Mill Lane. Round that long corner we are driven, and there in the distance are the school buildings. As they appear, a prolonged cheer goes up, from which I assume, wrongly as it turns out, that everyone is happy to be back.

Very soon, we are walking up that long passageway past Mr. Tim's study and to my astonishment I see as I approach it that the former entrance hall, which had seemed so neutral and nondescript on my last visit, simply an ante-room to Mrs. Workman's private quarters on one side and the central school corridor on the other, has somehow been transformed into something like the stage set of a cheerful drawing-room.

It is beautifully carpeted, comfortable easy chairs have been spread out here and there, and a lovely log fire burns merrily in the grate and throws out an inviting heat. Although I can already begin to hear Mrs. Workman's strangulated tones, the general impression is one of kindness and goodwill, and she and Mr. Tim are smiling cheerfully as they welcome a stream of children and parents.

Mr. Tim looks down at me when I reach him and says: "Graves, isn't it? Hello there, welcome to Copthorne! Did you have a good journey?" "Hello, Sir" I reply, politely shaking his hand and telling him that we had an easy journey across London. He looks baffled. "What was that?" he asks. "I can't make out what you're saying!".

"I'm afraid I'm wearing a plate", I say, after removing it from my mouth.

Mr. Tim looks very annoyed. "Oh dear, what a nuisance! I don't think your father said anything about a plate. Well, you'll just have to work hard on making yourself understood."

As he turns away to greet the parent who is next in line, his look of annoyance is replaced with another beaming smile. A moment later, I find that some hand or other is in the small of my back, pushing me through the door on my left, and expelling me from the cheerfulness and the warmth of the ante-room into somewhere altogether colder and less inviting.

END OF VOLUME ONE